Flashbacks

A Passion for Film

Peter Cowie

Sticking Place Books
New York

© Sticking Place Books 2025
© Peter Cowie

www.stickingplacebooks.com

ISBN 979-8-89976-007-5

Flashbacks

Contents

For my children
Monica, Felicity, and Robin

Peter Cowie, Laos, 2023

The past is part of my today.

Samuel Fuller

Memoirs and diaries are the concern of politicians, high-ranking military figures and sports celebrities. Like diaries, they evince a certain degree of vanity, an attempt to preserve the past in amber and to paint a personal portrait. Memoirs are best dipped into rather than read from start to finish. One of my favourites is Donald Richie's *The Japan Journals*—a blend of observations and daily memories over a period of half a century. During that time, the expatriate American Richie became the fore-most English-speaking interpreter of Japanese culture, and its cinema in particular. In his pages you can find descriptions of Yukio Mishima, Marguerite Yourcenar, Somerset Maugham and Francis Coppola.

This preamble simply means that I have no desire to write a traditional memoir. I have not kept a diary, except for a brief spell around the age of 20. I have no wish to discuss in public the intimate details of my private life. So why have I chosen to write this book? Perhaps it is because many of the people who crossed my path in life possessed an intrinsic interest of their own, often not associated with their celebrity. Perhaps also because you cannot comprehend the present without analysing the past. John Buchan, whose suspenseful books I devoured in my youth, entitled his autobiography *Memory Hold-the-Door*. Those who dismiss memory as a synonym for nostalgia are in effect slamming the door shut on their past. Memories offer a perspective on life by which we can measure the present and anticipate the future. All our experiences, great and small, seem inscribed on the hard disk of our mind.

The night before writing this, placing a pair of trousers on a clothes hanger stolen during the mid-1950s from the Centraal Hotel in Amsterdam, the sight of that name brought instantly to mind the taste of gingerbread slices. Served along with breads and toast at breakfast in the hotel dining room, that gingerbread seemed so exotic to me only a decade after the end of the Second World War. And it aroused in me an enthusiasm for all things

Dutch that would persist for years, shaping my travels and sensibilities in ways I could never have foreseen. That morning in the hotel dining room returns to me now not as a mere recollection, but as evidence that the past is never truly lost, and reappears at comforting moments throughout one's life. We filter out the boring everyday routine and strive to bury the painful memories, cherishing instead sensations that seem trivial at the time and yet acquire significance with the passage of time.

1.
Youth

Once evacuated from Harrow-on-the-Hill, where I spent my earliest months in wartime 1940, my parents settled in a rented house in Peachfield Road, Malvern, a proper little town nestling in the lee of the Malvern Hills in Worcestershire. Formerly the local golf clubhouse, it had a small garden, and my mother used a gigantic "copper" in which to wash clothes. My father devoted several hours each day to his writing. Poetry flowed from his pen, and eventually he would publish three volumes of collected verse, from sonnets to ballads. He had been about to take his entrance examination for Cambridge when, in 1928, his father was appointed general manager of a department store in Christchurch, New Zealand, and sailed to the southern hemisphere with his entire family in tow. My father then enrolled as a junior reporter on *The Press*, one of New Zealand's leading newspapers.

Impressions of happiness stir in the depths of my memory: walking with my mother across the Common to the shops in Great Malvern, she clutching her basket with one arm, and me with the other; playing day after day with my first friend, Michael, whose departure for Lichfield when I was five left me in tears; climbing on the hills of a Sunday morning, returning for a roast lunch prepared with such verve and skill by my mother; climbing into my parents' bed one morning as they developed their plans to launch The Tantivy Press, the firm that would eventually publish all my early books; and giving my father a pair of pliers on his 35th birthday in January 1946.

Both my parents had Scottish ancestry. My paternal grandfather had run away to London from the fishing village of Buckie, where his father owned a trawler. My mother, Ruth, had been born in Brisbane, Australia, where her father was the youngest mayor in the history of Toowong before being cut down by tuberculosis at the age of just 28. His widow married again, and the new couple took their two, and soon three daughters to Christchurch, where Fred Dudley was involved in some business venture.

This explains how my parents met, in their late teens. My father, Donald Cowie, detested the philistinism of the New Zealanders he knew ("poor, proud and pretty" he would say), and yearned to return to England. He and my mother married in 1933, and three years later had saved enough money to buy third-class tickets on a liner bound for Southampton. They were single-mindedly determined that my father would break through as a serious writer.

On many mornings, breakfast would be interrupted by the sound of the post arriving. My mother would hasten to retrieve the letters and bring them to my father. All too often, rejection slips lurked in the envelopes, and my father would fall into a depression. Ever since my parents' arrival in England in 1936, my father had typed scores of articles while spending his quality time on poetry and novels. During the war, he used his pen to help the war effort, writing books entitled *War for Britain* (Chapman and Hall), *An Empire Prepared* (Allen & Unwin), *The British Contribution* (Allen & Unwin), and *The Campaigns of Wavell* (Chapman & Hall). But when the war had ended, my father found himself caught in the void between the generation that had given their service and often their lives for their country, and the rising tide of young talented writers born a good decade after him.

So he decided to publish his own work, and then other books that were out of copyright and yet clearly appealed to a niche public, such as Wordsworth's *Guide to the Lake District*, a facsimile of the 1835 edition. It was a tacit admission of defeat, but also a gesture of defiance in the face of an intellectual establishment to which my father neither aspired nor belonged. There were moments of excitement, however, which kept my parents in a mood of optimism about my father's future as a writer. His comic novel, *The Indiscretions of an Infant*, was translated into Spanish in 1946, and in the following year 20th Century Fox took an option on his historical novel, *The Pioneers*, but nothing ever came of the project.

In old age, memories of earliest infancy sometimes well up, and long-forgotten faces and images lead one down the path of nostalgia. When I awake in what Cole Porter called "the still of

Age 7, with my parents Donald and Ruth,
in Littledean, Gloucestershire.

the night" and cannot sleep again, I summon up sequences
from my childhood. I must have been 6 years old, and we
were then living in a cottage above Littledean in Gloucestershire, overlooking the serpentine coils of the River Severn. Mill
Cottage could not have been a more romantic retreat for my
poet-father. Washed in pink, it had two rooms downstairs, and
two up. The bathroom was unusually large, however, and on
Sundays I would clamber into the huge metal bath with my

father, who would scrub himself and belt out the old music-hall hit, "Cabbages, Cabeans and Carrots." Meanwhile my mother, downstairs, was struggling to cook on two Primus stoves. They would often falter, and my father had to clear the wick, pour methylated spirits into the saucer-like receptacle at the top of the stove, light the fluid with a match, and pump vigorously for several seconds until the burner engaged. My mother was proud of these stoves, and would frequently clean their bases with Brasso.

Then the most cherished sequence comes back, with an exquisite clarity: I hear my mother's high-pitched, sing-song call from the kitchen—"Peter, Peter, lunchtime!" I am crouched in some undergrowth at the side of our front garden, playing with my snails. I have collected the unfortunate creatures according to the whorls and colouring of their shell. I pop them, squirming, into a jam jar and then with a skewer I pierce several holes in the lid so that they can breathe overnight. When my mother calls again, I leap up and scamper round the side of the cottage, past the ancient stone cider-press, past the crab apple tree, and towards the vegetable patch. Here my father is squatting down in his cord trousers and black rubber "gum-boots." He shows me, using a "dibber," how to make holes in the freshly sifted earth, in which seed can be dropped. A Freudian tinge to my memory, perhaps?

"Come on, Daddy," I cry, deciding to postpone lunch for as long as possible. I lead him by the hand to the back gate of our garden, beneath the enormous walnut tree, and then over a stile into the field that stretches down to the farm below. I race ahead of my father, skipping across the tufted grasses as though to the manner born. I clamber over a white five-bar gate and come into the farm itself. I pause for a few seconds at the pigsty, with two amiable sows wallowing in the mud. Then I enter the cow-shed, where Mary Wintle, the farmer's buxom, rosy-complexioned daughter sits on a three-legged stool, tugging away at the teats while the cows moo with relief.

My father and I, hand in hand, stroll down a rutted track, past the row of soaring poplars that sway against the sky, and into woodland. Finally we arrive at a clearing, and an open field dips into a gentle valley. Across the valley one can see sheep, dotted white against the lush pasture-land. I sit with my father for a few moments. The sheep seem so far away, the beauty of the grass and trees against an autumn azure sky so emblematic of paradise in a young boy's eyes. That is why, even in my eighties, I can still send myself to sleep by re-living this scene. Nothing I have witnessed in adult life—not the Pyramids, not the Taj Mahal, not Machu Picchu—can match the simple perfection of those sheep grazing peacefully across the sheltered valley in a remote part of the English West Country.

Although I had not been exposed to the cinema in those very early years, I am convinced that my happy childhood influenced my preference for the romantic film, rather than the cerebral, and for films that open up a far horizon, rather than for those that occur in airless, claustrophobic conditions—the Western, yes; Michael Haneke, no!

My parents kept in close touch with their Malvern friends, and we would often drive the thirty miles or so back to the old stamping ground to enjoy lunch with Charles and Vera Hinton. Charles was my parents' first bank manager in the area, and he was a joyous individual—large, with double chins that trembled in the wind, a delightful chortling laugh, and with a kindly disposition towards me, perhaps accentuated by the fact he and his wife did not have any children of their own. When he sensed that I was getting bored in the post-prandial haze of coffee in huge, soft armchairs, he would open a wooden trunk and let me gorge myself on past issues of the *National Geographic* (as yellow was my favourite colour, that magazine felt close to my heart).

We spent New Year's Eve with the Hintons, and as 1950 approached, my father was sent out into the moonlit garden to be the "first footer" to bring good luck to the household, ringing the bell just as midnight struck. To this day I can remember Charles Hinton lifting a glass and crying to all and sundry on the veranda, "Here's to the next half-century!" It sounded to my childish ears like an eternity stretching before us.

Not much further afield, the Forest of Dean spread across five hundred square kilometres. Once or twice a year, my parents would take me to the Speech House Hotel, in the heart of the forest, and enjoy an alfresco lunch before crossing into the woodland for a post-prandial walk. I little knew that Dennis Potter was in his early teens, growing up in nearby Coleford before gaining fame with *Pennies from Heaven* and *The Singing Detective*. Another weekend excursion was to May Hill, with its views towards Wales, and sometimes even to Bredon, where the poet A. E. Housman had gazed down upon "the coloured counties."

Although my parents took me with them on business trips (my mattress rolled and squeezed into the boot of the Austin Seven), they could not do so during school term. I would be billeted with the Wintles on their farm, first in Littledean, and then in Tibberton. My father wrote numerous poems about this family, and old Mrs. Wintle in particular. She had a serene, noble face, framed by carefully arranged grey hair, and for hours, it seemed to my childish eye, she would sit at the large table in the kitchen, preparing the vegetables, knitting, or on occasion reading:

> Now Millicent Mullock the ma of the farm
> As a countess she sits in the kitchen,
> And see how she plies that statuesque arm
> At the seat of the trousers she's stitching.

My bed upstairs was deep and soft, and the pillows were stuffed with feathers from the ducks and geese that prowled the yard behind the farm-house. In harvest month, my father would join the Wintle "boys," John and Cyril, and watch the square of corn shrinking and shrinking as the combine harvester roared inexorably around the field. Suddenly the hares could hide no more, and raced out, at which point the men would raise their shotguns and shoot as many as they could. Rabbit, or hare, was a staple on the menu of those days.

The winter of 1947 brought heavy snow to the United Kingdom. When the binder in Edinburgh sent bales of books to my father's address, they would arrive at the station in Newnham-on-Severn, two miles down from our cottage. I and my father would somehow get the bales on a sledge, and then my father would haul the sledge all the way up the road towards Littledean, slipping and sliding on the icebound surface. The sturdy paper around each bale was set aside, along with the string, and re-used to pack individual orders which, in turn, had to be taken down to the station for despatch.

In Tibberton, near Newent, where we bought a house in 1949, the garden was quite substantial, rich in fruit trees—Keswick apples, pears, red-currants, black-currants and, as at Mill Cottage, a walnut tree. Electricity came from a generator in the garage. From time to time it would fail, and we would be plunged into darkness. My father would take a torch to the garage and manage to start the engine again.

Most of my childhood images are of human beings who, inexorably, have all passed on. Mary, the farmer's daughter who helped my parents to pack books, and taught me to appreciate animals. John Lucas, the librarian in Malvern who admired my father's writing and whose gaunt, troubled face spoke of a prickly marriage; it was said that his wife would hurl cutlery at him during an argument. George Melly, the jazz singer, who came to stay with us from his family home in Liverpool, and wrote me long letters with amusing drawings in the margin, as he travelled around the British Isles. And "Jim" Evans, who was a schoolboy in Gloucester, strutting his stuff as Hamlet, when my parents met him. He recognised my father as a mentor when we had lunch at the Garrick Club half a century later. He was by then established as James Roose Evans, founder of the Hampstead Theatre Club and director of *84 Charing Cross Road*.

Most writers look back fondly to their relationship with one of their parents. I was incredibly fortunate to have both a mother and a father who stimulated my interest in life and the arts from earliest infancy. My mother taught me to read and write, and urged me to discover the classics of world literature, from *Children of the New Forest* to *The Count of Monte Cristo*. My father lacked the pedagogic intensity of my mother, but he would converse with me for hours about books, and history, and the secrets of good gardening. He kindled my love of poetry and novels, even as my mother had fostered within me the tools by which I could appreciate literature. My father typed a daily diary, over a period of more than fifty years, while my mother every so often wrote a journal (in elegant copperplate) tracing the story of her life with her parents in Brisbane, and then with my father in New Zealand and London.

There were my early schoolmates, nice and nasty, with names that linger—Glanville House, Maxwell Hathaway—and my primary schoolteacher Mrs. Groves who looked up at me after I had passed my "11-plus" exam and said "Now you are going out into the world," a remark that resonates with me still and that carried all the significance of an astronaut being told that he is soaring into outer space. Or Mr. Jordan, an earlier headmaster in Littledean, who cheerfully beat me for my transgressions, and then did the same to a bully who had thrust his fist into my face outside the schoolyard, an act of aggression fortunately seen by my mother. Or "Canon" Newth, who presided over the King's School in Gloucester, sweeping into the classroom in black suit and black gown, and with never a smile or a laugh to count his own. I still bear a long white scar on the lower palm of my left hand, sustained when I was pursued across Newth's playing fields by schoolboys who found my curly hair absurd. I ran and ran, but at last stumbled and fell, slashing my hand on a stout blade of grass.

My parents sent me to Dean Close Junior School in Cheltenham, preparatory to my entering Charterhouse. I survived with some difficulty, as I was bullied, due in part to my lack of sporting prowess. The headmaster, former Squadron Leader E. J. B. Langhorne, had served with distinction in the R.A.F. during the war, and would march around the school grounds with his pet Afghan Hound. During my final year, he would invite the boys into his lounge for readings from sinister, atmospheric books like Christopher Woodforde's *A Pad in the Straw*. From him I learned to articulate when speaking in public, although never with the same booming voice.

One other memory has stayed with me, of my housemaster, a choleric if not disagreeable man named Harwood, concluding Sunday night prayers with a quotation from Cardinal Newman: "May He support us all the day long, till the shades lengthen, and the evening comes, and the busy world is hushed, and the fever of life is over, and our work is done!" Never disposed towards doctrinal Christianity, I found myself touched by the cadence and poetry of Newman's words, and I consciously relaxed on hearing them. Now that the evening has indeed arrived, the memory of those words relaxes me even more.

I had always been, as one school report stated, "an omnivorous reader." Prompted by my parents, I fell like a glutton on any book that could stretch my imagination and keep me turning the pages, from *The Black Tulip* to *Poor Jack*, from *The Mill on the Floss* to *Kidnapped*. When I began to outgrow the "Powee! Zamm!" of those weekly comics, *The Dandy* and *The Beano*, my parents generously paid for me to subscribe to comics leaning towards storyline rather than knockabout comedy: *Tiger*, *Lion*, and, most luxuriously presented of all, *The Eagle*. Dan Dare and his struggles with his extra-terrestrial nemesis, "The Mekon," inspired in me an abiding affection for science fiction in all its forms.

For my eleventh birthday, my parents gave me a typewriter, a small portable that had been used by my father. I picked away at the keys, and was soon racing along. I still use two fingers, even as I tap out these lines in 2024, but I feel a certain childish pride in being able to type faster than many a touch typist. I wanted to write "a novel," and as my father was going through a phase of reading thrillers, my maiden effort would have to be a thriller too. I called it *The Dagger with Many Blades*, and the hero was one "Kane Karr of the C.I.D." Turning the yellowed pages of the 102-page typescript, I can recall how much I was under the influence of the pulp fiction writer James Hadley Chase, with his hard-bitten dialogue, snappy sentences, and continual bursts of action. The suspense of the BBC radio serial, Dick Barton, had also impressed me. I shared my father's taste for the thrillers of Eric Ambler, and Victor Canning; a generation earlier I suppose I would have devoured the work of A. E. W. Mason, Edgar Wallace or G. A. Henty. They were every bit as well constructed as the spy novels of Ian Fleming who, I dare say, would be as forgotten as Ambler, Chase and Canning, had the cinema not created an immortal hero in the character of James Bond.

Were I to have been born thirty years later, I should never have read so many books as I did, and as I continue to read. During my later years at Charterhouse, I even won the Thackeray Prize, named after one of the school's most illustrious authors, although I cannot recall the subject of my essay. I suspect that only a handful of boys entered for the competition. I embarked on more "mature" literature, racing through virtually all the novels of Thomas Hardy and Emile Zola, the short stories of Guy de Maupassant and W. Somerset Maugham, and the poetry of Rupert Brooke, Matthew Arnold and A. E. Housman (all three of whom I studied for my A level exams in English). Even in this area, I appeared non-conformist to my schoolmates who were dutifully analysing the work of Virginia Woolf, James Joyce or D. H. Lawrence, none of whom have ever captured my imagination. For a spell I found myself seduced by the Russians, by Tolstoy, Dostoyevsky, Turgenev and Chekhov. I cherished books that seemed to me to mark the summit of what writing could achieve: Aldous Huxley's *Point Counter Point*, Thomas Mann's *The Magic Mountain* and Thomas Hardy's *Tess of the d'Urbervilles*. During my Cambridge years, I leaned towards the Americans, to Ernest Hemingway even more than F. Scott Fitzgerald, to Edith Wharton more than William Faulkner, and much later to John Updike rather than Saul Bellow.

Violence in movies was not be celebrated, only tolerated under duress. My parents gave me, one Christmas, a splendid Western pistol, with mock-ivory handle and revolving chamber. I treasured it, as I did my model soldiers, cowboys and Indians, staging skirmishes around my model stagecoach and various improvised forts and stockades. Only learning to swim at the age of 13, I found myself fascinated, and terrified, by such Hollywood adventures as *20,000 Leagues Under the Sea* and *Underwater!* "Adult entertainment," however, bored me, and I recall enduring the laborious convolutions of *The Caine Mutiny*, *The Barefoot Contessa* and *Not as a Stranger*.

Not that I held the cinema in high intellectual regard. Throughout my childhood and teenage years, I felt that "going to the pictures" was like visiting the circus: entertainment pure and simple. If I did venture into London's West End, it was with a certain degree of guilty gratification to see new releases like *Night People* or *The Curse of Frankenstein*. Not all those films seen during an impressionable childhood have withstood repeated scrutiny. One of the joys of being a film critic is revisiting films every few years, and most of the Westerns seem as powerful today as they did when I saw them in the 1950s. Other genres, such as the Biblical epic, and the xenophobic political film, have not fared so well.

Foreign-language films were beyond my ken, which made my conversion all the more dramatic when it occurred, as late as early 1959, when I saw *The Seventh Seal* with my parents at the Royal cinema on Edgware Road. Bergman's medieval masterpiece had already long opened in London, but at the Royal, a revival house, it was the supporting feature to *I Am a Camera*, the screen version of Christopher Isherwood's Berlin stories. My father liked Isherwood, which is why we trundled along to the Edgware Road on that fateful evening, my mother and grandmother in tow. I fell in love on the spot with Julie Harris as Sally Bowles, but *The Seventh Seal* seized me by the throat and, to some extent, has never let go. Bergman asked questions that I had asked myself during sleepless nights—all those fundamental questions you ask when young and then spend the rest of your life trying to forget. His fears, his aspirations and, yes, his romantic agony, leapt from the screen.

When the witch was about to be burned at the stake, my grandmother said in a harsh whisper, "There's too much talk about Death in this film!" and with a clatter of seats announced that she was leaving. My mother followed her anxiously into the London night, and my father and I were left to consume the remainder of the film. When we, too, returned home around midnight, we talked about *The Seventh Seal* at length.

How fortunate I was to have a father who shared my passion for film and poetry. A creative man to the end of his days, Donald Cowie could never have total respect for my "non-fiction" approach to writing; each morning he could think of several plots for stories, and I often wish that I could have inherited his inventive approach to life. But he encouraged me as I leaned more and more towards writing about the cinema, and the spring and summer of 1959 were packed with screenings. I joined the National Film Theatre, and revelled in "The Passionate Cinema," John Gillett's season of Swedish films. My mother, more generous and spontaneous than her husband, had visions of greatness for me which I never fulfilled. Had I become an Ambassador, she might have been satisfied, but otherwise throughout the first eighteen years of my life, I was subjected to her mantra, "No, he'll never do well!" We had huge, explosive rows. Affection ran beneath these arguments, as it always does, and in old age she and I both relaxed more in each other's company.

Flashback: Max von Sydow

The first time I "met" Max was in May of 1959, when Bergman's stunning production of *Urfaust* came to London for
just one week in the World Theatre Season. Groupie of all
things Swedish that I was at the age of 19, I waited outside
the stage door at the end of the evening, and gathered the
signatures of Max, Gunnel Lindblom and Toivo Pawlo in my
programme booklet.

Not enough people know that Max was among the
most gifted stage actors of his generation, if not the most
gifted, and during his years at Malmö Municipal Theatre,
he appeared in nine productions under the direction of
Bergman, who said at the time: "Max is wonderful. You'll see,
posterity will consider him as one of the greatest actors of
our time."

We really only became friends in the early 1980s, when
Max played the Emperor Ming in Mike Hodges' version of
Flash Gordon and was stationed at Shepperton Studios for
a stint, and then one year later, during the shooting of Jan
Troell's *The Flight of the Eagle*.

To reach the "location" on *The Flight of the Eagle* you
endured a 50-minute ride across rough ice in a snowmobile just south of the Arctic Circle in the Gulf of Bothnia.
The Swedish explorer S. A. Andrée, played by Max, tried
to reach the North Pole in a balloon in 1897, and Troell
was having as much difficulty in launching the balloon
that day as Andrée and his companions more than eighty
years earlier. It lurched upwards, then lost height, and
Max was trapped between the ice floe and the gondola
basket. Soon the ice started breaking up, a helicopter was
summoned, and I was flown back to shore with Max and
two of the actors (priority for the star and the journalist!).
The rest of the crew were left to travel home as best they
could.

While darkness fell, a farmer's wife served coffee and
smörgåsbord to us all, not recognising Max. Then everyone
drove away in a Volkswagen minibus. Max nodded off in
the front seat. Once at the hotel, the makeup had to be
removed, and a late supper devoured. Long after midnight,
the producer moved among the tables, circulating the next

Peter
Cowie

CHAPLIN
film magazine
SPECIAL

Max
von Sydow

**from
The Seventh Seal
to Pelle the Conqueror**

day's call sheet. "9 a.m.," said Max gravely, and with his consummate professionalism, "Yes, that sounds acceptable."

In 1988, Max was invited to London to appear as Prospero in Jonathan Miller's staging of *The Tempest* at the Old Vic. He had an apartment in South Kensington, and there we would meet regularly to work on a small book I wrote about his work. Max invited me to see his friend Tim Pigott-Smith in *The Winter's Tale* at the National. I barely recognised Max in the foyer—coat collar turned up, and a cap pulled down over his dark glasses. After the performance, Max said he had promised to visit Tim in his dressing room. We went through security at the stage door, and as Max signed the visitor's book, a man in a dirty raincoat (literally) sprang up from a couch nearby and asked Max to sign a 10x8 glossy still from *The Seventh Seal*. "Certainly," intoned Max in that medieval voice of his. Halfway up the spiral staircase to the dressing-rooms, he turned and asked me: "Peter, how do you think that man found out that I would be here this evening?" I mumbled something about the price of fame, but he was clearly mystified.

It's all too easy to classify Max as a Bergman actor and not much else, but his work for Jan Troell was enormously fruitful. They made seven films together, at least three of which are classics—*The Emigrants*, *The New Land* and *The Flight of the Eagle*—and the last of which, *Hamsun*, featured a subtle and perceptive portrait of Norway's most notorious writer. Nor should we forget some of Max's Hollywood characterisations, such as the assassin in *Three Days of the Condor*, the defence attorney in *Snow Falling on Cedars*, and Father Merrin in *The Exorcist* ("Not many realise, Peter," he said to me, tongue in cheek, "that *I* am the Exorcist in that film!"). And what about his marvellously petulant painter in *Hannah and Her Sisters* and the scorn he puts into that memorable line: "Can you imagine the mind that watches wrestling?"

Max agreed to be the honorary president of my wife's new-born Scandinavian Film Society, and he attended the opening night of the first season, along with his only film as a director, *Katinka*. He would send us long, handwritten letters from locations such as Australia, where he was shooting *Until the End of the World* with Wim Wenders. Then he threw over the traces and embarked on a new life in France, with a new wife and family. Like most of his former friends, I found it difficult to reach him and when I last spoke to him, at a film festival in Lyon in 2012, he gave me a weird look and asked, almost rhetorically: "Have we met before? But that must have been a long time ago…" It was indeed.

During my freshman year at Cambridge, I quickly accepted that I could not transfer my thoughts into images, only words. Even if I want to draw something very simple, my hand will not obey my mind, and I envy those who can with a casual flourish produce a sketch that clearly represents what they want to draw. So filmmaking held no allure for me. I comforted myself—and still do—by saying that one does not have to be a composer to appreciate great music, or a painter to quail before a Rembrandt self-portrait. I gladly admit to having a prosaic mind. My father could compose a poem, or invent a tale, almost without hesitation; that is a gift I could never share. By the same token, the study of philosophy remains anathema to me. Terms like "determinism," "Cartesian," "Non-Cartesian," "Kantian" and "Hegelian" leave me perplexed—as does semiology. I had no such qualms about studying history, however, and in retrospect I can see that the historical method has helped me considerably in managing my research and my sources when preparing a book.

My first published piece on the cinema dates from February 1960. Charles Barr, an editor of *Broadsheet*, the Cambridge weekly arts magazine, came round to my rooms in Magdalene College saying that he quite liked the review of Bergman's *Wild Strawberries* that I had submitted on spec. He said that *The Face* (known as *The Magician* in the U.S.) was opening in the city the following week, and asked me to write a review. I did so, and it duly appeared. Charles and I became friends, and he introduced me to other contemporaries of his at King's College—Peter Graham, Alexis Lykiard and Corin Redgrave. I helped with the stapling of *Broadsheet*'s "roneo'd" pages, and sometimes with the delivery of the magazines to various outlets in the city.

Through the university network I met Ian Johnson, a cheerful, trainee TV editor from Loughton in Essex, who launched a film magazine called *Motion*. We had a friend in common, Allen Eyles, and together they persuaded me to prepare a "monograph"—that buzz-word of the period—on Ingmar Bergman. It appeared in December of 1961 and to my amazement and delight was mentioned in the major Sunday newspapers. "A work of love and scholarship," wrote Penelope Gilliatt in *The Observer*; "detailed and useful as well as enthusiastic," said Dilys Powell in *The Sunday Times*. Both critics included Ian's private address in their review, and he phoned me to say that the postman had struggled up to his front door with a sackload of letters ordering the booklet. A second edition followed in February 1962, and a third in August of that year. Even Foyle's in the Charing Cross Road devoted a window to my "monograph," a tribute more to Bergman's fame at the time than to my talent as a neophyte film historian.

Flashback: Ingmar Bergman

Ingmar Bergman, if not quite so secretive as B. Traven or J. D. Salinger, was hard to meet during the early 1960s, long before email, faxes and low-cost airlines. Thrilled, like so many of my generation, by *The Seventh Seal*, I wrote to the Great Man before going up to Cambridge at the age of 19. The first of Bergman's letters proved characteristically succinct. On June 6th, 1959 he replied: "I think it is much better that we meet for a personal talk next time you visit Stockholm." I never went that year, but when I published my first little pamphlet on Bergman's work, I sent it to him in Sweden. On February 9th, 1962, he wrote that he had read it "with the greatest pleasure." He had, he continued, "just finished *The Communicants* [*Winter Light*] and have started to cut the film. In that situation I never talk about my work. I am feeling too frightened." Another polite letter followed on September 4th, 1962. "I am unfortunately just in the final part of my film *The Silence* and my principle is and has to be not to meet anyone during the shooting. We can perhaps meet later this coming autumn."

Throughout the 1960s I visited Stockholm annually, writing about each new Bergman film. But I could never pin him down for an interview. He would send a couple of theatre tickets to my hotel, and his assistant took me to at least one dinner, but no Ingmar. My luck changed in Sorrento, near Naples, where a Swedish Film Week was held in the (elsewhere) tumultuous summer of 1968. There I met a Swedish journalist, Gunnel Hessel, who promised to introduce me to Ingmar next time I came to Stockholm. In January 1969, Gunnel arranged for me to attend a press conference at the Royal Dramatic Theatre, where Ingmar talked about his stage production of Büchner's *Woyzeck*. Afterwards she introduced us, and the ice melted. I had dinner with Ingmar at the nearby "Teatergrillen" and he chatted happily about his stage work, sudden thunderclaps of laughter punctuating his conversation. "I'm a fervent believer in the human imagination," he said. "We have become lazy because colour, stereo sound, and CinemaScope leave nothing to our imagination." Ingmar's regular table was discreetly placed out of sight of casual passers-by. Midway through our one-course dinner, the door opened and a vainglorious Swedish actor who would much later be used to good effect by Lars von Trier stood for a few moments waiting for all eyes to enjoy him. He was then at the height of his local fame, and Ingmar leaned towards me with a conspiratorial smile: "Let's hope that little shit doesn't come over here," he said. The actor made his royal tour of the various tables, and when he reached ours, Ingmar sprang to his feet and embraced him warmly. In that instant I realised that in the tight-knit world of stage and screen, expediency is always the better part of valour.

In 1971, I interviewed Bergman in his austere office high above the Royal Dramatic Theatre, with its upright chairs, its small, truckle bed, and mineral water to hand. He talked of *The Touch*—"It's probably the nearest of my films to reality but nevertheless a dream, full of sadness and desire." Did he still believe in his dictum that the theatre was his wife and the movies his mistress? "Forget it," he laughed. "Now I'm living in bigamy!"

Two years later we discussed *Cries and Whispers*. "I intended at first to write something about my mother. She's in all four of the women in the film. My feelings towards her were ambivalent. When I was little I felt she loved my brother more than she did me, and I was jealous."

The next time I actually met Bergman was in 1980, in Munich. He had taken refuge there after a nasty spat with the Swedish tax authorities, who in 1976 had accused him of declaring insufficient earnings. He was later exonerated, but when I interviewed him he had been shooting *From the Life of the Marionettes*, an anguished, sombre film that reflected his depression and deracination. During a Saturday afternoon chat at the Bavaria Studios, he maintained that "the cultural climate here in Munich is extremely stimulating and very varied. I miss that in Stockholm, where there is no life-or-death struggle in the cultural field." He wrote to me a week

At Bergman's grave on Fårö, 2022. Photo by Ari Aster.

or two later saying that it was "an indescribable relief to at last be free of this difficult and stressful film [*Marionettes*], which really cost me blood, sweat, and tears."

In 1982, I sat on the set of *Fanny and Alexander*, as Bergman directed Harriet Andersson in a dream sequence. He had been hailed by the Swedes like a prodigal son, and thanks to funding from Gaumont he could make what he declared to be his final film in a lavish, epic idiom. But he was—he claimed—retiring: "I want to stop. I want to stay on Fårö, and read the books I haven't read, find out things I haven't yet found out. I want to write things I haven't written. To listen to music, and talk to my neighbours. To live together with my wife a very calm, very secure, very lazy existence, for the rest of my life."

The following autumn, we enticed him to London's National Film Theatre. He told me quite candidly that he would not talk about his own work. "I have just made my final film, and it lasts 3 hours 14 minutes. It was meant to be 2 hours 45 minutes, but as it is my final production I think I can indulge myself just a little!" He agreed to the NFT appearance only if the discussion be devoted to his mentor,

Alf Sjöberg, who had just died. I concurred, but figured that I could gradually switch the conversation to Bergman's own films. Sure enough, after about twenty minutes on stage, we were chatting about the early days of Ingmar's own career, and everyone was delighted. Of course, my ruse was transparent, and Ingmar probably knew as much.

His career had overlapped with that of Sjöberg, and he told us on stage that when he first began directing Bibi Andersson in *Smiles of a Summer Night*, she had just come from working on one of Sjöberg's pictures. "We did one take, and another, and another," he said. "And I asked her what was wrong." Bibi replied that Sjöberg's method was to do thirteen, or fourteen or even fifteen takes, and when you have done it that many times you can really start to play the scene. "My method is the opposite," declared Ingmar. "I try to do just one, two or three takes, and to prepare in such a way that when we start to shoot, the actor knows exactly what to do, but he or she still has some freedom."

Although Bergman would resort to digital cameras for his swansong, *Saraband* (2003), he disliked technological advances. "I think it's quite tragic that electronics have taken over now [in 1982!]. Of course, it must be so. Film was invented in 1895, and we still work with it in exactly the same way. Something else has to happen, and I think that it's to be welcomed, but I don't want to be involved in it. I like to work with a screen and projectors, with the sound of the projectors and the shadows."

The NFT was absolutely packed that evening—understandably, for Bergman was loath to travel and felt ill at ease away from his routine at home in Sweden. Relaxed and smiling amid the adulation, he used my back as an impromptu desk for signing autographs after the interview. Later, at a restaurant, he had two beers with his meal. Ingrid, his wife, whispered happily: "Ingmar never has more than one beer. This is really something!" At some juncture during the dinner, Andi Engel (head of the British distribution company Artificial Eye) suddenly called out down the table, "Ingmar, why do you give so much time to this man Cowie?" Seated opposite me, Ingmar did not look at Engel, but instead fixed me with a hooded stare. "I think we trust each other," he said, more to me than to the impudent Andi. I remember wondering what would happen should I ever betray that trust.

A few weeks later, he wrote me: "The visit to London was in fact really nice, the first and until now only comfortable experience I have had in that city [referring probably to his clashes with Laurence Olivier when Bergman's production of *Hedda Gabler* was staged at the National]. It's difficult to say something subtle and substantial in a foreign language, and that evening just happened to be more 'foreign' than usual!"

As I left him and Ingrid in the lobby of the Savoy that night in September 1982, I had no idea that I would never see him again. We talked on the phone sometimes (friends were permitted to call him on Fårö around noon on Sundays), and in the late 1980s he gave me some nice quotes about Max von Sydow for the book I was writing on the actor. I forwarded various requests from festivals for Ingmar to travel here, there and everywhere. All were turned down politely, or not so politely. By the 1990s, he had slipped out of fashion, replaced in the arthouse pantheon by new names such as Nanni Moretti, Jane Campion and Quentin Tarantino. Even his status as God of the Nordic Cinema had been usurped by Aki Kaurismäki and Lars von Trier. Almost the last letter I ever received from him was about the biography I had written during the 1980s: "I get giddy when forced to turn and look back [over my career]. But as I understand that the tone of your book is friendly, then, despite everything I'm able to confront the irretrievable past."

Through Charles Barr I also met David Frost, who lived on the ground floor of a large house on the corner of West Road in Cambridge. When he was appointed editor of *Granta*, the venerable university magazine, Frost asked me to become its business manager. We would chat every day or two, and often I would arrive at his flat at around noon, and David would be enjoying a breakfast that consisted of cornflakes and Campari. He had already established a foothold at Anglia Television, and teemed with ideas and irreverent wit. When he asked me to contribute a book review, he wrote at the foot of my piece: "Controversial Peter Cowie, 21-year-old Magdalene cinemaestro, sang 'Roses of Picardy' in perfect tune at the age of eighteen months. An Editor of *Broadsheet*, he is no relation to Pete 'Cosh' Cowie, the Teignmouth hoodlum."

Where financial matters were concerned, David's reach definitely exceeded his grasp, and my parents grew increasingly anxious that I would end up in a bankruptcy court if *Granta* foundered. The printers, Foister and Jagg, had a soft spot for David, however, and respected the way he visited the plant to supervise the final proofs of the magazine. One day, we found that an advertiser had failed to send in copy. A white space needed filling—urgently. David took out his pen and scrawled, "Wellesley Nudilon Pantilets, 9s.11d, in Duro-Masturbene Luxipaks." The ad appeared, and aroused not a single comment.

In October 1960, Frost urged me to take advantage of the sporadic correspondence that I had developed with Somerset Maugham. "If you could meet him," he said, "we could do a profile in the 'Feet of Clay?' series in *Granta*." I baulked at the notion of one of my literary heroes being mocked, but I asked Maugham if I could visit him during one of his stays in London. He replied, inviting me to "take a dish of tea" with him at The Dorchester in Park Lane. A busy and memorable Friday ensued.

At 4 p.m. sharp I arrived at The Dorchester. A porter announced me by phone to the Maugham suite. I was met outside the lift by Alan Searle, who warned me that his master was a little deaf. When I went into the huge, very warm drawing-room, replete with paintings (or reproductions) by Leonardo and Canaletto, the aged man sat huddled on a sofa in a silk smoking jacket. He patted the cushion next to him and asked me to sit down. "I haven't been well lately," he offered, "so I'm very pleased to have someone to talk to."

The most striking thing about Maugham the man was his stammer. I had understood from articles in the press that this had long been cured, but I realised then that in Maugham's youth it must have just as terrible an affliction as Philip Carey's club foot in *Of Human Bondage*. He was far more charming than his critics maintained, and was delighted to speak on all subjects, from the Far East to the West End theatre, with a leaning towards malicious gossip. He gave the impression of a man immensely experienced in life and yet still eager to learn, of cultivated wisdom and yet of engaging frankness. With a satisfied smile he told the story of his meeting the distinguished writer Edmund Gosse, who approached him during a party several years after Maugham had become famous, and said, "Oh, my dear Maugham, I liked your *Liza of Lambeth* so much. How wise you are never to have written anything else!"

Searle sat on a nearby couch and watched over him like a wife. We had a frugal if attractively presented tea of toast and jam, and every now and then I had the impression that Maugham was scrutinising me like some bird, from the corner of his hooded eye. Knowing his powers of description, it made me rather apprehensive.

At 5 p.m. Searle declared that "Mr. Maugham" was "getting tired," but he was not too tired to sign my first edition of his *A Writer's Notebook*. When I asked what books I should read to develop my craft as a budding writer, Maugham urged me to seek out the French—Flaubert, Stendhal and Balzac above all. He shook my hand softly, and invited me to come and dine at his villa in Saint-Jean-Cap-Ferrat if ever I was down on the Riviera. Then it was a rush to King's Cross for the train back to Cambridge. When I told David Frost how much I liked Maugham, he quietly dropped the idea of a derogatory piece in *Granta*.

Benedict Nightingale, who would become drama critic at *The Times*, had been at Charterhouse with me, and also studied at the same college in Cambridge. When he became editor of the university's weekly newspaper, *Varsity*, he asked me to take care of the film department. Soon I had a full page, and sometimes two, at my disposal, for reviews, interviews and various squibs. This gave me the excuse to go down to London for press screenings, and my studies during the Michaelmas (autumn) Term must have suffered due to my constant commuting to the National Film Theatre for the London Film Festival.

Flashback: François Truffaut

One morning in October of 1961, I attended the press screening of François Truffaut's *Shoot the Piano Player* at the NFT, a full month prior to its opening in France. Truffaut was there, and he explained that he had collected the very first wet print from a lab in Paris at dawn (it was then around 10.30 a.m.) and had not even seen it yet himself. He looked gaunt and pale, and it seemed clear that he

Graham Petrie's book about Truffaut, published in 1971 by Tantivy.

feared a negative reaction from the British press, perhaps because this riff on the traditional film noir marked such a change from *The 400 Blows*, which had rhymed very much with the prevailing British screen adherence to social commitment. A polite silence prevailed as the lights came up after the credits. Truffaut, confused, asked Richard Roud, the director of the London Film Festival and his good friend, "Why the silence?" Roud explained that the reaction was quite normal and did not reflect any disapproval on the part of the critics. (British journalists have always been reticent at press conferences, in contrast to their French, Italian and American confrères.)

Intrepid, I put up my hand to ask Truffaut why he had opted for Dyaliscope in his first two films, but I cannot recall what he said in response, which says more about my youthful self-esteem than it does about Truffaut's timidity on that chilly morning. Yet *Shoot the Piano Player* met with a pretty civil reception from the mainstream London critics, which was just as well, for you had a feeling that Truffaut might remember and catalogue every review he received. During the years that followed, he grew more confident in dealing with the fourth estate, and would double-check every press book before it was issued.

As an exhibit at the Cinémathèque française demonstrated many years after his death, Truffaut hoarded like a squirrel every document that entered his daily life, from movie ticket stubs to press cards and casting notes. This archival instinct joined forces with a restless efficiency, ensuring that Truffaut replied with alacrity to every letter he received. He wrote to people outside France on creamy, lightweight rice paper. His assistant translated into English as required, and also typed some of his business correspondence. Truffaut, like many autodidacts, adored the act of writing, using a thick-nibbed pen and a jet-black ink that withstood time's attrition. His earliest letter to me, dated July 13th, 1971, began with a formal "Messieurs," and advised me to contact his literary agent, Don Congdon, in New York concerning my offer through the Tantivy Press to publish André Bazin's *Jean Renoir* in English. He also said that he appreciated the book by Graham Petrie (*The Cinema of François Truffaut*) that we had just released.

In January 1973, he wrote in French, "I have not forgotten your interest in the book by André Bazin, which is why I am sending you his work on Orson Welles, which has just appeared in France." As well as being the spiritual heir to Bazin, Truffaut served as his assiduous literary executor.

Three years later, we published the book *Surrealism and the Cinema* by Michael Gould, and when Truffaut received it, he responded with enthusiasm and promptly dispatched four titles that he felt would interest me, among them his screenplays for *The Story of Adèle H.* and *L'argent de poche* and a couple culled posthumously from Bazin's manuscripts.

How I had been promoted by that stage from "Monsieur" to "Mon Cher Ami" I am not quite sure. It may have resulted from our only meeting of consequence—in the early 1970s, when I plucked up the courage to buttonhole him on the Croisette in Cannes and said how happy I was that he had featured one of our Tantivy titles, *Hitchcock's Films* by Robin Wood, among the books to be burned—or saved—in *Fahrenheit 451*.

With his artfully wrapped scarves (long before they became de rigueur for French politicians and intellectuals), the discreet and courteous Truffaut raced through the streets, as he did through life, like a hero of 19th-century literature. He found other languages impossible to master, although he did manage to make one or two charming speeches in English in the United States, notably when he won the Best Foreign Language Film Oscar for *Day for Night*.

Truffaut directed only twenty-one features, but their range of emotion and setting is surprising. The Antoine Doinel films (from *The 400 Blows* to *Love on the Run*) may have appeared to the public at large to be his most autobiographical works, but their quirkish and increasingly genteel textures conceal a personality that ran deep and was driven by restless passions. *The Soft Skin* encompasses marital infidelity in cinematic terms that are audacious and unorthodox: around one thousand shots, of which virtually half are close-ups of Jean Desailly. The literary adaptations (*Shoot the Piano Player*, *The Bride Wore Black* and *Confidentially Yours*, to cite but three) reveal his knowledge of the American pulp thriller, while he brought an acute, almost anguished gaze to bear on such themes as book burning (*Fahrenheit 451*), social intolerance (*The Wild Child*), and death itself, as refracted through the sensibility of Henry James (*The Green Room*). And none but Truffaut could have transfigured Henri-Pierre Roché's delicate writing into those abiding masterpieces *Jules and Jim* and *Two English Girls*.

In January 1980, he sent me New Year's greetings and wrote that the following week he would begin shooting *The Last Metro* (which would become a poignant tribute to artistic courage under the Nazi yoke). In late 1983, while I was living and working in Finland, a friend who was organising the annual congress of the International Federation of Film Societies in Helsinki told me that she had received a telex from France saying that Truffaut had fallen ill and could not attend in his capacity as president. Less than one year later, he was dead, cut down by a brain tumour at just 52 years of age. A tireless romantic, he had loved life—especially women—almost as much as he loved the cinema.

In early 1962, I took the train down to the West End to attend the press screening of *Last Year at Marienbad*. Both Alain Resnais and Alain Robbe-Grillet were there, and afterwards I buttonholed them in the lobby of the now defunct Cameo-Poly arthouse on Upper Regent Street. Robbe-Grillet, known up to that point only for his experimental novels, such as *The Voyeur* and *Jealousy*, was far more mercurial and voluble than Resnais, gesticulating furiously to emphasise a fact or opinion.

He claimed that the cryptic initials of the characters in *Marienbad* (A, X, and M) had no special significance, "just as in *Hiroshima mon amour*, where the lovers have no names." He admitted that although many of the tracking shots in the film were outlined in his script, Resnais made them at once more complicated and practical. Robbe-Grillet's opinions were precise and dogmatic—he hated Bergman ("too metaphysical"), loved Orson Welles, and thought Jacques Demy's *Lola* the best film of 1961. On the literary side, he admired James Joyce (though Resnais smiled and admitted he had never read him) and Virginia Woolf, and immensely enjoyed the detective fiction of Graham Greene.

Flashback: Alain Resnais
Like Albert Einstein, Alain Resnais remained throughout his life an extraordinary mix of intelligence and playfulness. But when I first met him in 1962, he struck me as grave, if not quite austere. At that time, he stood at the apex of French cinema, the cerebral master behind *Hiroshima mon amour* and *Last Year at Marienbad*. He seemed a pole apart from the antic innovators of the New Wave. Of course, he was a full decade older than Truffaut, and eight years senior to Chabrol and Godard. He had already won an Academy Award in 1949 (for his short *Van Gogh*) but didn't embark on

his maiden feature until ten years later. "Although I was not fully part of the New Wave because of my age," Resnais told me in 2002, "there was some mutual sympathy and respect between myself and Rivette, Bazin, Demy and Truffaut. I did not know Rohmer so much, although I liked what he wrote. Chabrol too, as I shared his passion for Hitchcock and Fritz Lang. So I felt friendly with that team."

He also looked different from the average intellectual at the turn of the 1960s. He held himself so erect that he seemed taller than he really was. His full head of luxuriant hair was always impeccably brushed, and beneath his trademark anoraks he wore semiformal attire. This gave Resnais a detached, somewhat forbidding air, despite his old-world courtesy.

On that wintry morning in 1962, as he stood in the lobby of the Cameo-Poly with Robbe-Grillet at his side, he answered questions with precision and without a hint of condescension or facetiousness. Resnais spoke of travelling to Germany in search of a hotel for *Marienbad*, and about the 2.35:1 widescreen format, which he had used for the first time in a feature. He also talked about his work as a documentarist and said he would probably not make any more of these short films: "It's a problem of finance. There is no assured distribution for them, and in any case they have to be commissioned by various societies." *Plus ça change…* He added with a smile that *Le chant du styrène*, a documentary in CinemaScope and colour, took him almost as long to shoot as *Hiroshima mon amour*. Then he turned to his pet project, *The Adventures of Harry Dickson*, based on the quasi-American dime-novel detective popularised by Belgian writer Jean Ray in the 1930s. Resnais was planning to make that one in black-and-white, he said: "I think one can only use colour when a film is down to earth… *The Adventures of Harry Dickson* will be a bit like a fantasy."

Early in 1963, I met with Resnais again, at Fouquet's on the Champs-Elysées in Paris, to talk about *Muriel ou Le temps d'un retour*. Now a nearly forgotten film, shot on location in Boulogne-sur-Mer, it explored the emotions and reactions of Hélène Aughain (played by Delphine Seyrig) during a fortnight's visit by her former lover. Resnais had switched to East

THREE MONOGRAPHS BY **PETER COWIE**

Michelangelo

ANTONIONI

Ingmar

BERGMAN

Alain

RESNAIS

PUBLISHED BY
INTERNATIONAL FILM GUIDE **7/6**

My first book, published by Tantivy in 1963.

mancolor, he said, "because with the different shades one can, as with ceramics, create a fragmentation of colours, or, if you like, a mosaic." We talked of our mutual love of Welles, and of Antonioni ("I've always liked his films, right from the earliest days"), and of the feature projects that had eluded him during the 1950s, among them an adaptation of a novel by Roger Vailland, although he did not say which one. He still appeared dispassionate, but his face broke into broad smiles when he again spoke of *Harry Dickson*, no longer, apparently, in black-and-white. "If all goes well," he said, "I'll start shooting at Christmastime. I've had a script ready for quite a while, and the film will be in colour like *Muriel*. Dickson was a kind of Sherlock Holmes, and in fact we'll be shooting partly in London."

Then, in the early 1970s, I was staying at the Hotel Manhattan on Eighth Avenue in New York, and who should I find in the breakfast cafeteria but Alain Resnais? Why was he there? I can't remember, exactly, although it may have had to do with *The Year 01*, the portmanteau comedy he made with Jacques Doillon and Jean Rouch. He was altogether more relaxed and less intimidating as he chatted away about his love of American comic strips. *Harry Dickson* still simmered on the back burner... For the first time, I felt I glimpsed a puckish sense of humour beneath those rigid features and that penetrating gaze.

Almost three decades later, in 2002, in preparation for my book *Revolution!*, about the explosion of world cinema in the late 1950s and '60s, I made an appointment with Resnais in Paris. Two months shy of his eightieth birthday, he walked in with the confident stride of a much younger man. Gone was the chilly elegance, displaced by funky trainers and a shabby wind-cheater. When I asked if I could record the conversation, he looked askance, and then relented. "Bob Fosse, one of my idols," he smiled, "would always bring his own tape recorder for interviews, to double-check everything that was said." After he had replied to my questions about filmmaking in the 1950s and '60s, the subject of DVDs came up. "I don't approve of voiceover commentaries by directors or scriptwriters," said Resnais. "I think it takes all the magic away. On the other hand, I like making interviews with extracts of scenes; that I find good."

Reflecting on his long career, he said, "When people ask me why I make films, I always answer that *'je tourne pour voir comment ça tourne.'* I make films to see how films are made. I'm proud of that phrase. I'm curious to see what will become of the script, because there are always surprises, and in the end the film does not resemble what one initially expects, generally speaking."

My very first book (a slim paperback) was devoted to, and entitled, *Antonioni-Bergman-Resnais.* I admired the work of Antonioni, I adored utterly Bergman's films, and yet Resnais... what appealed to me in him? It must have been his mathematical control over his material, and the way in which he held you at arm's length for long periods, only to touch the heart with that seemingly endless shot of the gigantic mounds of human hair found in the Auschwitz of *Night and Fog*. Who could have forecast that the severity, even solemnity, of his early work would give way to a flair for musical comedy and late-flowering whimsy? Or that at the age of 91 he would give us yet another feature film, *Aimer, boire et chanter*, based on a play by his beloved Alan Ayckbourn? A film, moreover, that earned him another major festival prize, at the Berlinale, just two weeks before his passing.

On leaving Cambridge, I wrote, in a farewell piece in *Broadsheet*, in June 1962: "Certainly beauty and intelligence are the two qualities that thrill me most in films, and when asked to justify my passion for the cinema I can only mention a handful of scenes that I carry carefully in my mind: the serene sequence in *The Seventh Seal* where, on the hillside, the Knight describes his simple, universal emotions to the wandering players; the final minutes of *L'avventura*, as one of the screen's immortal heroines comes to terms with her disillusion in the grey dawn and the lofty corridors of a vast hotel; or the staggering intensity of Emmanuelle Riva's *cri de coeur* in *Hiroshima mon amour* when, moved by Delerue's beautiful waltz, she exclaims, 'Oh, how I was young once!'"

I also referred to the closing scene of Fellini's *Cabiria*, as Giulietta Masina, with her whimsical, ingenuous face, is encouraged by the playing of the children around her in the road, to accept life's deceptions yet again. I mentioned the "snatches of lyrical melancholy that crop up in the most unexpected places in Truffaut's *Shoot the Piano Player* and *Jules and Jim*, radiating, as Scott Fitzgerald would say, 'That divine vagueness that helps to lift beauty out of time.'" I concluded, in the faintly pompous manner of the final-year student, that "All these moments give me the same proverbial shiver down the spine as the best poetry, music or painting, and make me willing to wade through the mud of innumerable spectacles, B-thrillers and inept British comedies in the hope of suddenly encountering them." I should also have mentioned the film that touched my heart more than any other in that period: Marcel Carné's sublime *Les enfants du paradis*, with its screenplay by Jacques Prévert, and an array of memorable actors bringing to life the tumultuous world of the Paris boulevards in the 19th century.

After graduation, I began to ask myself if, by writing about the cinema, I could achieve fulfilment while performing a useful role for the movie buff. I thought about the job of the critic—the danger of drawing too much attention to oneself with flowery prose, the diminishing return of imposing one's opinions on the reader, the duty to inform, to guide and not pontificate. The critic's work is justified if he can shed some light into the tunnel that links the work ("work of art" is, alas, not always relevant) with the audience. A good review should yield its fruits when read both prior to viewing the film concerned and afterwards, when the spectator's mind teems with his own thoughts and feelings about what he has just watched.

My inspiration as a writer came not from eminent film journalists so much as the poets and authors I admired with such fervour in my late teens. Many years later I had grown to like and admire film critics like Dilys Powell, John Coleman, Andrew Sarris and Michel Ciment, but clearly any kind of elegance of form was anathema to the average journalist assigned to write about movies. Most wrote as though speaking aloud, without any attempt to polish their prose, none more offensive in this regard than the much-vaunted Pauline Kael. I respected Hemingway and Maugham for their ability to produce sentences that were lucid and not so much graceful as euphonic. Then, as now, I often thought of opening sentences and phrases, and would, on waking, transfer them to the typewriter or iMac. I find it much easier to write in the morning than in the afternoon or evening, and by noon I am ready to turn to other activities.

However, in the early 1960s I had little time in which to shape and burnish my own sentences. When reviewing for F. Maurice Speed's weekly, *What's On in London*, I would return from a Wednesday morning press show to the magazine's offices off Oxford Circus, only to find the phone ringing on my desk. It was the printer in Chesham. "Peter, can you just dictate me your first sentence, so we can get that into type, and then you can call in the rest in half an hour or so..." At least one learned to write quickly, and to shrug off the repetition of adjectives or the occasional misspelling of names when *What's On* appeared on the Friday morning.

When Maurice fell victim to a prolonged bout of glandular fever, he asked me to replace him as lead film reviewer, and this I did for some three years, between 1965 and early 1968, starting with reviews of *The Sandpiper* and *Darling*. In September 1965, I warmed to the skills of John Schlesinger in *Darling*, noting that "he catches emotions in the street rather more easily than he catches them in bed." That same week, Renoir's *Boudu* was released in Britain for the first time since 1932. Three months later, in Christmas week 1965, I first saw the young Judi Dench, in *Four in the Morning*, directed by the all-too-soon forgotten Anthony Simmons. In May 1967, I enthused about Coppola's comedy, *You're a Big Boy Now*, writing that "the dialogue has an offbeat, ebullient wackiness about it, and witty observations flash like sparks as Bernard chases a kite through Central Park or fights to subdue an over-productive milk machine in the library canteen." Then there was Kurosawa's *High and Low*, with its "final confrontation between Gondo and the kidnapper, so that the two men's faces seem to merge one with the other, and sum up in a scarifying image the film's basic theme—that both men are motivated by the same instinct, greed for cash and power."

As the 1960s advanced, there was an appetite for films that has never been surpassed, before or since. But not for Hollywood blockbusters, rather for films that aspired to some kind of artistic stature, films that asked questions about society and its shortcomings, about human relationships, and about the means of cinematic expression. So many of the filmmakers of that time acquired lasting fame and respect. The very names evoke the period: Godard, Truffaut, Malle, Chabrol, Bresson, Resnais, Sautet, Demy, Melville, Fellini, Antonioni, Visconti, Bertolucci, Rosi, Bergman, Carlsen, Kalatazov, Chukhrai, Kurosawa, Ozu, Mizoguchi, Satyajit Ray, Lindsay Anderson, Reisz, Schlesinger, Makavejev, Widerberg, Skolimowski, Wajda, Kawalerowicz, Polanski, Munk, Forman, Jancsó, Schlöndorff, Wenders... I could go on, but those thirty-six directors alone would outrank the pantheon of any other decade.

When *Films and Filming* assigned me a monthly column in which I would cover films in production at the studios in and around London, I found myself able, for the first time, to encounter filmmakers, actors and technicians for brief but privileged moments. A publicist would pick me up with a driver at around 8 a.m. and I would spend the entire day on one or more sets in Pinewood, Shepperton or Elstree, the three most active studios of the time.

During 1963, this gig afforded me some memorable interludes, such as watching Sean Connery and Daniela Bianchi making love in a saffron-sheeted bed on *From Russia with Love*, while the camera recorded what Ian Fleming called the couple's "Arabesque" contortions; then Connery at last coming to sit beside me, tearing off a kind of prosthetic "chest-piece" that made him seem even more hirsute than he was in reality, and telling me that "We're even keeping the little touches—Bond's gunmetal cigarette case and lighter, for instance," while a telephone directory for Istanbul on the table next to him stressed the accent on authenticity. He agreed, even then, that "it could become dangerous if one were to play Bond all the time."

Then it was to lunch with director Terence Young in the panelled dining room at Pinewood. Young, tall, aristocratic and debonair, he had been at Cambridge with, among others, Robert Hamer and Ken Adam, and had worked as a prop-boy during the vacations. He saw James Bond as the Bulldog Drummond of a new generation and felt that Connery was the first British actor since Laurence Olivier to stand some chance of earning world stardom. "It's great fun making these films," he said. "It's all right to keep your tongue in your cheek provided you don't poke it out at the public." He had directed, and then supervised the editing, on *Dr. No* and had deliberately accelerated the pace. "Ian Fleming said he thought *Dr. No* was a better film than it was a book," he smiled with pleasure. A technician approached our table and squatted down deferentially beside the director. "For the gypsy fight this afternoon, Mr. Young, what sort of clothes do you want the girls to wear?" Young took a sip of wine and, barely glancing at the man, replied, "Nothing whatsoever," before turning to me and resuming our conversation. The technician slunk away. The women in fact wore ragged bikini tops and bottoms.

Anthony Asquith's *The VIPs* commanded a huge stage at Elstree in order to recreate a terminal at a fogbound London

Airport. Elizabeth Taylor and Richard Burton were scheduled
to give me a few minutes during my day in at the studio, but
apparently the lovers had enjoyed a ferocious squabble in the
Dorchester the previous night during which she suffered a black
eye and he a bruised ankle. Thus Asquith was obliged to film
madame from the waist downwards and monsieur from the
waist up, and neither actor was available for interviews.

Flashback: Anthony Asquith

For too long languishing in Hitchcock's burly shadow, Anthony
Asquith (or "Puffin," as he liked everyone to call him) was a
charming maverick who emerged from one of Britain's most
patrician families. His father, Herbert, the Earl of Oxford, had
been Prime Minister from 1908-16, and his mother, Margot
Asquith, was a celebrated socialite and aspiring writer. Puffin
studied at Oxford, and, a reluctant aristocrat, then journeyed
to Hollywood to study the film industry in the mid-1920s,
staying with Douglas Fairbanks and Mary Pickford for three
months in their palatial home.

Immediately on his return to England, Puffin wrote the
screenplay of *Shooting Stars* (1927), a satirical melodrama
directed by A. V. Bramble. Puffin served as assistant director
and also as editor. "One prided oneself at not needing a
musical accompaniment," he recalled, "but we did a musical
soundtrack because the film appeared just as sound was
coming in."

By 1929, his reputation was assured, and he made his finest
silent movie, *Cottage on Dartmoor*. The script was based on a
story that had appeared in the *Weekly Dispatch*, "but, except
for the actual escape, we concocted the sequences ourselves,"
said Puffin. "The last sequence is a sort of Liebestod edited
in the style of Eisenstein and Pudovkin." This succès d'estime
introduced the richest decade in Asquith's career, culminating
in *Pygmalion* (1938). "I wanted to include a scene of triumph
at the Ambassador's Ball, so I arranged a lunch with Bernard
Shaw, and for some reason or another Shaw liked my line 'She
came up the stairs with the frozen calm of a sleep-walker,'
and he wrote the scene for us." Three endings were shot for
Pygmalion, with Professor Higgins' removing his hat in the
final shot being a touch invented by Puffin, who also told me

that he was proud of having written the line, "In Hertford, Hereford and Hampshire, hurricanes hardly happen." In fact, he added, "*My Fair Lady* is really closer to the film than to the play." Higgins was played by Leslie Howard, whom Puffin remembered as "a brilliant technician. He could repeat a shot half a dozen times and his eyebrow would be raised to exactly the same degree."

The Browning Version (1950) remains Asquith's most poignant achievement. He seemed to be on exactly the same wavelength as playwright Terence Rattigan, with whom he made several films. "I'd wanted to do this play for years," said Puffin. "Fortunately, [the American film producer] Earl St. John fought on my behalf against the entire Rank board—and won." Michael Redgrave's performance as the tortured schoolmaster justly earned him the Best Actor award at Cannes the following spring. Asquith was, like Rattigan, a closet gay whose tense features and social timidity suggested that he felt ashamed of his disposition.

The Importance of Being Earnest (1951) proved to be Asquith's greatest box-office success, and arguably the smartest screen adaptation of any Oscar Wilde play. "I insisted on 'curtain up,' 'curtain down' so as to preserve the stage conventions." Who can forget Edith Evans as Lady Bracknell, her tone forever interrogatory, her comportment a regal passage of purple plumage across the drawing-rooms of one fashionable house after another. "I remember we were told that the Americans didn't know the word 'perambulator,'" smiled Puffin. "And so we decided to say 'baby-carriage' instead. But Edith drew herself up and pronounced magnificently, 'As a Dame of the British Empire, I protest against this!'"

In late 1957, Asquith's plans for making a film about Lawrence of Arabia came tantalisingly close to fruition. Rattigan wrote a script, later converted into the stage play entitled *Ross*, and Paramount, followed later by Rank, had agreed to back the project. "I'd been to Iraq and found the locations," said Puffin wistfully, "and we were thinking of Bogarde, Guinness or Burton for the title role. I'd met Lawrence once at my sister's house. He was so small physically, and the most striking thing about him were his blue eyes."

In early 1963, while Asquith was shooting *The V.I.P.s* at Borehamwood Studios in north London, *Films and Filming* commissioned me to write a profile of this most English of directors. I visited the set, and Puffin grew excited at the prospect of such attention in a "serious" publication. His leg in plaster due to cartilage problems, he deprecated his work on *The V.I.P.s* at every opportunity: "I didn't work on this script," or "One doesn't feel that it's quite one's own child," and "The difficulty of this production is that I'm constantly having to shoot round all sorts of characters." He fretted over shooting in CinemaScope: "It's frightfully limiting—you can't concentrate, and it's much slower because your eye has time to wander." To my surprise, he arranged for me to see almost all his important films on a succession of weekday mornings, in the tiny viewing theatre above the NFT on London's South Bank. More often than not, he would attend. Like most critics, I'm averse to having to watch a film with the director sitting nearby, but Puffin was so self-effacing, so utterly lacking in arrogance, that my enjoyment of his work was enhanced by his presence.

When my survey of his career appeared in *Films and Filming*, Puffin sent me a charming letter. He was relieved that I had not slaughtered his efforts. Accompanied by an aristocratic woman of a certain age and whose name I have long forgotten, he treated me to lunch at the Hyde Park Hotel in Knightsbridge, and gave me an exquisite book on the history of ballooning, one of the few subjects Puffin himself had not essayed in his screen work. Only two tidbits of wisdom can be found in the notes I made afterwards: "The point of a close-up is not that it's 'close' but that it isolates," and "I've never been an actor, so I don't have any temptation to instruct them!" Highly strung, seemingly frail and almost too gentle to have survived in the film business across six decades, Puffin Asquith gave you the impression that he really needed your opinion of his work. Pretty rare, for a film director.

Around the time of *The V.I.P.s*, Elstree also welcomed Robert Wise's *The Haunting*, with its elaborate, two-storied sets spread over the largest (18,000 square feet) stage at the studios. Julie Harris played Eleanor, one of the researchers into what is now called "paranormal activity" at an old dark house. I had a crush on Julie from the moment I saw her magical performance as Sally Bowles in *I Am a Camera*. Like Naomi Watts, Julie Harris always looked younger than her years (she was, for example, almost 17 when she played 12-year-old Frankie Addams in *The Member of the Wedding* in 1952), and as I entered her trailer beside the set, she seemed utterly pristine. When Wise first discussed *The Haunting* with her, she offered to learn the whole script by heart. Called on set by the assistant director for a rehearsal with other actors, Julie entered a kind of trance, apparently oblivious to the technicians and makeup team around her.

Occasionally I would visit a film on location. Harold Pinter's play, *The Caretaker*, was being brought to the screen by Clive Donner, and I clambered up to the attic of an aged house near Hackney Downs to meet him, the lighting cameraman Nicolas Roeg, the actors Robert Shaw and Alan Bates, and of course Pinter himself, bobbing and peering in the cramped confines of the garret-like "set." The playwright relished his pomp, with Joseph Losey directing his screenplay for *The Servant* down in Shepperton, and the sublime script for *Accident* a few years in the future. He enjoyed discomfiting a young interviewer like me. When I asked about the sociological implications of *The Caretaker*, he looked quizzically at me and said, "Society? I don't know what 'society' means. What do you think?" He continued in enlightening vein: "This is just a particular film about particular people in particular circumstances." He remarked, en passant, that Noël Coward had joined more than two dozen others in squeezing into the attic the previous day.

Another excursion took me to Box Hill, a patch of sharply undulating scrubland near Dorking in Surrey, and the location, almost four decades later, for the opening battle sequence in *Gladiator*. Here Carl Foreman, the screenwriter and producer, flushed with the box-office triumph of *The Guns of Navarone*, was directing his first film, *The Victors*. The story traced the fortunes of a squad of American soldiers through the Second World War, from the Battle of Britain to the peace in 1945. For what seemed like hours I stood on the windswept ridge, flanked by George Peppard and George Hamilton. Peppard, the heart-throb lead in *Breakfast at Tiffany's*, and Hamilton, the world's "most eligible bachelor," proceeded to conduct an informal "auction" for my grey woollen overcoat. For some reason they loved the leather buttons and large lapels. It did seem more protective than the khaki blankets they had been given by the crew, though I can report that I held on to my coat at the end of that bone-chilling day in Surrey.

The form, or should I say formula, of the *International Film Guide*, stemmed from my father's annual *Antiques Yearbook*, which he had conceived, edited and published at the end of the 1940s. In short, an annual book that would engross anyone interested in the subject. We would include reviews of new films, profiles of directors, a guide to film magazines and to bookshops specialising in film, and so on. The knack in the first year was to attract sufficient advertising to pay for the printing and production, thus leaving one net revenue from the sales of the book itself. This in turn meant that we could sell the *Guide* at a very reasonable price (around $18 in today's money). I even copied certain attributes from my father's creation—a distinctive yellow cover, for example, and a publishing schedule in the late autumn, with the following year's date on the cover, thus prolonging the shelf life of each edition.

Gaining support for the *Guide* proved more difficult in my home country than it would in Europe. One always remembers the few who contribute support when all one has to offer is charm and promises. Charles Cooper was my first target. He ran Contemporary Films in Soho Square, and released the work of masters like Eisenstein, Kurosawa and Satyajit Ray. He listened patiently to my patter, but his telephone rang every few minutes, and he answered it with the same protracted courtesy as he extended to me. I thought he would never make a decision, but at last, when he replaced the phone for the fourth time, he said quietly, "Of course, we'll need a full page." With Contemporary on board, I could persuade other leaders of the arthouse field, like Connoisseur Films and the Curzon and Academy cinemas, to take space in a book that did not yet exist.

My wife and I toured Germany in search of business for the upcoming *IFG*. I was determined to include as many countries as possible in our world survey section, and so I made contact with DEFA, the East German film authority. They sent me a letter on wafer-thin airmail paper, telling me that

ESSENTIAL NEW CONTENTS, including surveys of films from 15 countries, with complete guide to Festivals, Animation, Sponsored Films, Specialist Cinemas, Books & Magazines. 110 Illustrations. "Excellent value" - SIGHT AND SOUND

International

FILM GUIDE

1965

Only 8s.6d. (7 Frs.) for 304 Pages

Directors of the Year: Fellini, Malle, Buñuel, Kubrick, Satyajit Ray

EDITED BY PETER COWIE

The cover of the second edition of the annual
International Film Guide.

I would need to show the correspondence to the border agents when crossing into East Germany. I duly arrived at Checkpoint Charlie at the foot of Friedrichstrasse in Berlin, and after being waved through by the West German guards, I reached the East German frontier and had to surrender my passport along with the letter from DEFA. For some twenty minutes I was kept in a windowless waiting room. Every so often a small shutter was lifted and I could see a pair of eyes scrutinising me. Eventually my documents were returned and I entered the austere streets of East Berlin. I took the subway to Milastrasse, where DEFA had its headquarters. During the journey I noted how virtually all the other passengers were reading *Neues Deutschland*, the state daily newspaper. Their gaze was fixed, as though hypnotised, and for a time I felt that I had stumbled into some kind of sci-fi conspiracy. At DEFA, the personnel were cordial and happy to support the *Guide*. I emphasised that I would write the reviews of their films and that I could not reprint "official" declarations about cinema in the "German Democratic Republic." As dusk fell, I was relieved to pass through Checkpoint Charlie without undue delay.

Visiting Paris in the first days of October 1962, I made a pilgrimage to Studio des Ursulines, the world's first "arthouse" cinema, founded in the Quartier Latin in 1926 by Armand Tallier and Laurence Myrga. Man Ray, André Breton, Fernand Léger and René Clair attended the maiden screening. I found myself irresistibly attracted to the arthouse as an institution. These little temples of discovery and delight treated the cinema with respect, showing "original versions" (not dubbed into French), and often involving the audience in a discussion of a film's merits after it had been screened. France could boast of more than a hundred genuine salles d'art et d'essai, forty-two of them in Paris alone, so the main thrust of my annual *International Film Guide* in its early years was a celebration of the arthouse movement across Europe. My then wife Elisabeth and I drove through Holland, Germany, Switzerland, and later Denmark and Sweden, interviewing the proprietors and programmers of each cinema. I persuaded several of them to support the *Guide* by taking a small advertisement. Whether or not they did so, I still wrote a review of their activities, trying to pin down their special atmosphere and tradition.

Many of the Parisian arthouses were run by women: Line Peillon at the Ursulines, Yvonne Decaris at La Pagôde, Danièle Wasserman at Studio Acacias. None of these cultural entrepreneurs struck me as prosperous. Even with government subsidies, the margins for an arthouse were tight—and are even more so today. Yvonne Decaris, with her elegance and old-Saint-Jean-Cap-Ferrat world courtesy, had made La Pagôde into one of the most appealing cinemas in Paris. She invited me to a reception one evening. I cannot recall the film that was screened, but I was most impressed at being able to have a spontaneous chat with Irish émigrés Samuel Beckett and Peter Lennon, Beckett the shy one, backed into a corner of the crowded room, his hair springing luxuriantly from that gaunt, sensitive head of his. I quickly found that creative celebrities (or celebrated creators) do not want to touch on the profound when talking to people they have never seen before.

My first hotel in Paris was on the rue de Lille, in the 7th arrondissement. The room was clad with cobwebs, and one washed in a bowl of chilly water. With mobile phones not even a pipe-dream in 1962, my only way of contacting clients was by visiting the main post office on the Champs-Elysées. There one waited for a cabin and made one's calls. Or one could buy a beer or a hard-boiled egg at a café, and ask the bar-man for a jeton, a metal token that enabled one to make a local call from the bowels of the café, usually next to the toilets.

Certain exhibitors linger vividly in my memory. Pierre Braunberger, for example, a diminutive, bullet-headed man who had worked with Irving Thalberg and Jean Renoir in the late 1920s and who, when I met him, was producing films by Truffaut and Godard. He ran an arthouse called Le Panthéon and, although he refused to take an advertisement in the *International Film Guide*, he introduced me to other exhibitors and, when we met again at the Hyères Festival in 1965, to Louise de Vilmorin, the elegant screenwriter of Louis Malle's *Les amants*. Then there was Henri Ginet, a gracious, moustachioed gentleman who might have strayed from the pages of Stendhal or Flaubert, and who programmed Le Ranelagh, in the heart of bourgeois Passy. Ginet mounted exhibitions of modern and surrealist art in a gallery adjacent to the cinema, and sought out interesting shorts to accompany the main feature.

The Dutch welcomed my youthful enthusiasm from the outset. One day in early 1963, I was asked to visit the offices of Cecil Cattermoul in Broadwick Street in London's West End. There a balding, elderly man of considerable girth told me that the Netherlands Government Information Office would like to welcome me to Holland as soon as possible, so that I could write about the latest short films and their directors. I received an air ticket from KLM, and was welcomed at the airport by a cigar-puffing Portuguese Dutchman who would act as my guide over three days. The visit began with a lunch at the Châlet Suisse in The Hague, hosted by a discreet, meticulous man named S. I. van Nooten. I warmed to him immediately, and for many years he would remain a staunch advocate of the *International Film Guide*. Driven from town to town, studio to studio, in a haze of cigar smoke, I met and liked such neophyte film-makers as Paul Verhoeven, Frans Weisz, Nikolai van der Heyde, George Sluizer and Pim de la Parra & Wim Verstappen. The quiet, ambitious Jan de Bont was a budding cinematographer, shooting films like Adriaan Ditvoorst's haunting *Paranoia*, a few years before commencing his long collaboration with Paul Verhoeven. His formidable career included the cinematography on *Basic Instinct* and the directing of two nail-biting thrillers, *Speed* and *Twister*.

In Holland I was also introduced to the great Bert Haanstra, then in his fifties and at the peak of his artistic career, having won an Oscar for *Glass*. The director with whom I stayed in contact until his death in 2007, however, was Fons Rademakers, a man of considerable vision and versatility. His *Village by the River* had been the first Dutch film ever nominated for an Academy Award, and in 1976 he would win the Oscar in the same category for *The Assault*.

It was in the Netherlands that I found the first mentor of my adult life. Dick Vriesman was a Dutchman who had, with a trio of friends, established *Excerpta Medica* in 1946. This medical reference source has survived and flourished under the aegis of Reed Elsevier and more recently Adelphi. Dick's hobby was the Leidsepleintheater, a 400-seat arthouse in the heart of Amsterdam. He appreciated my commitment to the cause so much that he persuaded the Confédération Internationale des Cinémas d'Art et d'Essai, of which he was Chairman at that period, to recognise *International Film Guide* as its official publication—an endorsement I proudly trumpeted on the front cover of our 1967 edition. Dick, having enjoyed financial success early in life, took great delight in introducing me to the pleasures of Dutch genever. Not to excess, but to an exact timetable. Precisely at 5 p.m., I would arrive at his home close to the Rembrandt House, and he would go to the fridge for a tall, chunky bottle of Bokma. The "Young" Bokma, not the "Old" genever (which, frankly, I rather preferred). This would be dispensed in small glasses, to the accompaniment of salted almonds. And after the second glass, with the candles lit for the encroaching dusk, one felt that all was right with the world.

The late Donald Richie wrote that "A journey is always also something of a flight. You go to reach, but you also go to escape." I never became a festival junkie, and I nurse a secret admiration for those like my colleagues Dan and Edna Fainaru, who led a nomadic existence throughout the year, flying from one festival to the next while never appearing fatigued or even dishevelled. However, for the next half century I attended at least three or four film festivals each year, and such trips, it is true, do involve something of an escape from the routine of home.

I attended my very first festival in Locarno in August 1963. Locarno was under the direction of Vinicio Beretta, a suave, unflappable individual who wore an eye patch. An apocryphal rumour suggested that he was forever planning a retrospective of the work of John Ford, Raoul Walsh and André de Toth, all of whom shared the same disability as Beretta himself.

I watched Visconti's *The Leopard* on the vast screen erected in the gardens of the Grand Hotel, then drove out of Locarno at about 10 p.m. Thanks to clear roads and a determination to stay awake, I reached Calais around noon the next day, collapsing on to the car ferry and eager to get home. Even though I have now lived in Switzerland since 2002, I only recently returned to the Locarno Film Festival in 2016, in part because it occurs in August, the one month in which one is most likely to meet friends and family for some kind of holiday, and in part because, like Browning's thrush, I feared that I never could recapture the first fine careless rapture.

The Swiss actor Michel Simon visited the Locarno event, and at a party in the Grand Hotel I talked to him about *Boudu Saved from Drowning* and his relationship with Renoir, about whom he was polite. One sensed that at 68, his antic ferocity had diminished, even if his physical size and satyric head remained impressive. Lotte Eisner, the great specialist in Murnau and Lang, and chief archivist for Henri Langlois at the

Cinémathèque française, took me under her wing and regaled me with stories of the silent era in German cinema. A Jewess who had fled to France in 1933, but had been caught and held in a concentration camp in Aquitaine, she had no hesitation in proclaiming during an alfresco lunch in Locarno: "I hate ze Gairmans!" Thanks to Lotte, I could visit the Cinémathèque on subsequent trips to France, encountering Langlois' muse, Mary Meerson, and even the notorious man himself. The magpie of film preservation, Langlois collected every reel within sight. He would keep them in sundry locations, including his bathtub and his refrigerator, and he cared little if Victor Sjöström's *The Outlaw and His Wife*, for example, was projected to the public without subtitles. To be fair to Langlois, a young Volker Schlöndorff had in earlier years been asked to sit in the front row and offer impromptu translations of German dialogue and inter-titles for the audience.

Flashback: Jean Renoir and Michel Simon

La chienne epitomises the brief if incandescent partnership between Jean Renoir, a director just reaching maturity at the close of the 1920s, and Michel Simon, a Swiss-born actor who kowtowed to no one. They were born less than a year apart, but they came from vastly different milieus (Renoir grew up around the artistic and intellectual friends of his father, Impressionist painter Pierre-Auguste Renoir; Simon was the son of a Swiss sausage-maker), and although they both made their way into military service, their experiences in the Great War could not have been more divergent. Renoir had been wounded at the outset of hostilities, and then returned to the Western Front as a lieutenant in the French Air Force (which inspired Jean Gabin's character in *Grand Illusion*). Simon, however, had been conscripted into the Swiss Army, and then swiftly dismissed for suffering from tuberculosis, and because he was regarded as disobedient and recalcitrant.

Each man came to the cinema via a different route. Renoir worshipped the genius of Chaplin, much admired Griffith, and when he met and fell in love with an accomplished actress working under the name "Dédée," he resolved to embrace the movies as a career. Catherine Hessling, as Dédée was known socially, became Renoir's wife and starred in his first few features—*Backbiters* (1924), *Whirlpool of Fate* (1925) and *Nana* (1926). Michel Simon, by contrast, had plunged into the legitimate theatre, gaining an early role in a Swiss production of Shakespeare's *Measure for Measure* in 1920, and then in stage productions of works by Shaw, Wilde, Pirandello and other playwrights of the time.

Although Renoir had been in touch with Simon since 1928, when he made *Tire au flanc* (*The Sad Sack*) and gave the actor his first starring role, their collaboration burned most intensely during a twenty-month period from late 1930 to 1932, during which they made three pictures together, including *La chienne*. Their second collaboration was *On purge bébé* (Renoir's first sound film), released in 1931, followed that year by *La chienne*, and in 1932 by *Boudu Saved from Drowning*, in which Simon had performed in the original 1925 Paris stage production. Of course, Simon would appear in memorable work by other directors, including Jean Vigo and Marcel Carné, but his performances for Renoir bore an undertow of danger and folly that set them apart.

Had the Second World War not intervened, I think Simon would have made even more films with Renoir. As it is, he starred as the Baron Scarpia in Renoir's adaptation of *Tosca*, which was completed by Carl Koch after Renoir fled Mussolini's Italy in 1940 (Simon, with his Swiss passport, could stay on unimpeded). As late as 1965, Renoir briefly considered casting Simon in a project entitled *C'est la révolution*—which mutated into the made-for-television movie *The Little Theatre of Jean Renoir*, and four years later in an uncompleted film that would have been entitled *Julienne et son amour*, revolving around a prostitute in pre-1914 Paris. Simon would have played Julienne's best customer.

He could be ingratiating, sinister, sadistic, vulgar, witty, and even violent (he once threatened Renoir with a gun after the accidental death of his beloved Janie Marèse, his co-star in *La chienne*). Renoir wrote in his autobiography that Simon "was exceptionally penetrating in his condemnation of the stupidity and bad taste of our time." He noted Simon's love of animals, and monkeys especially, his belief in health foods, and the fact that his friend and colleague "was reputed to be particularly interested in unorthodox sexual practices."

When I met Simon at Locarno in 1963, he had the presence of an ex-pugilist. His nose, protuberant like Depardieu's, seemed to have absorbed a lot of punishment. His smile reminded you of a child obliged to eat a lemon. His hair had remained relatively luxuriant, adding to his height in a crowd. He listened courteously when I asked him, for some reason I have long forgotten, if he had ever appeared on-screen with Annabella, another star of the 1930s. He replied, with infinite patience, that in fact he never had. We were then interrupted by Valerio Zurlini, who declared that the Italian cinema had remained the same since 1945. Simon quipped that in France the opposite applied—everything had changed with the New Wave.

In the autumn of 1967, the London Film Festival screened *La Marseillaise*, which had slumbered almost unseen since the 1930s. Renoir bustled cheerfully onstage, telling us how the film had been misunderstood upon its first release. He had shot it on the basis of many months of detailed research. He had, he said, written very little dialogue, and had drawn the essential gist of the film from documents dating from the 1790s. Renoir's ebullient personality literally beamed off the stage. The great head hunched forward, the voice husky from half a century's worth of cigarettes, and the hands gesticulating like Stokowski at his peak. Some of us had gathered at the side door to catch his arrival and were rewarded with a quick, almost gentle handshake. By then, the maestro was in the evening of his career, with only *The Little Theatre* ahead of him, and he and Simon would never again work together.

Some memorable screen moments still lay ahead for Michel Simon, however—notably, that very year, as the crusty, politically incorrect grandpa in Claude Berri's *The Two of Us*, which won him a Silver Bear at Berlin. In 1964, he played the aged engineer condemned for sabotage in Frankenheimer's *The Train*, and in 1970 he portrayed a crusty, retired professor in *The House* (directed by Polanski's screenwriter, Gérard Brach). Two years later, he was the lascivious "Master" in Borowczyk's *Blanche*.

Simon died in 1975, at the age of 80, just a few days after the release of *The Red Ibis*, his final film; Renoir would pass on four years after his friend, the erstwhile right-wing anarchist who had somehow bonded with the greatest of all French directors and a committed supporter of Léon Blum's left-wing Popular Front. When he heard of Simon's death, Renoir wrote to Claude Beylie that "the sun has turned darker..."

I met some of my early life's principal friends and acquaintances at that Locarno festival of 1963. Felix Bucher had been born and bred in Lucerne. Orphaned far too early, during the Second World War, he had been raised by his maiden aunts. His right hand was malformed, but Felix took gleeful advantage of the fact to introduce himself to all newcomers, thrusting a prehensile, webbed forefinger and middle-finger into your hand for a vigorous shake, accompanied by a broad smile of complicity worthy of Fernandel. We found from the outset that we shared the same sense of humour, with nothing sacred and even the most miserable prospect transformed by laughter into a glowing horizon. His knowledge of classical music was rivalled only by his passion for the cinema. Many years after our first encounter, he compiled a formidable dictionary of German cinema which we published at Tantivy. It remains a standard work. I admired my new friend's ability to mix with all manner of people. Felix could, as Rudyard Kipling would have appreciated, walk with kings and yet not lose the common touch. He was loyal without question, and not just to his tightly-knit Catholic circle in Lucerne.

Felix and I would meet at festivals in Cannes and Berlin. I still have a snapshot of him at a seminar held in Budapest, seated near me and two other friends from that era, Arne Svensson and Gerald Pratley. Felix and his close chums Hans and Eugenia Bolli would come over to Glyndebourne every summer, always accompanied by fine wines and cognac that would be enjoyed on the sloping lawns of that country mansion. Then, in October 1988, I received a phone call on the *Variety* stand at the MIFED in Milan. Felix had died unexpectedly. He was just 50 years of age.

Another journalist at the Locarno festival, the Austrian Goswin Dörfler, appeared some ten years older than I. Gentle, and speaking in the soft tones of Vienna, Goswin sat next to me at meals and, during the hot afternoons, sunbathed beside the lake at the Hotel Palma au Lac where most critics were accommodated during the festival. One day I asked him, disingenuously, how he had acquired the deep, white scars that ran across his shoulders. With no hint of embarrassment, he said that he and some friends would often go out at weekends into the woods around Vienna. There he would be tied to a tree and lashed by his friends with whips until the blood ran and Goswin could abandon himself to an exquisite frenzy. I discovered later that he spent more time in the clubs of Berlin than he did at screenings during the Berlinale. But, like Felix, he had a scholarly bent, and wrote articles for Tantivy's magazine *Focus on Film*, and contributed an annual round-up on Austrian cinema for the *International Film Guide*. We exchanged Christmas cards, his always ecclesiastical in nature, until his death some forty years later.

The *Variety* journalist Gene Moskowitz at first intimidated me. He entered the hotel dining room in Locarno like an urbane mafioso—midnight-blue blazer wound around his barrel-like girth, sunglasses beneath the dark, curly, carefully gelled hair, cigar in hand. Yet beneath this hands-off exterior dwelled a man of immense warmth and discriminating vision where films— and particularly European films—were concerned. He reviewed thousands of new titles for *Variety*, and despite his eminence had the gift of listening to the opinions of others. Stricken by leukaemia while still in middle age, Gene retained his sang-froid to the very end; friends would take turns in pushing his wheelchair into screening rooms and through the streets of Cannes during the festival.

Unlike Cannes or Venice, the two pre-eminent West German festivals of the 1960s had neither beaches nor starlets to compensate for the unremitting hours of projection. The Oberhausen Short Film Festival in the Ruhrland was a working festival, a vital smoke-filled forum for discussion of the problems facing the future of short films, and a shop-window for more than eighty of them. Here one discovered the tart, magical draughtsmanship of cartoons from Zagreb Film, the graphic mastery of Polish animators like Jan Lenica and Walerian Borowczyk, the puppets brought to life on screen by Jiří Trnka, and Chris Marker's haunting journeys into unfamiliar lands, none more poignant than *Le Mystère Koumiko*, the director's tribute to a gravely beautiful young woman from the Unifrance office in Tokyo during the 1964 Olympics.

In Oberhausen, during those chilly February nights, I met film buffs who would become acquaintances, and some-times friends, for life: Gerald Pratley, the courteous and much respected film critic from Canada; Ronald Holloway, a lapsed priest from Chicago who had made a new life as a film critic in Germany; and Leo Dratfield, the quiet, chuckling distributor from New York's Contemporary Films.

When I read that Orson Welles would be shooting parts of *The Trial* in Zagreb, I had to consult an atlas to find the loca-tion of that offbeat name. It was of course in the heart of Tito's Yugoslavia, the only Communist state readily accessible to Western Europeans. So when in the mid-1960s Želimir Matko, sales manager at Zagreb Film, visited my office in London and declared his admiration for the *International Film Guide* and the section we had devoted to animated film, I welcomed him happily and took him to lunch in Soho, where he requested a large portion of cottage cheese. He spoke fluent English, and made constant jokes at his own expense, urging me to visit the studios of Zagreb Film. I never did, but I was able to meet many of the animators annually at Oberhausen. I remember taking a bottle of whisky to give him when he invited me to the Pula Festival in Croatia in 1968. With a hearty laugh he explained that he was president of the teetotallers association of Yugo-slavia—but that there were only three members!

The Zagreb animators were fast gaining a worldwide repu-tation on the arthouse circuit with their cartoons built on a succession of incidents and wicked jokes. Each had a distinctive personality. The satirically-minded Dušan Vukotić had won the first Academy Award for animation from a country other than the United States, with *Ersatz* in 1961. Some years later he made *A Stain on His Conscience*, combining live action with anima-tion to create a weird and terrifying atmosphere. There was the witty and poetic Žlatko Grgić, the background painter Žlatko

Ronald Holloway's study of Zagreb animators,
published by Tantivy in 1972.

Bourek, the protean designer Boris Kolar, the fluent script-writer Dragutin Vunak, and the observant humourist Borivoj Dovniković, who all attended the Oberhausen Short Film Festival and expressed their pride in the studio. My favourites were Nikola Majdak, a photographer whose subtly-coloured *Time of the Vampires* enchanted me, and Nedeljko Dragić, whose *Tamer of Wild Horses* was a prodigious animated paradigm for misguided oppression, all flowing movement and twilight colours—animation serving as inspired shorthand, no less.

In a single year towards the end of the decade, no fewer than 857 copies of Zagreb cartoons were screened in the cinemas of 45 countries. In 1972, I published *Z is for Zagreb*, by Ronald Holloway, a guide to the leading lights at the studio.

If Henri Langlois with his magpie instincts was committed to cinema as an archivist, then a majority of the key directors of the early 1960s were driven by a now-faded kind of idealism. Everything needed fixing: Africa, north and south, suffered the agony of colonial and post-colonial struggles; south-east Asia twitched in the hands of dictators or corrupt administrations that the Americans, Russians and Chinese strove to exploit. In my own country the Macmillan years may have proved prosperous, but could not disguise the need for innovation in the arts, in everyday cuisine, and in transportation. That innovation sprang from the roots of society, not from its governors. The Beatles, and then the Rolling Stones, transformed the soundscape of popular music. André Courrèges in Paris and Mary Quant in London introduced the mini-skirt and gave everyday clothes a brightly-spangled zest in contrast to the grey, postwar orthodoxy. Terence Conran brought to his Habitat stores a flair he had discovered while traveling on "the continent," as Brits condescendingly described other parts of Europe.

The inaugural edition of the *International Film Guide* had gone to press, which in those days involved a long process, with each illustration rendered by means of a copper plate nailed to a block of wood and tapped into place within the signature frame (areas of 16 or 32 pages arranged so that when eventually printed they could be folded and bound in sequence). In November 1963, the *International Film Guide* was printed and bound in Holland (where, until the devaluation of the pound in 1967, prices for printing were less expensive than in the U.K.) The books arrived in crates at the Port of London. Clearing the merchandise involved several trips to dingy offices, in which the precious "Bills of Lading" were scrutinised and initialled by humourless customs officers. So as to integrate the stills into the text, we had chosen a quite expensive coated paper which, if not as fine as the art paper you found in luxurious books about painters, still struck my friends as unusual. When I took one of the first copies with me to a press show at the small MGM theatre in St. James' Street, Tom Vallance (a colleague on *Films and Filming*) opened the book as wide as possible and put his nose deep into the spine, sniffing that special odour of print and paper.

This maiden effort was greeted with enthusiasm by the press. Dilys Powell, in *The Sunday Times*, said she "stretched out an eager hand for [this] new survey edited by Peter Cowie: indices to the work of chosen directors, data on international production, magazines, specialist cinemas, festivals—it looks readable too." Brenda Davies in *Sight and Sound* wrote: "Excellent value at a very reasonable price is offered in this pocket-sized volume, which contains a range of information formerly to be found only in expensive and inaccessible reference books." *Films and Filming* said that "for a first edition it shows promise of becoming as essential to the filmgoer as the Michelin to the bon vivant." I was tickled, too, by the review in the French monthly *Cinéma 64*, which ended its positive comments with, "Même à ceux qui manient sans brio la langue de Shakespeare, cet aide-mémoire bien informé rendra plus d'un service." ["Even for those who handle Shakespeare's language without flair, this well-informed reference guide will be of great help."]

Flashback: Lindsay Anderson

Lindsay Anderson, the perennial outsider in English film circles, remained the clarion-caller for his generation. Contemporaries like John Schlesinger, Tony Richardson and Karel Reisz sooner or later all responded to the seductive appeal of the studios, but Lindsay (like his younger compatriot Ken Loach) refused to go to Hollywood. He was fond of Matthew Arnold's great poem "The Scholar-Gipsy" and the poet's urging the wandering scholar to pursue an independent path far from "the sick hurry and divided aims" of modern life.

I first met Lindsay in late 1963, under the eaves of the Royal Court Theatre in London's Sloane Square. That was his spiritual home, where he directed such indelible productions as *The Long and the Short and the Tall* and *Serjeant Musgrave's Dance*. He found it easier to experiment in the theatre, where budgets were not so vast and a pool of new talent lay readily to hand. I was surprised at how affable Lindsay was to such a young journalist as myself, and he sat back in his chair and chatted freely. He stressed that *This Sporting Life* (released that year) had been something of a miracle. "Tony Richardson had often asked me, 'Why don't

you make a film for [my production company] Woodfall?'
I read the book by David Storey immediately it was published,
but Woodfall was outbid in a rush for the rights. Independent
Artists won and asked Karel Reisz to direct it. But he said no,
partly because it wasn't his kind of subject, and partly because
he wanted to get exposure as a producer, if I directed it! So
there you are." Lindsay remarked that while he didn't like the
films of Alain Resnais, he admired him as a stylist, and especially the audacity of his montage. "What he's done gave
us courage in one or two places in *This Sporting Life.*" He
added that the entire structure of the film was created stylis-
tically in the poetic realism tradition of Humphrey Jennings,
the British documentarist he so admired.

Over the years, Lindsay and I would exchange letters and
run into each other at the bar of the National Film Theatre.
"My chief objection to filming abroad," he confessed, "is
that one tends to work where one has one's roots. I would
be extremely hesitant to make a film [in America] unless the
subject matter was something I felt I could really come close
to" (which happened much later, with *The Whales of August*
in 1987, though hardly a studio film). He cherished the idea
of filming *Wuthering Heights*, with Richard Harris as Heath-
cliff. "Buñuel had wanted to make it in his surrealist days, but
by the time he did so in 1954 he'd rather lost the feel for it.
Wyler's version was a well-made commercial picture." The
project had gathered momentum while he was shooting *This
Sporting Life* up in Yorkshire, but, like so many of his plans,
it foundered.

To a large extent, Lindsay was forever haunted by the
failure of the Free Cinema movement of the late 1950s. He
described it tersely: "Half-a-dozen would-be filmmakers
combined to present work […] at the National Film Theatre,
coined a provocative title and wrote a coat-trailing manifesto—filmmakers against a constipated, class-bound British
cinema which in no way reflected the realities of today."
Lindsay spent the next four decades striving against the
current, sporadically giving birth to films that laid bare the
hypocrisy of a conservative society: *This Sporting Life*, *if....*,
O Lucky Man! and *Britannia Hospital.*

In September 1981, he wrote to me about *Britannia Hospital*: "Another all out, crazy and unfashionable venture which our highbrow friends at the [British Film] Institute will intensely dislike and have pleasure in putting down, but to Hell with them. Onward!" His fears proved all too accurate, and in February 1983 he said that, "It's been extraordinarily disappointing that the film has had so little support in Britain. I don't refer to the attacks and the dismissals—those I have learned to expect. But it has been truly discouraging to see the centres of resistance contract, and the outposts of dissidence and independent thought fall, one by one."

Garrulous and acerbic without ever quite slipping into cynicism, Lindsay enjoyed decrying all things trendy. In the late 1960s I asked him to compare *Sequence*, the magazine he and others had started at Oxford in the 1940s, with the modish *Movie*, for many years a British equivalent of *Cahiers du Cinéma*. "*Sequence* was based on enthusiasm," he replied. "In *Movie*, they simply give judgements—nearly all of them second-hand."

For all the savagery of his satire, Lindsay could also be sentimental, to the point of preferring Ford's *My Darling Clementine* and *She Wore a Yellow Ribbon* to the harsher mood of *The Searchers*, and therein may have lain his rejection at the hands of the critical "establishment" in Britain. When I asked him in 1983 to write a piece about British cinema for the *International Film Guide*, he referred to "the whole, useless army of institutional, over-subsidised academics," adding that he found it difficult to write about British cinema "without seeming (and perhaps being) a bit personally jaundiced."

We celebrated the 25th anniversary of the *Guide* in 1987, and Lindsay gladly came along to the NFT to introduce *if....*, which I had chosen to open the season accorded to us by the BFI. He was all too nice about my book, describing it as "like *Wisden* to the cricketer, *Spotlight* to the casting director, *Debrett* to the snob: a rich and indispensable source of entertainment and information." He concluded his speech with an eloquent dig at the Thatcher-Reagan years: "The 1960s remain both a threat and a reproach to the 1980s." And he was right.

Less than a year before his death in 1994, he still looked to the future: "I have been trying to get a film financed," he wrote in his final letter to me. "Not easy nowadays, especially if one is in no way an entrepreneur, as I'm afraid I never have been. But keep looking forward—you never know!" Maverick of mind, waspish of tongue, efficient in daily life, and a loyal friend, Lindsay Anderson will, I believe, endure as an uncompromising auteur.

2.
The Prime of Life

There had always been books about the cinema. First editions of early classics like Terry Ramsaye's *A Million and One Nights* (1926) and Paul Rotha's *The Film Till Now* (1930) were already coveted by collectors when I commenced publishing in 1963. Across the Channel, French studies of directors (Rohmer and Chabrol on Hitchcock, for example) had been widely quoted in Anglo-Saxon journals. Pierre Leprohon, at Seghers, had launched an excellent series of paperbacks on directors, some of which were, much later, translated in the United States. Nearly all the French publications, however, neglected the reference aspect, and suffered from embarrassing inaccuracies and lacunae.

Apart from Roger Manvell's splendid initiative through Penguin in the 1940s, a really lively series of paperbacks at reasonable prices did not exist in Britain until we began operating. In 1963, the situation was difficult for anyone trying to promote such a range of film books. Too many established publishers could point to unsold stocks of the movie titles they had issued from time to time, and, perhaps reasonably, they rejected the argument that a new, younger and more enthusiastic audience was coming forward in the wake of the New Wave in so many national cinemas.

I believed that original paperbacks, presented with a reasonable number of illustrations, were most likely to succeed. They had to be inexpensive (although because the market was undeniably a specialised one, they could never be so cheap as Penguins or Pans). They had to be durable and not fall apart at the spine like a flimsy thriller bought to while away a train journey. Above all, they must offer a knowledgeable text, supported by filmographies and bibliographies that would prove useful to the cinephile long after his first reading.

One of the best-selling, and perhaps the least respected, movie monthlies of the period was *Continental Film Review*, which had been launched in 1952. But beneath its glut of semi-pornographic photographs of stars and starlets, there lurked the occasional article and interview of real interest. The editor, Gordon Reid, talked to me at press shows, and soon asked if I wanted to contribute pieces. He had a particular fondness for French cinema, and for the good looks of Brigitte Bardot, Mylène Demongeot, Françoise Arnoul and Martine Carol. He also happened to be a talented saxophonist. In 1965, Gordon suggested I cover the Cannes festival for the magazine, and I accepted without hesitation.

By virtue of *CFR*'s surprisingly high circulation, I was given free accommodation at the newly-opened Cannes Palace, with all of its four stars. In fact, the hotel was far from the action, situated to the west of Cannes, beyond the Martinez, but at that time the Palais des Festivals stood where today the J.W. Marriott Cannes Hotel extends its brazen frontage. This proved a crucial trip for me, widening my circle of acquaintances in the film world. Long before the dubious era of low-cost flights, one would take the "Blue Train" overnight from Paris. Awaking at dawn, drawing down the carriage windows, one was met by the fragrance of herbs and lavender. The Riviera really did seem like another planet by comparison with a grey and rainswept London. The festival bore little resemblance to the media circus of today. During the mid-1960s, until the harsh upheaval of May 1968, one could stroll the Croisette and meet personalities as diverse as François Truffaut, Rock Hudson and Richard Lester. In the intimacy of the Salle Cocteau, the veteran critic Georges Sadoul would introduce discoveries from Eastern Europe and the U.S.S.R. A former surrealist, then communist, Sadoul died early, in 1967, but his history of world cinema was one of the few general studies available to my generation.

Europe was still the crucible of world cinema and its inventiveness, even if the ensuing four decades would see the bravest of new films emerging from Asia, Latin America, and the Middle East. But in 1965 the critics were discussing the work of Czech, Polish, Romanian, Hungarian, French, Swedish and British directors. Only Japan, with a trio of remarkable films in contrasting idioms (*Kwaidan*, *Tokyo Olympiad* and *Onibaba*), breached the American and European walls that year at Cannes.

One day in 1965, a young Australian named Bernard d'Abrera came to my office in New Bond Street. He adored the *International Film Guide*. Bernard said that the Sydney Film Festival lacked life and initiative, and he and his friends were planning to launch a rival event, called the New South Wales International Film Festival, under the auspices of the University of NSW. As they would be using our book as a guide to selecting their films, they felt that I should be present at the inaugural event. I would be furnished with a return air ticket with Lufthansa, and they suggested I fly out via New York and Mexico City, and return via Bangkok and the Middle East. It seemed too good to be true, but true it was, and in August 1966 I left on my first inter-continental journey.

I stayed a couple of days in Manhattan, at the Hotel Edison, then a flea-ridden hotel that was subsequently used for the scene of Luca Brasi's murder in *The Godfather*. When I reached Mexico City one evening, it was too late to go into the city, and I slept fitfully on a bench in the terminal. Early the next morning I was picked up by a most cultivated Mexican, who was in the process of publishing in Spanish my books on Orson Welles and Swedish cinema. The sun shone, and my impressions of Mexico City, in the hands of such an amiable and sophisticated guide, were rich and positive. The magnificent Museum of Anthropology in Chapultepec Park, with its roof in the form of a gigantic umbrella, had opened less than eighteen months earlier, and I was stunned by an architecture far removed from that of London.

However, the next leg of my journey proved harrowing. We ran into a heavy storm between Mexico City and Acapulco, and the Qantas pilot told us with sardonic candour that even he could not see the mountains. The plane lurched and veered alarmingly. Drinks were tossed into the air and the occasional scream could be heard above the roar of the engines. The twenty-minute flight seemed to last hours. At last we set down in Acapulco, and after taking on more fuel, the plane droned on through the night to Fiji. We landed for an hour or two, strolling through a balmy night to a tiny terminal surrounded by mighty palm trees. Local women placed garlands of flowers around our necks, and the anxieties of that journey across Mexico were forgotten.

The next stop was Auckland. My father's brothers still lived in New Zealand, and during our brief halt I managed to phone my uncle Alan, who was desperate to come down to the airport to meet me. But I could not go out through customs, and, alas, I never again had the chance to talk with him. In Sydney I was accommodated at the fashionable Sebel Town House in King's Cross, an area that had become known across the decades for its whores, artists and musicians. Here I did manage to meet one of my relatives, my mother Ruth's cousin, Leighton Woods, who came to the hotel lounge bar and asked eagerly for news of her and her life in England. He had known her during her early youth in Brisbane.

Bernard d'Abrera and his team made a valiant effort to match the glamour of the Sydney Film Festival, but could not quite succeed. I introduced a few films (notably during the tribute to Joseph Losey's work) and was fêted at receptions. I was galled to miss the world premiere of Michael Powell's *They're a Weird Mob*, which had been filmed in Australia, but at least I had the schoolboy satisfaction of sitting a few rows behind the star of the movie, Walter Chiari, on the long flight to Rome. While in Sydney, I was befriended by three journalists, Charles Higham, John Baxter and Joel Greenberg. They urged me to publish a series of paperbacks on Hollywood, each devoted to a particular decade. Higham and Greenberg brought the films of the 1940s to life in the first volume, and Baxter followed suit with the 1930s. Comprising eight books, the series proved one of the most successful of all Tantivy's ventures. I also met David Stratton, a young British émigré about to galvanise the Sydney Film Festival by inviting a succession of prominent directors to attend the event, and also to become my Australian correspondent for the *International Film Guide* for many, many years.

Bernard d'Abrera would soon be accepted as one of the most respected lepidopterists in the world, and his festival colleague Michael Robertson made some feature films in Australia. My visit Down Under took place at a time when Australians felt isolated culturally from the rest of the world. "We're seven hours from anywhere," lamented one film buff. Airlines such as Etihad, Virgin or China Southern had not yet brought about the era of (relatively) inexpensive air travel.

Even I, who at the age of 26 had accomplished very little, was regarded in Sydney as a link with a burgeoning, almost exotic European cinema that only occasionally reached local screens.

Flashback: Orson Welles

Orson Welles was frequently in Britain during the 1960s, acting as much as possible to accumulate cash for his next production. It must have been early 1963 when, bent on writing a book about his films, and reading that Welles had had arrived in London, I phoned the Ritz Hotel, where the switchboard said that Mr. Welles was not accepting any calls. I waited thirty minutes and then rang back, adopting a fake Spanish accent and shouting, "This is Madrid! I have an urgent person-to person call for Signor Welles!" It worked. A P.A. informed me in cut-glass tones that Mr. Welles was very busy but that she would talk to him about my request for even a brief meeting.

Two days later, I was interviewing Anthony "Puffin" Asquith for a profile in *Films and Filming*. As we talked, a male secretary crept into Puffin's Thurloe Square drawing-room and said that there was a call for Mr. Cowie. "Who's it from?" I asked. "I believe it is Mr. Orson Welles, sir." Asquith, who had directed Welles in *The V.I.P.s* the previous year, jumped to his feet and said I should take the call at once. In fact, it was Welles' P.A., who had tracked me down via my home and informed me glacially that Mr. Welles would receive me at the Ritz the following afternoon. I trusted he would not be in the basement barber's salon, where I had met Louis Malle a year or so earlier, lying supine, his face covered with shaving lather, and a cigarillo in his mouth, answering my questions as the barber scraped his way across that aristocratic terrain.

Then my knock on the suite door, and Welles himself opening it, massive and somehow mythic, part Arkadin, part Advocate from *The Trial*, with an endless cigar jutting forward as he bid me welcome. We talked of Kafka and the abandoned railroad station in Paris, the Gare d'Orsay, which Welles had used as his main location in *The Trial*, long before it was converted into a museum for the Impressionists. When I praised his use of the Albinoni Adagio, he sought for the right adjective: "Yes... it's very... NOBLE music... noble."

The 1973 revised edition of my book about Orson Welles,
first published in 1965

He spoke gently, with dignity and a deep-purple resonance. When I remarked that much of K's dialogue in *The Trial* verged on the cynical, he demurred: "No, I'm a pessimist," said Welles. "I'm not a cynic—I hate cynicism.

Welles advised me to write him with any questions and assured me he would reply. He did indeed, dictating his letters at the Hotel Suecia in Madrid. When I requested permission to reproduce some of his screenplays, he responded: "I am fundamentally opposed to this and have always refused to grant such permission, since I feel that the only real existence of screen writing is on film. I'll be happy to let your publishers have some excerpts from different scripts, particularly if I can have a hand in choosing them, but no full texts. This isn't as bad as it sounds. In fact I think really interesting chunks from all of my films would make more interesting reading than the full versions of just two or three."

In a subsequent letter, however, he confessed that he did not "have the scripts of any of my films. There are a few somewhere in Rome, but here I am in Madrid." Then he replied to the kind of detailed questions that only a young man asks—how long did the script of *The Trial* take to write ("about six weeks") and, "The picture of the Judge in *The Trial* was originally painted by a commercial artist from a photograph. I then worked over it."

When I made the mistake of asking him about the significance of the nuclear mushroom rising over the landscape at the end of *The Trial*, he baulked: "About the cloud, and all other subject matters, I must hold firmly to my rule of never explaining anything." He also jumped on my jejune admiration for the "aged" look of the newsreel at the start of *Citizen Kane*. "There is no particular secret to aging and graining film. The stuff for the newsreel in Kane was worked over several times before we got it right, but the process is standard and represents no innovation. When the picture opened in Italy right after the war, a lot of people booed and hissed and even shook their fists at the projection booth. Because they thought this old newsreel stuff was bad photography."

Welles did furnish me with some specific comments about films like *The Magnificent Ambersons* and *The Stranger*. "I never expected to have control over the editing of *The Stranger*, since Sam Spiegel was the producer," he wrote on July 10th, 1964. "This is the only picture I have made in which I did not at least expect to function as producer (in the American sense of the word). The best stuff in the picture was a couple of reels taking place in South America. Spiegel cut it out entirely. There was also a famous fight about a close-up. He wanted to cut into a scene for a close reaction of Loretta Young. I was opposed to this and, remarkably enough, Miss Young took my side in a heated debate involving Spiegel, her agent and a number of other officials. Because the female star demanded that she should not have a close-up, we won the day."

As for *The Magnificent Ambersons*, "five, maybe six reels of *Ambersons* are exactly as I cut them before leaving for South America, with the exception of a single cut in the middle of a very long travelling shot. The cut involved a couple of remarks about 'olives'—a novelty in the town. Don't ask me why they wanted it out. The result was a useless jump in an otherwise unbroken scene. I also cut the last part of *Ambersons*, but it was completely re-done after a preview. About forty-five minutes were cut out—the whole heart of the picture really—for which the first part had been a preparation. The closing sequence in the hospital was written and directed by somebody else. It bears no relation to my script."

Women adored Welles, from Sylvia Syms, who told me how affectionate he'd been on location for *Ferry to Hong Kong* in 1959, to Jeanne Moreau, who had fallen under his spell in 1950. One evening, Maurice Bessy, a French journalist who later became the director of the Cannes Film Festival, came to her dressing room and said that Welles wanted to meet her. "I was then playing Bianca in *Othello*," said Moreau when she met me more than half a century later. "My first husband, Jean-Louis Richard, was jealous and did not want me to go, but I did. Orson sat opposite me at the table, and many years later he reminded me that when he'd dropped me in the street outside my apartment, I had been too shy to say anything, and that he'd been dying to kiss me." She would go on to star in four of the Master's films, none better than *Chimes at Midnight*, where she capers cheerfully over his corpulent Falstaff.

Ruth Warrick was another out-and-out admirer. Welles had welcomed her into his company at the Mercury Theatre, and persuaded her to appear on screen as Mrs. Charles Foster Kane. When a bevy of us, including Beatrice Welles,

Orson's daughter, and Suzanne Cloutier, the Canadian actress who had played Desdemona, gathered in Marrakesh in 1992, to pay tribute to Welles on the fortieth anniversary of the shooting of *Othello* in Morocco, Ruth regaled us with stories of how Orson had nursed her through the early days of the *Citizen Kane* shoot. "He was always there to put an arm around me and dry my tears when I was hiding in the wings, feeling I just couldn't go on set for the first take." In fact, he was just two months older than his protégée, but it seems that for everyone who met him, Orson Welles was the elder statesman.

By the mid-1960s, the Tantivy Press series of film books had gathered momentum. I retained the almost-square format that I had admired so much in Pierre Seghers' series of books on film, poetry and philosophy. Some of the covers were designed by Allen Eyles, who had joined Tantivy in 1965 as my assistant editor, and others by Stefan Dreja, whose gift for unconventional imagery exactly suited the tone I needed for the series.

I searched for new authors, writers who had written the occasional magazine article but who had not yet embarked on the full-length book or monograph. Talents like Robin Wood and Roy Armes began to emerge. Indeed, when Wood's *Hitchcock's Films* appeared from Tantivy in 1965, Philip French wrote in *The Observer* that it set "an altogether new standard for critical books on the cinema in this country." The jewel in our reference crown proved to be Peter Graham's compact *A Dictionary of the Cinema*, released in 1964 and reprinted before the end of the year. Peter's most original idea, allied to a fastidious, meticulous researcher's instinct, was an index to every film (some 5,000 titles) referred to in the dictionary. It occupied a lot of space, but attracted widespread praise from readers. "This little book," wrote Peter Baker in *Films and Filming*, "is quite the most fascinating and valuable published about the cinema in recent years."

We were able to accelerate to an output of eight to ten titles per annum thanks to two developments: in 1967 I sold my interest in the firm to Thomas Yoseloff, a publisher from New Jersey who had the courage to invest in an expanded list; while Zwemmer continued to believe in our enterprise and to pay for their 4,000 copies of each new title within 2-3 months, thus diminishing our risk. Brian Doughty, manager of the Zwemmer bookshop on Charing Cross Road, devoted a window display to each of our new titles. He sold around two hundred copies of each new title within a week of publication; if one added the dozens that were purchased in Foyle's and Better Books, then both flourishing in the same street in Central London, it became clear that a hearty appetite existed for reading about movies.

Yoseloff had imported my father's annual *Antiques Year-book* for sale to the book trade in the United States. During one of his visits to my parents' house in South Kensington, he shook hands with me and seemed intrigued by my ambitions to launch a similar annual on film. Thus his company, A.S. Barnes & Co., bought a consignment of 2,000-3,000 copies and, joy of joys, paid for them upon receiving bills of lading, which enabled me to send sufficient money to our Dutch printer to sustain our line of credit. For the next four years this procedure never faltered. I would rush to an accountant's office in the Charing Cross Road, where a senior clerk would inspect the bills of lading and then issue a certified check for the entirety of our invoice.

In 1967, Thomas Yoseloff asked my wife and I to supper at the Chanterelle Restaurant in the Old Brompton Road. It proved to be a memorable evening. Tom Yoseloff could, on a bright day, have been mistaken for President Harry Truman — petite, dapper, pork-pie hat, glasses and a ready smile. He had started life as a journalist in the American Midwest, then developed a publishing concern that functioned most efficiently. He never had a best-seller, nor did he covet one; instead, he concentrated on selling a few thousand copies of a great many non-fiction titles. Soon he was also publishing books on behalf of various university presses on the East Coast.

During the meal, he commissioned me to compile a kind of history of film, which appeared in 1969 under the title *Seventy Years of Cinema*. He then proposed an even more seismic development. By that stage, Barnes & Co. was buying four titles each year from Tantivy. Yoseloff pointed out that if we joined him, we would have sufficient funding to accelerate to eight or even twelve books per annum. I argued that I was quite happy with the current situation as I wanted primarily to write about cinema, and was using the publishing simply to retain my independence. Yoseloff grinned at me across the table: "You can do both, you know!" And so I was beguiled, and in fact never regretted my decision to sell Tantivy to A.S. Barnes & Co. I received a long-term contract, and began to supervise the sale of Yoseloff titles in the United Kingdom and the continent. By the early 1970s our warehouse contained small quantities of literally hundreds of titles, ranging from cookery to sport, from horticulture to the history of the Civil War.

I had concluded the sale in Yoseloff's suite at the Waldorf Astoria Hotel on Park Avenue, and it was agreed that I should visit New York at least once or twice a year for meetings. These trips enabled me also to create a beachhead in the United States where the *International Film Guide*'s advertising revenue was concerned. Indeed by 1970 I had become friends with Bill Becker and Saul Turell at Janus Films, and began writing catalogue notes for their library of classic European films. Janus led to the Criterion Collection, and more than half a century later I continue to write for them.

The Yoseloffs invited me to their horse farm in Colts Neck, New Jersey, each weekend during my New York trips. I would take a bus from the Port Authority terminal and alight in Freehold, where Tom Yoseloff awaited me in a Cadillac. I was much taken by his young wife, Lauretta, who resembled Lily Tomlin in her prime, and their small daughter, Tamar, who would practice the *Moonlight Sonata* while I relaxed between meals in the luxurious sitting room. Tom Yoseloff had two grown sons by his first marriage, one of whom, Julien, gradually began to manage the daily affairs of A.S. Barnes & Co. in nearby Cranbury. But I had the feeling that I was regarded as some kind of surrogate scion, and that my passion for work and for all things literate reminded Tom of his own vanished youth.

In confident mood, we launched a quarterly magazine, called *Focus on Film*. My assistant editor, Allen Eyles, had dreamed of doing this for years, and in January of 1970 we published the first issue. Allen chose a landscape format, reflecting the widespread studio migration to widescreen CinemaScope. His aim was to provide historical articles and profiles of lesser-known or forgotten stars alongside reviews of new films, accompanied by detailed filmographies – a mix that no other British magazine was delivering. Allen adored compiling lists and statistics where film was concerned, and did so with unfailing accuracy. The magazine endured for 37 issues, and built a small but loyal readership. We even sold binders so readers could keep their copies in pristine state. The first issue established an eclectic tone, with tributes to Bob Hope, Tuesday Weld and Edward Everett Horton, alongside reviews of films as diverse as *True Grit* and *Ma nuit chez Maud*. We featured interviews with Casey Robinson and Burgess Meredith, Walter Lang and Maureen O'Sullivan. My favourite number of *Focus on Film* was devoted entirely to a dictionary of great cameramen, a project that involved meticulous and exhaustive research.

Flashback: Otto Preminger

I first met Preminger in late 1970, in his suite of offices at the top of the Columbia Building on Fifth Avenue in New York. As I entered, he was sitting at a vast desk that seemed about a mile away across the petrol-blue shag carpet. I was soon to publish a book about Preminger's career written by Gerald Pratley, the Canadian broadcaster and journalist who had frequently visited Preminger on locations and earned his trust. Now I had come to ask for help with obtaining illustrations. "Listen," he barked in his not unfriendly Austrian accent. "I don't mind vot you say about my films. But if you toucha my vife or my kids—I kill you!" With that caveat out of the way, he became most cordial, and suggested we go to lunch. As we entered the elevator, he drew a small electric razor from the pocket of his blazer and ran it over his domed head to ensure that no fuzz would mar the elegance of his image. He offered to commission Saul Bass to furnish us with the colour logos of some of his most famous productions, so that we could use them on the cover of the book. Bass had also created a font for the words OTTO PREMINGER, with each capital letter slit discreetly from top to bottom, and this became an emblem close to Preminger's heart. The Bass version of his name even adorned the white door of the office on Fifth Avenue.

When our little book appeared, Otto invited Pratley and me to dinner at his Manhattan townhouse in November of 1971. The rooms were huge, all-white, with black as a secondary motif. A single couch could seat a dozen guests. As I admired a Picasso (or was it a Gauguin?), the painting

Gerald Pratley's study of Preminger,
published by Tantivy in 1971.

began to tilt outward, and then upward, to reveal a beaming
Otto at his wet bar behind the wall. Clearly delighted with our
astonishment, he mixed drinks for everyone. A Giacometti
sculpture dominated the patio, and a Henry Moore stood,
spot-lit, outside the dining room window. More pictures
lined the walls of the corridors, and deep carpets reduced
all movement to a whisper. The other guests were the comedian David Steinberg, young, eager and then at the height
of his fame, and David Schoenbrun, the veteran CBS reporter
who had worked with Ed Murrow in the 1940s. Schoenbrun

dropped names like confetti throughout the meal: Arthur (Miller), John (the Pope, of course), and Edgar (Faure, the French politician). After a meal cooked and dispensed by a French couple, we climbed the stairs to the Preminger screening room. Otto's wife served coffee and brandy while mine host fiddled at a console and gave the order for the projectionist to start a 35mm screening of John Schlesinger's *Sunday Bloody Sunday.* A screen descended to cover the shuttered windows. Schoenbrun dismissed John Schlesinger's movie with a few suave and lethal words. Otto and I defended the picture, to little avail.

At the end of the evening, a little the braver for booze, I asked Preminger if life had become difficult in the years since he had enjoyed a box-office hit. "Listen," he intoned, "early on I discovered that in order to have some freedom I had to become my own producer. And if you are your own producer, you get a fee irrespective of what happens at the box office." When he had first arrived in Hollywood, the "town" was run, he recalled, by "six or seven studios with the head of every one being a dictator. The stars were the only people they had to cater to."

By becoming his own producer, Preminger also ensured that he had final cut as a director. In so doing, Preminger placed himself in the vanguard of change in Hollywood during the 1950s, a time when actors like James Stewart and Elizabeth Taylor were kicking against the pricks of a studio contract. He dealt with drug addiction in *The Man with the Golden Arm*, with the birth-pangs of Israel and the partition of Palestine in *Exodus*, and with the shenanigans of Washington politics in *Advise and Consent*. Like his contemporary producer-director, Stanley Kramer, he believed that the public would respond to a "message" movie. He knew that the studios shied away from contentious issues. His pioneering courage opened the way for filmmakers like Arthur Penn, Bob Rafelson, Francis Ford Coppola and Martin Scorsese.

I last saw Preminger at the Tehran Film Festival in 1973. He was checking into the Hilton, and I suddenly heard him shout, "Vair is my sveet?" The concierge explained that all the suites in the hotel were occupied—apart from one. "Who has zat?" asked Preminger. "Buster Keaton," replied the concierge. At this, Preminger seemed ready to explode. "Buster Keaton," he said dismissively, "has been dead for years!" The concierge, imperturbable, gestured to a poster on the wall behind him. "There, you see, the Buster Keaton retrospective is taking place this week." Preminger, stunned, paused and then said firmly but not harshly: "I am going to the restaurant to have some caviar. If my sveet is not ready when I return, I vill fly back to New York."

That evening I saw Preminger enjoying what appeared to be a relaxed meal with colleagues. I asked Hagir Dariush, the director of the festival, how he had resolved the problem. He shrugged and said with an icy smile: "I simply told the concierge that if the suite was not ready in ten minutes, he would be in chains."

This incident underlined the dictatorial control exercised by the Shah of Iran, but also showed how Preminger had determined to get his way. He had learnt in the first instance from Darryl Zanuck at 20th Century Fox, and he had realised that to survive in Hollywood one had to have an iron will and an unquenchable optimism. The irony remains that his most enduring picture, *Laura*, was made within the constraints of the studio system against which he later rebelled. This masterly, intricately-constructed thriller reflected the duplicity and hypocrisy against which Preminger fought throughout his life.

Flashback: Miloš Forman

Even in his early thirties, Miloš Forman gave off an air of formidable gravitas and authority. Burly, dimple-jawed, speaking in measured tones with that gravelly voice that never changed, he represented all that was most durable in the Czechoslovak New Wave of the 1960s. That is when I first met him, in May of 1966. His second feature, *Loves of a Blonde*, opened at the diminutive Paris-Pullman cinema in London's South Kensington. We journalists were crammed into a tiny business office at the back of the theatre for an after-screening drink, and Forman stood there like an unassuming prince, his friend and co-screenwriter Ivan Passer beside him. Across the subsequent decades our paths would cross many times, in various countries from Switzerland to the United States, and it was Forman who persuaded me to distribute in the UK the English-language edition of Josef Škvorecký's compelling book about the Czechoslovak New Wave, *All the Bright Young Men and Women*.

Poland had dominated the arthouse scene more than any other Eastern European nation during the late 1950s and early 1960s, but by 1965 the Czechs had taken over, cocking a snook at the Communist bureaucrats who managed their film affairs, and doing so, moreover, with a sense of irony. So many talents emerged: Věra Chytilová, Evald Schorm, Jan Němec, Jiří Weiss, Karel Kachyňa, Karel Zeman, Otakar Vávra, Juraj Herz, Jiří Menzel, Ivan Passer, Elmar Klos and Jan Kadár…

But only the versatile Forman endured through four more decades as an auteur of exceptional stature. Like a chameleon, he could adapt to different cultures and different climates. He made a mere dozen or so feature films, but even his shorts were idiosyncratic and amusing (for example, his segment of the 1972 Summer Olympic Games documentary *Visions of Eight*). Forman was in Paris when Russian tanks rolled into Prague to stifle the Prague Spring in August 1968. Fired by his studio in the grim, authoritarian period that ensued, he moved to the United States. He filmed there, in France, in Spain, and of course eventually back in the Czech Republic for his most lauded work, *Amadeus*. Who would have thought that the films of such a dyed-in-the-wool European could capture no fewer than eight Academy Awards? (Not forgetting that both *Loves of a Blonde* and *The Firemen's Ball* received nominations as Best Foreign Language Film.)

After joining FAMU, the freshly founded and soon famous Czech film school, in 1950, Forman had spent several years making documentaries for the national television network. He collaborated on screenplays, and also served as director of the Laterna Magika Theatre. He told me in 2002 that from 1956, after Khruschev came to power and denounced the dictatorship of Josef Stalin, "suddenly the political situation loosened up a little bit, and that created an absolutely ideal situation. We were allowed to make our films the way we wanted, and we were the bosses." Nonetheless he waited, with some circumspection, until his early thirties to shoot his first film; and with the featurettes *The Audition* and *If Only They Ain't Had Them Bands* in 1963, Forman immediately showed his flair for observing ordinary mortals in much the same compassionate vein as Ermanno Olmi was doing in Italy.

Forman, like Polanski and so many others, had lost both parents in the Nazi camps during the Second World War, yet his early work shook off the burden of war and from the outset boasted a wry sense of humour. One of his first discoveries, Vladimir Pucholt—he appeared in *The Audition*, *Peter and Pavla* and *Loves of a Blonde*—brought an antic mournfulness to his roles as the archetypal Forman hero, the youngster bewildered by adult life. Miroslav Ondříček, the young cinematographer of these early films, would remain faithful to Forman for many other features, including *Amadeus*. Their technique in the early films was very much that of cinéma vérité, with Ondříček wielding two long-lensed cameras in the streets and dance-halls of northern Bohemia, the brass bands refracting the petty pomp and circumstance of the Communist regime.

Forman's move to the United States taught him to accelerate the narrative pace of his films so as to reach a wider public. Allying his talent to the satirical writing of John Guare and Jean-Claude Carrière for *Taking Off* in 1971 enabled Forman to export his quirkish observations from the music halls of Bohemia to the streets of Manhattan, and in Buck Henry he found an actor who reflected the absent-minded and emotionally myopic personalities of Forman's Czech years.

One Flew Over the Cuckoo's Nest (1975) reaped an unexpected Oscar harvest. Forman's subsequent films in the United States did not always hit the bull's eye, but they were almost invariably on-target. He committed himself wholeheartedly to each new project, but with hindsight I think it's clear that his soul is most evident in those early Czech comedies. He dwells tenderly on the tribulations of young people trying to survive under a totalitarian regime. He forgives them their clumsy approach to love because they have not yet become petrified in the conformism of their elders.

His romantic situations unfurl in a slow-burning, but never ponderous, tempo. Films like *The Audition* and *Loves of a Blonde* were light years removed from the sombre if technically dazzling work of Andrzej Wajda and the young Andrei Tarkovsky.

Forman always believed that his characters struggled through life at the mercy of a complex, bizarre system of social codes. Everyone, even a Mozart, even a Goya, let alone a Larry Flynt, comes into conflict with the rigorous conformism of his times. In *The Firemen's Ball* (1967), what should be a cheerful occasion crumbles into a kind of poignant farce, as the members of a provincial fire brigade celebrate their annual ball, complete with tombola, booze, and even a beauty queen. The firemen's "committee" inevitably evokes the Politburo of the period, and the stealing of prizes from the tombola display evokes the pilfering that Forman said was endemic in Czechoslovakia under Communism.

The Firemen's Ball aroused the consternation and anger of party officials in Prague, but Jan Němec smuggled a print out of the country just as the liberal Alexander Dubček was assuming power, and Forman submitted the film to Cannes. When the festival collapsed under the weight of protests in the context of May '68, Forman told me that "this was the most absurd day for me, because here I was at the festival with the filmmakers who I not only admired but respected. And suddenly I see these same filmmakers trying to put up a flag which all the young intellectuals in Communist countries were trying to tear down!" Perplexed, Forman agreed to withdraw his film from the competition.

The themes adumbrated in Forman's early work would recur in almost all his major-league movies of the next forty years. Youth in the battle to stave off conformity (*Taking Off*, *Hair*, *The People vs. Larry Flynt*); the bitterness and confusion of old age (*Amadeus*, *Goya's Ghosts*); the creative outsider in a puritanical society (*One Flew Over the Cuckoo's Nest*, *Ragtime*); artistic and public rivalry (*Man on the Moon*, *Amadeus*).

When I interviewed him in 2002, he reflected: "You are always under pressure in the film business. In the Communist countries you were not under commercial pressure, but you were under strong ideological pressure. Here in the United States you are not under ideological pressure at all, but you are under commercial pressure. To be honest, I prefer commercial pressure, because then I am at the mercy of the taste of some audience. Under ideological pressure, I am at the mercy of one or two idiots!"

Only a filmmaker of exceptionally generous spirit could have approached personalities as disparate as Mozart, the Hustler publisher Larry Flynt, and comedian Andy Kaufman with such relaxed sympathy and bonhomie. Patient as Job when required, Forman auditioned more than a thousand applicants for the cast of *Hair* (1979).

Our final conversation took place at the Zürich Film Festival of 2010. Then in the evening of his career, he could reminisce about his work with every kind of performer: "Actors are very fragile instruments. So my philosophy is, the less I talk to the actor, the less I confuse their head!" Fine cigars were one of his few concessions to the luxury that his success could have afforded him, and to the end of his life he remained gracious and tolerant. Forman never warmed to intellectual circles, and he eschewed the glamorous brand of hero or heroine. His characters comprised the good and the not-so-bad, the plump and the slender, the shy and the vulgar, and they flourished in Forman's benign pursuit of everyday truth.

How fortunate we were to have been publishing at a time when each new monograph was almost always the first of its kind in English—Carl Dreyer, Andrzej Wajda, Orson Welles, John Frankenheimer and Otto Preminger. Other houses followed our lead. Ian Cameron at Studio Vista edited an excellent series of beautifully-designed paperbacks, and Secker & Warburg collaborated with the British Film Institute on the "Cinema One" collection, which included studies of Godard, Hawks, Wilder, and Pasolini. By the turn of the 1970s, the field had grown crowded, with auteurs like Losey and Resnais already the subject of three books or more. Further, publishers began to take larger risks, issuing hardbound books that were costlier to produce and buy than the modest paperbacks we had been doing. There was competition for the rights to publish screenplays. Comprehensive reference books on the cinema began to emerge in both Britain and the United States. Reading about movies became *l'air du temps.*

Some auteurs reacted with suspicion to our suggestion of publishing a monograph about their films. Joseph Losey and Stanley Kubrick surprised me with their need to control what was written about them; apparently Robert Bresson also fell into this category. Losey's *Accident* had been shot in the summer of 1966, and James Leahy, a contemporary of mine at Cambridge, approached him about a book. Losey graciously agreed to give him several interviews, even though he was in the thick of post-production work on the film. He offered to do a foreword for us. It was long and rambling. When I sent the proofs to Losey (at his request) he phoned to summon me to his house in Royal Avenue, Chelsea. He opened the Georgian door of number 30, and I thought for a few moments that I was entering the very setting of *The Servant.* Losey grinned. "Everyone thinks that," he said, "but in fact we shot the film in an almost identical house across the avenue." He then proceeded to tell me, in language as rambling as his own foreword, that the entire piece would have to be re-written. He said he would do it quickly. In those days, all type was set in metal, and each correction, even to a single word, cost money. I winced, and agreed.

A large man, with a patrician, almost Roman profile, Losey startled me with his brusque, somewhat abrasive manner and way of talking, at odds with the sensitive mind that must have created those finely calibrated analyses of the British class system such as *The Servant, Accident,* and, four years later, *The Go-Between.* All three films were scripted by Harold Pinter, whose contribution can be seen, in retrospect, to be very significant. I had the impression that beneath his bluster cringed a man whose appalling experiences at the hands of the McCarthy witch-hunt had made him uncertain of his own significance as well as of his neo-Marxist convictions.

Losey did not retype the text, but added chunks of new material, even as he excised other sentences. I pointed out that this would cost a great deal of money, and quite frankly, we did not have that kind of budget. He then abandoned the idea of the foreword, and wrote a mercifully brief encomium to the screen-

James Leahy's book about Losey,
published by Tantivy in 1967

writers and technicians with whom he had worked, concluding
with an ambivalent evaluation of "young James Leahy's"
monograph: "As for his opinions—some of them I share, others
I would strongly disagree with, and some I must confess I do
not understand."

Losey did at least permit the book to appear, and it was
well received, even if, despite the brilliance of certain films, this
expatriate Midwesterner never commanded the awe in which
directors like Bergman, Fellini, or Truffaut were held during the
same period. With Stanley Kubrick, however, we ran full tilt
into a wall. At 27 years of age, I still cherished a naïve belief in

the sublime tolerance of the artist for his critics. I sent a copy of the *International Film Guide* to Kubrick at Hawk Films while he was shooting *2001: A Space Odyssey*, and to my amazement he ordered MGM to take a full-page advertisement for the film in our 1968 edition, which appeared in November 1967. It remains a lost icon, for the artwork was never again used in promoting the movie.

So when a young critic and aspiring playwright named Neil Hornick came to our offices and suggested we do a book on Kubrick, I accepted with alacrity. "Let's ask him if he'll give you an interview," I said. Again, to my surprise, the response was almost immediate. Ray Lovejoy, Kubrick's editor and, it seemed, a kind of front-man at the time, visited me dressed in an elegant suit, which I thought odd for a technician in 1968. Suave and reassuring, Ray told me that "Stanley admires your work, Peter, and he'll be happy to give Neil an interview." He then explained that Stanley would like to see the finished manuscript, just to check that there were no factual errors of the kind that crept all too frequently into studies of his work. "But he won't ask the author to change anything fundamental, will he?" I asked. "Peter," came the smooth-as-syrup response, "we both know Stanley well enough to say that nothing like that would ever occur to him."

We received a brief letter of contract from Kubrick's lawyers in Lincoln's Inn. A tiny alarm bell sounded far in the back of mind when I read that Kubrick would have "absolute discretion" to accept or reject the manuscript, but I did not protest. Hornick's manuscript was duly delivered to him, and within a few days I received a curt letter from the lawyers saying that the manuscript was "unsuitable for publication." Baffled, I replied, asking if we could have more details of Kubrick's objection so that the author could consider them and perhaps make changes. We were told in no uncertain manner that Kubrick did not wish the book to be published by Tantivy or by any other publisher anywhere in the world, and that if it were, he would pursue me, Peter Cowie, personally.

Eventually, a mixture of exasperation and fear compelled me to seek legal advice myself. I instructed Rex Harrison's lawyers in Lincoln's Inn, and a partner listened sympathetically to my description of the situation. Within a few weeks, he had settled the affair over lunch with Kubrick's attorney. Tantivy agreed not to publish the book, and we licked our expensive wounds. Neil Hornick subsequently consented to place his manuscript in the archives of the British Film Institute where it might be consulted by legitimate researchers. A mere two years later, Alexander Walker published his elegant *Stanley Kubrick Directs*. I bought it as soon as I saw it, in a bookshop in Manhattan. I spent that evening in my hotel room, combing the book for clues as to why Walker's monograph had been acceptable to the Great Man, but not Hornick's. Suddenly I stumbled on the answer. Walker's beautifully illustrated text contained only passing mentions of *Spartacus*, a film that Hornick had praised at length. Kubrick's relations with Kirk Douglas, his producer—and star—on *Spartacus*, had deteriorated past the point of no return and in some way he had shut the film out of his world-view. Had we ever met face to face, I am sure that Kubrick and I could have reached a compromise, but the icy, formal legalese extinguished what could have been an important book at a time when no other on the subject existed in English.

Fortunately, Neil's manuscript was resurrected and published in 2024, to widespread recognition in the press. He died the following year.

Animation, that unique art-within-an-art, was an important pillar of the burgeoning European film scene during this period. The animated film knew no bounds in Eastern Europe, notably in Poland and Yugoslavia. It needed no dialogue, no off-screen narration, to communicate its message or its emotion. At Tantivy, we were surprised when Ralph Stephenson's paperback entitled *Animation in the Cinema*, published first in 1967, soon went into a second edition. Animators sprang up in countries as far apart as Japan and the Netherlands, Canada and Czechoslovakia. Cartoons, puppeteering, stop-action, collage—the many faces of the animated film traversed national and linguistic borders in the blink of an eye.

Flashback: Richard Williams

London was a powerhouse for animated film in the 1960s. George Dunning produced and directed the animated version of the Beatles' *Yellow Submarine*, Bob Godfrey made

The Do-It-Yourself Cartoon Kit, a satire on the burgeoning world of animated TV spots, and John Halas and Joy Batchelor still basked in the accolades for *Animal Farm* (1954). In the very first edition of the *International Film Guide*, I had written about the artistry of Richard Williams, arguably the most talented of all the London animators. Tall, good-looking, quiet-spoken, he did not quite fit the shaggy-haired image of a young man in the time of the Beatles. Dick Williams had come from Canada to make his reputation as a designer and animator at exactly the right moment. TV commercials were booming, and agencies were clamouring for inventive animation.

He had learned the technique of animation at the age of 12 at the Ontario College of Art. "But by 15, I had given it up," he confessed wryly. He painted until he was 21, and had spent two of these years in Spain. There the idea for *The Little Island* was born. It caused an upheaval in his life, and he decided to take animation seriously all over again.

The Little Island, a satirical fantasy in which Truth, Beauty, and Goodness fail to live together in harmony, ran half an hour, and made brilliant use of the CinemaScope format. The animation was bold and sweeping. Williams was still only 24, and indeed looked that age for almost the rest of his life.

When I first met him in 1963, he was teeming with ideas for original animated films, among them *I. Vor Pittfalks*. "It's as serious as *The Little Island*," he told me, "and it ends in calamity. The tone is rather Hitlerian. Everything everybody says comes out in shapes. Everything I. Vor says comes out in black. We've used a 75-piece brass orchestra for the music." Along with studio colleagues Tony Cattaneo and Charlie Jenkins, he completed some ten thousand drawings for the first six minutes of the film.

Another project was an adaptation of Gogol's *Diary of a Madman*, for which Williams drew romantic, delicate portrayals of Sophia, the aristocratic woman who beguiles Poprishchin. When he sat at his desk, his hand would follow his mind with unerring precision.

You never quite knew who else would be hunched over the drawing-board when you visited Dick Williams in his capacious townhouse studio in Soho Square. It might be the gravel-voiced Ken Harris, who had worked at Disney before the Second World War, and then on Merrie Melodies and Bugs Bunny. Or Art Babbitt, who had been a major contributor to *Snow White and the Seven Dwarfs* at Disney, in particular creating the character of Goofy. Or Grim Natwick, then in the sunset of a glorious career that had seen him develop the figure of Betty Boop during the 1930s. Bringing these legends of Hollywood animation out of retirement delighted Williams, for he felt a strong kinship with the tradition of Walt Disney, Max Fleischer, UPA, Hanna Barbera and other studios.

Even in the midst of completing numerous commercials, Williams always found time to sit on a high stool and chat about any number of topics. Ebullient, optimistic and with an enviable gift for translating his visions into graphics and moving images, he soon shifted into a higher gear. He would go on to create the credit sequences for such features as *A Funny Thing Happened on the Way to the Forum*, *The Charge of the Light Brigade* and *Return of the Pink Panther*. He reached the pinnacle of his profession as animation director on *Who Framed Roger Rabbit*.

I shall always remember Dick's seething energy. He could work through the night to fulfil a deadline, and he could also lose himself in jazz, forming a Dixieland ensemble that proved a popular attraction at venues in London. Academy Awards came his way, but he never lost sight of his personal dreams, producing animation of exquisite audacity and finesse. Besides, he was a loyal friend and an indefatigable supporter of what we were trying to do with the *International Film Guide*.

In May 1968, I was attending the Cannes Festival for the fourth time, paying my own expenses and staying in a one-star hotel called the Pullman, where the loo and the shower were shared among the four or five rooms on each floor. It was conveniently just around the corner from the legendary Petit Carlton café. Here I met fellow journalists and also directors like Dušan Makavejev and Henning Carlsen, who enjoyed the smoke-filled atmosphere of the place. The Petit Carlton was presided over by an astute man who looked like a cross between Danny

DeVito and Napoleon Bonaparte. He sat at a cash desk over-looking the café, writing the checks in a hand so spidery that one simply ignored the details and went to the scribbled total, hoping one had sufficient cash to cope with it. Every so often someone would sneak out of the front door without paying, only to be brought to heel by a sharp bark. Meals were, shall we say, unpretentious, with omelettes a staple of the menu, served swiftly for those wanting a bite between screenings. If the tables downstairs were full, one could clamber to the mezzanine, although for someone tall like myself it was essential to bend from the waist in order to avoid hitting one's head on the low ceiling, and a sharp ledge jutting out above the head of the stairs meant that one also ran the risk of being trepanned if one rushed down too quickly.

I have written about the events of May 1968 in my book *Revolution!* (2004), and what remains most vividly in my memory is the opportunism of protesters and directors alike. I watched from the gallery of the old Palais des Festivals as critics from *Cahiers du Cinéma* vied with Truffaut and Godard for control of the microphone, haranguing the festival as well as one another, jostling for power in a dangerous vacuum caused by the breakdown of government credibility and authority throughout France. Would this upheaval have the same impact as 1789? Scarcely, for the only tangible consequence of May '68 at Cannes was the creation of the "Directors' Fortnight," in opposition to the "official" programme. The following year some guests even wore tuxedoes when entering the Palais, a practice that the *soix-ante-huitards* had condemned as quasi-fascist.

Panic, often ill-suppressed, began to seep through the three Dante-esque "circles" of Cannes: filmmakers, business execu-tives, and journalists. Maximilian Schell was seen in the lobby of the Martinez Hotel, offering hard currency to anyone who could furnish him with a car. His voice took on a braying despair that reminded me of Richard III at Bosworth Field, for whom "a horse, a horse" must have been the 15th-century equivalent of a car.

I constantly checked the diminishing amount of cash in my wallet, as banks had closed and credit cards were dismissed scornfully by shops and hotels. My friend Felix Bucher knew a Swiss exhibitor, and arranged for the British journalist John

Gillett and me to accompany them in a long journey overland to Geneva. The portly exhibitor planted a large bottle of marc next to the shift stick, and we set off via Draguignan. As darkness descended, and a cloudburst enveloped the mountains, a tyre blew out. The only light available was John's pencil-torch that he used for taking notes during screenings, and we crouched down beside our host as he wrestled with the jack and various levers. The wheel eventually changed, we limped into Grenoble, then on into Switzerland.

Flashback: Liv Ullmann

The Swedish Film Week in Sorrento in 1968 offered screenings as well as alfresco suppers and excursions to Capri and Pompeii. Ingmar Bergman was expected, and he and Liv Ullmann were assigned a luxurious villa for the duration. But Ingmar pleaded an ear infection, and Liv was left to cope with the paparazzi, as well as a showing of *Shame* and some formal receptions with Princess Christina of Sweden.

We had not met, but one evening I was taken to Liv's villa by Gunnel Hessel, at that time a Scandinavian equivalent to Hedda Hopper or Louella Parsons. Liv received us in a vast, sombre salon that might have suited Garbo in all her solitude. She appeared ill at ease with her duties in Ingmar's absence, although her natural charm overcame her embarrassment and uncertainty. Here was a woman clearly under the gun, reluctant to embrace celebrity.

Flash forward to the winter of 1972. I had visited the offices of Paul Kohner, a veteran Hollywood agent who represented Bergman and his actors in America. When I returned to my hotel the phone was ringing. "Would you like to introduce *Cries and Whispers* at a special Academy screening for the foreign press tonight?" asked Kohner. "But I haven't even seen the film yet," I protested. "No problem," purred Kohner, "You can talk about Liv."

So I fumbled my way through the presentation, keenly aware that this was the first film Liv and Ingmar had made together since their breakup at the end of the 1960s. At a dinner at Skandia restaurant afterwards, a journalist approached Liv's table and "accused" her of lesbianism. I'll always remember Liv's red-faced indignation—"Just because Ingrid [Thulin] and I caress each other...!" She was more poised, but still getting used to the brazen attitudes of Hollywood. And she was never, one felt, happy in fluff like *40 Carats* and *Lost Horizon*. Instead, she has adored the theatre—"the moment of absolute quietness—then there's real communication between and an audience," she told me long ago. None who saw it can forget her greatest triumph in the United States, playing Nora to Sam Waterston's Torvald in *A Doll's House* at Lincoln Center's Vivian Beaumont Theatre.

Flash forward to December 2004. The European Film Awards in Barcelona, and a conference on the craft of acting in European cinema. Liv delivers the keynote address—a magnificent, eloquent speech that for months afterwards would be cited by actors and critics alike. "In my profession as an actor," she said, "my material is the life I am living and the life I am watching, the life I am reading about and the life I am listening to." Finally she was at ease, gracious and forthcoming, having achieved so much as actress, writer and director. Her memoirs, *Changing*, matched Ingmar's own *The Magic Lantern* for candour and perception. And so long as Bergman's *Persona* and *Scenes from a Marriage*, or Troell's *The Emigrants*, are screened, Liv's stature will be unquestioned. Almost imperceptibly, she did indeed "change" from a passionate, ingenuous girl to a mature and sagacious personality.

When my biography of Bergman appeared in 2023, Liv flew over to Oslo, where my friend Jan Erik Holst had arranged a launch for the book. We were interviewed together on stage prior to a screening of *Persona* and reminisced about Ingmar and his team. Liv was once again the most natural of stars, her inner beauty shining through the wrinkles she had chosen not to disguise. She was at home, in her Oslo, and chatted with anyone and everyone.

In 1972, Groucho Marx came to the Cannes Festival to receive an award from the French government, albeit a minor gong compared to the Légion d'Honneur meted out later to valiant performers like Sharon Stone and Michael Douglas. As he shuffled off the stage after a screening in the Salle Cocteau, wearing brown-rimmed glasses, a blue turtleneck and his trademark

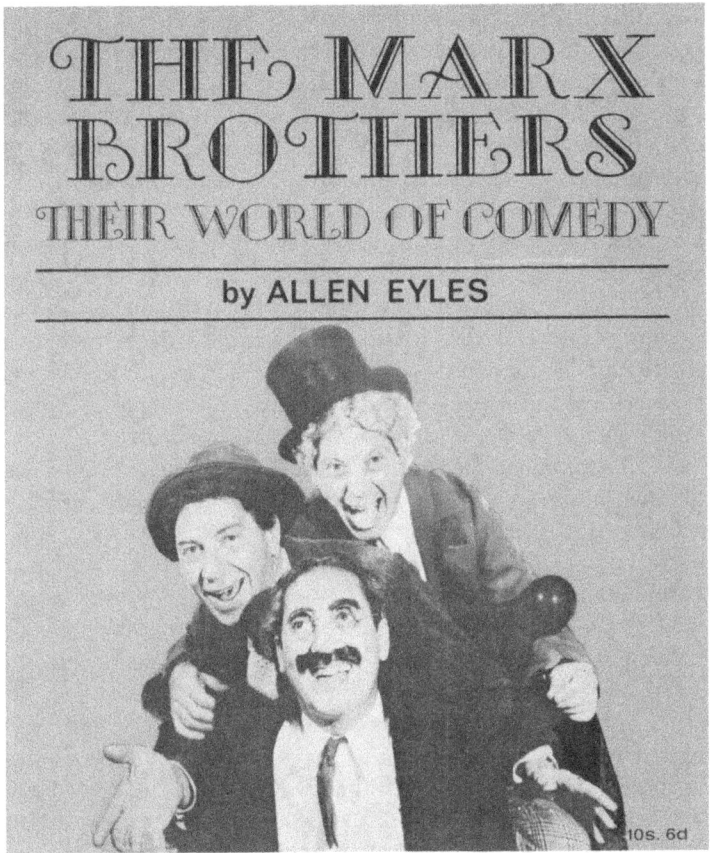

Allen Eyles' book about the Marx Brothers,
published by Tantivy in 1966.

beret, I pressed into Groucho's hand a copy of Allen Eyles'
paperback *The Marx Brothers and Their World of Comedy*,
which had sold very well for Tantivy. Without missing a beat,
he drawled, "Hey, this book looks kinda square, but really it's
pretty good!" His moustache was white, and he cheerfully
recalled his youthful work in vaudeville: "In those days almost
everyone wore a false moustache. You had several performances a day and it was easier to put on greasepaint. Sometimes I wore a real moustache, so that I wouldn't be recognised
in the street."

Admitting to a fondness for Woody Allen, Groucho reflected: "I don't think you can be a good comedian unless you're a good writer. I'm not amused by clowns." He railed against America's military involvement in Vietnam. "We should end the war," he declared. "We were opposed to the government, and that's why the kids today still like our films."

By 1972, I could write in my notebook: "In ten years I have launched more than sixty titles on film. Ten of those have been the annual editions of the *International Film Guide*, an amalgam of articles, facts, reviews, illustrations, and advertisements that has grown to almost six hundred pages in length. To achieve all this has required a dedication—or more, an addiction—to the cinema that most people would consider selfish and debilitating. Never have I wanted to abandon this bizarre field of endeavour.

"Occasionally, the pressure of administrative chores or the damning indifference of my English colleagues has drained my initiative and slackened my restless drive towards that mirage, perfection. But the respect and enthusiasm shown by friends abroad, the innumerable reviews of our books, and the concomitant sense of a need being filled by our efforts, have always revived my spirits. I return from my foreign trips determined to improve our standards of criticism and presentation."

Thanks to the long-established editor, Penelope Houston, I began to creep into the pages of *Sight and Sound* in the 1970s. Penelope herself had written *The Contemporary Cinema* for Penguin, an excellent primer to the new waves of filmmaking in Europe and elsewhere, and I found her less intimidating than did some of my colleagues. Educated at Roedean, continuing to a Double First at Oxford, she edited the legendary postwar magazine, *Sequence*, alongside names like Lindsay Anderson and Gavin Lambert. She struck me as a fugitive from the early 1920s, with her fierce independence as a woman. Using an elegant cigarette holder, she smoked incessantly, from need rather than for enjoyment, and her principal passion was horse-racing, followed closely by golf. Penelope was an early advocate of Antonioni, Wajda, Resnais and especially Buñuel, whose films, she wrote, were "like raw spirit poured straight on to an open wound, a stinging, cauterising therapy of shock." In 1988, two years before she retired, she gave my career a two-page splash in *Sight and*

Sound under the title "Framed." I'm not sure that her more highbrow contributors altogether approved.

Tantivy's reputation as a publisher of film books had reached into the industry itself. One bright morning in 1971, a tall, well-dressed American with a gravelly voice and patrician bearing came to my offices in New Bond Street. This was Ray Harryhausen, the legendary wizard of stop-action animation and special effects, in the days before CGI was available to all and sundry. He showed me the mock-up for a scrapbook devoted to fantasy in the cinema. He had gathered scores of original drawings, models and stills which in their ensemble traced the development of such classics as *King Kong*, *Mighty Joe Young* and *Jason and the Argonauts*. Ray proved to be one of our most congenial authors, and I enjoyed visiting him and his wife at their home in Holland Park, filled with some of the model dinosaurs and other creatures that had made Ray's reputation. We hesitated at first to reproduce the scrapbook in exactly the format he had conceived, but he was persuasive, and he was right, for Ray Harryhausen's *Film Fantasy Scrapbook* quickly went into a second edition, and delighted his fans around the world.

The 1970s proved to be the engine-room of my career. During that decade I took on more staff; launched two other annuals commensurate with the *International Film Guide*, one devoted to classical music, the other to cycling (racing, touring, recreational); wrote three books on aspects of Scandinavian cinema; and dealt with the release in Europe of around one hundred new titles from A.S. Barnes (many on film, and not all outstanding).

The *Guide* (or *IFG* as it became known to our staff) remained the backbone of our operations. Each year more pages were added, more countries covered, more advertisements sold. I began to delegate some of the business activities. In 1970, I hired Julia Palau, who at just 21 years of age radiated a joie de vivre and an eagerness to learn. She soon became popular with our clients, and when I took her first to the Cannes festival, she worked from morning to night. We stayed as usual in the tiny Hotel Pullman, around the corner from the Petit Carlton café. To make appointments with potential advertisers, Julia would use the one available phone, in the hotel lobby, and would not rest until she had tracked down the executives who made the decision we needed. Julia stayed at Tantivy for almost five years, before moving to a post at Lew Grade's ITC Entertainment. Soon afterwards, she decided to establish a sales company with Michael Ryan, a fellow sales representative at ITC. Their venture, known as "J & M," became a significant player in the independent film world of the late 1970s, '80s and '90s.

A succession of salespeople (mostly women) followed in Julia's path at Tantivy; some were diligent, some charismatic, but all enabled me to concentrate on my own books as well as dealing with our growing status as a publisher. Although I did not admit it at the time, I felt a twinge of guilt when an advertiser asked about the circulation and effectiveness of *IFG* as an advertising medium. We never sold more than about 8,000 copies each year, a circulation that seemed derisory to the agencies that handled the ad budgets for the major studios or film entities in the U.S. and Europe. My argument was that the quality, rather than the quantity, of the book's circulation would bring results. Sure enough, evidence of exactly this surfaced with sufficient regularity to persuade our regular clients to renew their advertisements each spring. For example, Želimir Matko, the Sales Manager at Zagreb Film in Yugoslavia, sent me a postcard from the United States, saying that "your little book works miracles here," as he sold numerous animated shorts to American distributors who knew the Guide.

On the editorial side, Allen Eyles, a contemporary of mine who had joined Tantivy as early as 1965, copy-edited many a manuscript. Allen was quiet and unassuming. Behind his discreet exterior, however, was a prodigious knowledge of certain areas of film history, in particular the Western genre and the Marx Brothers. His book on that formidable comedy team was arguably the best ever written on the subject, and yet I never once saw Allen even smile, let along guffaw, when he described the antics of Harpo or the witticisms of Groucho.

A majority of our book covers were, as mentioned earlier, designed by an imaginative young artist of Polish descent, Stefan Dreja, who could use bright colours and audacious draughtsmanship to enliven, and sometimes transcend the traditional black-and-white film stills. He executed all his own artwork, and was always working against deadline. On one occasion,

SCREEN TEXTBOOKS

PRACTICAL MOTION PICTURE PHOTOGRAPHY
compiled and edited by Russell Campbell

Russell Campbell's book was published by Tantivy in 1970.

I needed some cover artwork to take to our publishers in New York, and Stefan, running late, had to jump into his own car and rendezvous with me in Hounslow just before I checked in at the airport.

Our range of film books diversified with each passing year. The London International Film School approached us to publish a series of textbooks on film technique. The School would guarantee to buy a large quantity of each title, thus effectively subsidising the enterprise. I was fortunate enough to find an editor for these Screen Textbooks. Russell Campbell, a lanky New Zealander, devoted himself with a will to creating each new book, based on interviews with technicians and his own knowledge as a neophyte filmmaker. After launching the first two titles, Russell returned to his native country in 1972 and was succeeded by a Canadian named Terence Marner, another graduate of the LFS. Unfortunately the school endured some rough times in the mid-1970s, and we could publish no more than five titles in the series.

Visiting the United States brought me in contact with a wide range of film personalities. These were not stars or A-list directors so much as distributors, exhibitors, and fellow critics. One of the first men I met, Gary Crowdus, had launched a magazine called *Cineaste* in 1967, and even as I write these lines he is still alive and kicking, at the helm of the magazine, which is perhaps the last remaining reliable print magazine that covers arthouse cinema and filmic trends in the U.S.

Prior to the video era, the 16mm market in America was dominated by the thousands of universities and colleges that possessed film societies, and where film was taught as part of the curriculum long before the practice evolved in Europe and elsewhere. Student draft deferments led to a massive increase in college enrolments during the Vietnam War period. Janus Films would make available not just the classic films of Kurosawa, Bergman, Fellini and Welles, but also themed catalogues and study guides, some of which I was requested to write.

And there were other companies that took advantage of the arthouse era. Leo Dratfield's Contemporary Films had a reputation for acquiring edgy, often experimental works from European cinema, and I would spend many a happy hour with Leo at the short film festival in Oberhausen, West Germany. Dan Talbot, of New Yorker Films, had introduced filmmakers like Fassbinder and Carlos Saura to the United States, as well as programming one of the most celebrated of all arthouses, the New Yorker repertory theatre, on the Upper West Side. I would go upstairs to his small office and exchange opinions on recent films we had seen. He unfailingly supported the *International Film Guide.*

New Line Cinema sported an extraordinary mixture of classic and contemporary foreign, experimental, American independent and porno films. Bob Shaye was the guiding light of this pared-down enterprise, located in a grungy office off Union Square in Manhattan. Bob looked on me with a kind of condescending amusement; he took the least expensive of ads in the *Guide* and took months to pay the invoice. Little did I know at the time that Bob would become one of the most powerful producers in Hollywood, with New Line Cinema years later giving birth to Peter Jackson's great *The Lord of the Rings* trilogy. But I already respected Bob as someone who had the courage to distribute Kinugasa's *A Page of Madness*, Herzog's *Fata Morgana* and Chabrol's *Ophelia*.

During the 1970s, "films for young people" (educational films) were all the rage in the United States. A host of companies, large and small, fought for a share in the market, and periodically gathered in their hundreds at the AECT Convention to meet the thousands of audio-visual educators who did such sterling work from one side of the States to the other. Collectively, they offered a vast selection of educational films on every conceivable subject—fiction, non-fiction, animation, even filmstrips of the most elementary kind.

There, Julien Bryan took me under his wing. Son of an elder in the Presbyterian Church, Julien had built up his International Film Foundation in the postwar years, having visited (and filmed in) such remote regions as China, Georgia and Outer Mongolia back in the 1930s. He was in Warsaw during the siege of 1939, and brought back remarkable footage from the ruins of the Polish capital, as well as from Gdańsk in 1946. Julien found that his ad in the *International Film Guide* yielded results, and he liked my British mien (whatever that was). He invited me to attend the AECT Convention, first in Minneapolis, and then in Atlantic City, and even found space to accommodate me, along with his staff, in a vast hotel suite. Through him I met Richard Leacock, and heard his stories of working with Flaherty on *Louisiana Story.*

A generous man, Julien once invited Murray Grigor and me to his club off Fifth Avenue. There we swam with men at least twice or three times our age, and swallowed oysters with bourbon while sitting, nude, on leather stools at the poolside bar. It was a memorable evening.

My most generous client in this field was the Learning Corporation of America, founded by Bill Deneen, and offering an up-market selection of instructional films for theatrical and television release. I mention the fact because the marketing manager, a hearty, intelligent woman of a certain age, took me to lunch each year, and immediately ordered martinis. She downed her first round in less than a minute and before I knew it we were about to consume a third martini as the entrée arrived. Over the years I learned to ask her if she would renew her two-page spread in the *Guide* before I reached that stage of the meal, as the remainder of the lunch would dissolve in an alcoholic haze. American barmen make the driest of martinis, none better than in the tiny Blue Bar at the old Algonquin Hotel on 44th Street, serving the lethal cocktail in petite, shapely glasses.

In 1970 I had begun writing programme notes and booklets for Janus Films, the most distinguished importer of foreign films in America. An earnest, restless, and engaging young man named Peter Meyer suggested that Janus should arrange a lecture trip for me, visiting the university societies that screened foreign films on 16mm. Through Peter I met Sedgwick Clark, who worked in the marketing department at the Philips classical label in New York. Both became lifelong friends. Sedgwick managed to get front-of-stalls tickets for Peter and me at Covent Garden, where Colin Davis was conducting some rare performances of Berlioz's opera, *The Trojans*, featuring Janet Baker and Jon Vickers. Philips had just published Davis' version on LP in a box-set. I shall never forget that evening. Having scorned opera until that point, I found himself enthralled by the drama of the subject, and the majestic, melodic score by Berlioz.

My passion for classical music must have struck those around me as odd, for I could play no instrument, could not read music, and had no ear for distinguishing chords and keys. The emotional texture of the music reached me very acutely, however, and I empathised with composers like Beethoven, Sibelius, Haydn and Schubert, all of whom dared to approach their fears and aspirations through the classical forms of symphony, sonata, concerto and quartets.

In 1971 a studious young man named Derek Elley, 22 years of age and fresh from Cambridge, where he had read Classics, applied for a clerical post with us. He seemed content to deal with orders that came through the mail, entering the customer's name and details meticulously in one ledger after another. He talked to me about the cinema, and also about music. We began to buy LPs from a company in North London named Opus, and compared notes on the quality of the recording, the approach of the conductor, and so on. Derek played the 'cello every Sunday with some friends. Soon he became my assistant editor on the *International Film Guide*, and in 1975 we conceived of a sister annual dealing with classical music.

This period marked the heyday of classical music's commercial appeal. Stores like HMV in Oxford Street, or Harold Moores in Great Marlborough Street, plied their trade to a loyal public, while in New York, emporia such as Sam Goody on Sixth Avenue, Tower Records near Lincoln Center, and specialist outlets like Discophile in Greenwich Village meant that independent record labels could flourish along-side the established giants (RCA, Decca, Deutsche Grammo-phon, Philips, and CBS). Derek accepted the responsibility of editing this book, which we called *International Music Guide*. Although he sometimes exasperated me with his quest for accu-racy and arcane detail, I valued Derek's talent and intelligence. He would become a film reviewer first with *Films and Filming* and, much later, at *Variety*.

The alliance with A.S. Barnes & Co and Thomas Yoseloff meant that we needed to fulfil a rapidly increasing number of orders. Warehouse space was expensive, and at first we negoti-ated with specialist companies, such as Tiptree Book Services in Essex, to store our books and invoice and despatch orders to the trade. We retained small quantities of the film titles for sending out from our own offices in New Bond Street. I had learned how to pack books from the age of 16, working alongside my parents, and I always enjoyed standing at the bench, folding the cardboard and paper, tying the string, and seeing the pile of parcels accumulate before the Post Office van arrived and took them away in red hessian sacks. Everyone, including my then wife Elisabeth, went to work with a will, and in the late 1960s I advertised for a full-time warehouse manager.

A stocky, cheerful Indian from the island of Mauritius presented himself to me, wearing a canvas belt of the kind issued by the British infantry, its buckle brightly polished. Davis Gopala had worked in the field for some years, and I immediately took a liking to him. He served Tantivy for a great many years, and nothing was ever too much trouble for him. Intensely loyal and trusting, he told me that when he retired he would go back to Mauritius and live on the cache of money he had saved and buried beneath the roots of a large palm tree on one of the more deserted beaches of that tropical island. When we decided to cut out the expensive service organisations and store and sell our books ourselves, I had no hesitation in letting Davis take charge of a rented warehouse in the City of London. In 1975, however, we found premises at 136-148 Tooley Street, on the south bank of the Thames between London Bridge and Tower Bridge. The top floor contained plenty of space for offices, and the floor below, even larger, could house the many hundreds of Yoseloff titles we had imported.

I would ride by racing bike from my home in East Sheen to Tantivy's HQ in Tooley Street. The trip took about 45 minutes to an hour, depending on traffic along the Embankment, and I was soon very fit, consuming enormous quantities of carbohydrates on my return home in the evening. We remained in SE1 for a full decade. The offices had been refurbished to a reasonable standard, and the only drawback was the small lift, which had a tendency to break down, obliging me to yank my bike up six flights of stairs.

During the 1960s and '70s, when film festivals burgeoned like mushrooms across the world, gradually replacing the arthouse as a source of nourishment for the film buff, I was approached by various events to advise or help them. Most have vanished into oblivion. One of the most colourful was held in Rochester, in the north of New York State. Famed as the home of Eastman Kodak, and the George Eastman House archives, this industrial city had also prospered thanks to the success of Xerox and its copying machines, and Bausch & Lomb and their lenses. Rochester's film festival was launched in 1970. Two men hustled and bustled during the months before the opening. Fred Mintz was a would-be entrepreneur who believed in my *International Film*

Guide and arranged my first lecture trip to the States. He subsequently produced the Joe Don Baker action movie, *Speedtrap* (1977). Bill Creighton wore well-cut suits and worked in a modest capacity at Xerox (some sneered that he was in effect a janitor, but that was probably unfair). Bill knew naught about films, but adored glamorous parties, while Fred contacted the local intelligentsia and arranged to fly in consultants like me and Murray Grigor, then head of the Edinburgh Film Festival.

The first festival suffered the usual teething pains. I had just introduced on stage George Pal, the legendary animator and producer. We returned to our seats, the lights dimmed, and the projection of one of Pal's early animated shorts commenced. But the curtains refused to open. I tried to signal to an attendant in the aisle that all was not well, but the projectionist had probably gone to sleep, because for almost two minutes the film could be seen only vaguely through the curtains. Pal put his face in his hands, and at length I was able to push past the people in neighbouring seats and have the lights switched on and the projection re-run.

Most of the Rochester festival's guests seemed as puzzled as I was to be wined and dined (albeit rather sporadically). There were actors like the chubby-faced comedian, Chuck McCann, and the handsome young Robert Forster. Rouben (*Love Me Tonight*) Mamoulian attended, spending most of the time in altercation with his feisty spouse. Ina Balin, John Wayne's squeeze in *The Comancheros*, behaved with grace under pressure. And there was Peter (*The War Game*) Watkins, then at the height of his notoriety as an uncompromising, if somewhat humourless, director. When Murray and I hastened to meet him across the nylon carpet of the newly-open Holiday Inn, our rubber shoes created such a charge that there were crackles and flashes of electricity as we shook hands with Watkins, who regarded us thereafter with dark suspicion.

Murray and I made an appointment to see Louise Brooks, who was living in retirement in Rochester. She welcomed us with all manner of witty, often caustic remarks about Hollywood in the silent era. We ran into her again later in the week, in a shopping mall, and thereafter I wrote to Louise, and received letters from her, at least once a month for several years.

Flashback: Louise Brooks

For years, I had assumed Louise Brooks to be dead. That iconic face staring out of posters for *Pandora's Box* and *Diary of a Lost Girl* seemed, like some fly in amber, a prisoner of the vanished 1920s. When my friend Peter Graham suggested that we use her image for the front cover of his *A Dictionary of the Cinema*, which I published at Tantivy Press in 1964, I grew intrigued. Soon afterward, after reading in *Cahiers du cinéma* that she had been rediscovered by James Card, the film curator at George Eastman House in Rochester, New York, I plucked up my courage and sent her a copy of the little book.

Almost instantly, she typed a letter to me: "Becoming a star thirty-five years after I was pronounced nothing is very heady stuff. It was a great honor to be your cover girl. Your book is evidently a huge success. I have received five copies from all over and could have had ten more from admiring friends." These remarks disguised the fact that Louise was by then a loner. True friends were thin on the ground, although Kevin Brownlow had become one, after he tracked her down for an interview for his book *The Parade's Gone By*.

Six years later, I was invited to "consult" on a new festival in Rochester. It had been arranged without Card's involvement and proved a near disaster, but the highlight of my week was a pilgrimage to Louise's modest apartment on North Goodman Street. I was accompanied by Murray Grigor, then galvanising the Edinburgh International Film Festival. We had been told by a local film buff that we should take half a pint of gin as an offering, and Louise was thrilled. "I always drink it in a tooth glass, with milk on the side," she explained with relish. She drew us into her bedroom, and as we sat on the bed beside her, she showed us a file of production stills from her work in the silent era. Two days later, Murray and I were killing time in one of the city's ineffable shopping malls when Louise materialised, gliding toward us in a long skirt, her even longer hair descending gaily to her waist. She was petite, like so many great stars, and her features had weathered the years well, while her voice, rarely noted, had an authority that broke continually into peals of laughter.

My tribute to Louise Brooks
was published in 2006 by Rizzoli.

More than forty years later, Kevin sent me a letter he had received from Louise in the wake of our visit. "I liked Peter at once, although he didn't like me [sic!]. He thought I was being grand not going to lunch or to dinner or to the film festival. But then by accident on the day he was leaving we met in the Midtown Plaza, and he glowed at me like a porcelain stove which is so cold-looking from a distance." Ah, the Englishman abroad! Indeed, in October of 1970, Louise had scribbled a note to me, saying, "You must know that I don't [not] go out because I think I am somebody, that is not true—it's because I know that I am nobody."

During the 1970s, Louise and I corresponded pretty much every three weeks. She delighted in dishing the dirt on silent Hollywood, with Garbo the actress she most loved to hate: "She was always positive about not wanting to play whores kicked around by men, but her absolute lack of intellectual discipline prevented her from being positive about what she wanted to play." In another letter, she noted that, where Garbo was concerned, "genius seems to balance the pressures put upon it. Here was a big husky dyke who found in Hollywood her escape into the most feminine of women. Her enemy, Louis Mayer, thought to kill her off with *Queen Christina*, so obviously lesbian, but he had to wait till *Two-Faced Woman*, with the help of the whole staff, exposing that cruel lesbian face, blotting out her genius."

As her articles revealed, Louise had a flair for writing that she should perhaps have indulged from the outset of her career. "My purpose in writing," she said in a letter in 1972, "is to search out those often unnoted incidents which shape life." She read books, magazines and newspapers with omnivorous zest. When she had her apartment repainted, she had "a wonderful time in reshaping the shelves, throwing out fifty books. To every book I said, 'Will I ever need you for reference?' When the answer was 'No,' out went Father's Homer, Carlyle's letters, bang, thump, dust— I love getting rid of things."

She adored provocation, telling me that "of course, Mr. Pabst directed the opening sequence of *Pandora* to direct the audience's attention to the penis-in-erection—showing me swinging on the wrestler's flexed arm." And yet it was only with the advancing years that Louise started to swear like a trooper. She wrote to me once, "Whatever shock value 'fuck' and 'shit' retain for the dainty, they have no value at all in revealing character. My articles have lost nothing by rejecting them." When she worked with the likes of William Wellman and W. C. Fields, she maintained, "Louise Brooks did not swear. It is part of the obscenity of old age."

Louise gave me one of the best compliments I have ever received. "You are the only person I know who speaks the truth to me," she wrote in January 1975. "And the truth makes me laugh. It isn't that other people would not like to speak the truth, but they have grown up in families in which speaking the truth brings punishment. I did not. And I must say this: in childhood is established truth or lies."

The last I heard from Louise was a card in which she thanked me for my review of her memoir *Lulu in Hollywood*, which had appeared to acclaim from Knopf in 1982. Of course, the Louise I knew in the 1970s was light-years away from "Brooksie," the flapper girl who had seduced Chaplin in the summer of 1925. Her antic, often brilliant mind surfaced only in middle age, and the iconic "girl in the black helmet," as Kenneth Tynan had called her, remained tantalisingly beyond reach for my generation. If she had lived to see my book *Louise Brooks, Lulu Forever*, published by Rizzoli in 2006, she would probably have made some scabrous comment about its being too kind.

My travel schedule appeared punishing, but I relished the arrival at every airport. While New York remained my most frequent destination, I also discovered countries like Italy, Finland, Poland, Iran and India. Plying the lecture circuit in the United States was an attractive sideline for innumerable European film directors and critics during the 1970s. The universities could afford to pay for one's appearance (the check ritually handed over as one left the stage) until the advent of Reagan and his acolytes, for whom culture was both anathema and subversive. The National Endowment for the Arts found itself maimed by the mid-1980s, having supported so many initiatives and performances across the country.

My initiation occurred in 1971. The same neophyte entre-preneur who had invited me to the Rochester festival, Fred Mintz, insisted that I could be successful as a lecturer on arthouse figures like Orson Welles and Ingmar Bergman. Few things are more chastening for a lecturer than facing a nearly empty hall—when just half a dozen earnest faces gaze back from the vastness of an auditorium built for 1,800. Making the best of such circumstances, one must plead with these loyal subjects to come down to the front so that one can shed one's mike and spend the next hour chatting rather than proclaiming, and learning each person's name instead of gazing out at a mass of anonymous faces. As Orson Welles reputedly exclaimed, in similar circumstances, "Why are there so many of me and so few of you!"

During the next few years I was despatched, first by the Swedish Institute, and then by Janus Films, to some twenty states of the Union. If it was Tuesday, it must be Columbus, Ohio. The pace was relentless. To the airport in the morning, lunch with one's host professor, a tour of the university, then back to the hotel or motel to prepare for the evening. Cocktails with the faculty, followed by the lecture and a screening. Finally, a buffet supper at the home of some munificent supporter of the university, then to bed to prepare for the next morning's depar-ture.

On arrival in Iowa, I trudged off the plane to find myself confronted by a banner stretching across the full width of the terminal: "Welcome to Des Moines. You're looking great!" I knew that I must have truly landed in the Midwest. Some of the country's brightest professors, however, can be found in the least expected of locations. For example, Richard Dyer McCann, my earnest host at the University of Iowa, had already published numerous books on the theory and history of the movies, and gave impetus to the much respected Society for Cinema Studies. Edwin Jahiel presided over a busy film schedule at the vast campus occupied by the University of Illinois at Cham-paign-Urbana. The multilingual, chain-smoking Edwin would become the only American honoured by France up to that time as an Officier de l'Ordre des Palmes Académiques, and exuded passion for every kind of film. We would enjoy Greek cuisine cooked by his wife Lenrose, exchange opinions, and indulge in

such harmless word-games as the linking of movie titles. He would say "*Citizen Kane*," and one's response might be "*The Caine Mutiny*," to which, with a gleeful smile, he would reply, "*Mutiny on the Bounty*," and so on.

A highlight of my trip in 1972 was being present in Ann Arbor, at the University of Michigan, on the turbulent night when Richard Nixon was re-elected to the presidency at the expense of the hapless George McGovern. Sometimes the lesser colleges proved more stimulating than the Ivy League establishments like Harvard and Cornell, where visitors like myself were two a penny. In October 1975, my lecture trip took me from Philadelphia to Carbondale, Illinois; from Cleveland, Ohio, to

Buffalo, New York; and from Lancaster, Pennsylvania to the Walker Art Museum in Minneapolis. I flew in small planes operated by such now-vanished airlines as Ozark, Piedmont and Mohawk.

Such a compressed travel schedule resulted in some tense moments. In the late 1970s I toured several of the Scandinavian Studies departments across the U.S. For example, I talked about my staple topic, Ingmar Bergman, at the University of Colorado in Boulder. Next morning, under a flawless blue sky and amid the snow-capped Rockies, I took the bus down to Denver Airport. By the time I arrived, a blizzard was in full spate. Planes were delayed. I was due to speak at UC Santa Barbara that evening at 7 p.m. Instead of reaching southern California in the early afternoon, I found myself forced to change flights, and rush from terminal to terminal in Los Angeles. I finally bolted off the commuter plane in Santa Barbara at 7.15. My host explained that my audience was waiting patiently. Twenty minutes later I was walking up the aisle of a crowded lecture hall, and had to start talking the moment I reached the stage.

And yet that traumatic evening changed my life in the short term. I was entertained to a civilised supper by Torborg Lundell, a lecturer in Swedish at UCSB. She had gathered a number of faculty members, who shared a love of European film. As he dropped me at the Faculty Club for a night's rest, Patrizio Rossi, an Italian who headed the unofficial film studies unit, casually suggested that I return to teach at the university. Within a few months, I received an invitation to take up a Regents' Lectureship at UCSB, established "to bring to the campuses of the University [of California] persons who have achieved distinction through other than the traditional academic avenues." One's duties were not exactly onerous: two formal lectures on subjects of one's choice, and a willingness to attend various functions and dinners hosted by prosperous and culturally-inclined figures in the community. My fellow Regents' Lecturer was Frederic Raphael, the cynical aesthete who had scripted two films by John Schlesinger (*Darling* and *Far from the Madding Crowd*) and would eventually help Kubrick with *Eyes Wide Shut.*

Awaking at dawn in the Faculty Club after the long flight from Europe, I could see students already flicking their frisbees

languidly to one another across the manicured lawns. Daily
life began early and ended early; most restaurants closed by
9 p.m. My first appointment was scheduled at noon with Patrizio
Rossi. "He's at the pool," a receptionist told me. There, almost
alone in the massive pool, Rossi was crawling lap after lazy lap.
At last he hauled himself out of the water to sit beside me. When
I remarked that the rhythm of life seemed very different to that
of European academe, he responded with words that epito-
mised the ethos of Southern California: "Why work a full day
when you need only work for half a day?"

During the weeks that followed, I enjoyed the company of
Dr. Rossi. Bruno Bozzetto, the Italian animated filmmaker, was
a friend of his and had apparently borrowed his name for his
favourite cartoon character, "Signor Rossi." Patrizio showed me
the area behind the town of Santa Barbara, and we hiked among
the hills. One morning, I was walking just ahead of him along
a trail and a rattlesnake barred the way, emitting that sinister,
unmistakable cough. I froze. Behind me I could hear Patrizio's
sibilant voice, calm as a lullaby: "Don't worry, Peter. He will
move away." And with that, he tossed a large twig down in front
of the snake, which instantly scuttled away into the brush.

When I returned in 1981 to teach a summer session at
UCSB, any pretensions I might have had were dashed on
my first day as a lecturer. As I looked at the steeply-banked
amphitheatre, with its students reminding me of the spectators
watching the catechism of Victor Sjöström during that nightmare in *Wild Strawberries*, I asked them, "So when was the
last time anyone saw a Bergman movie?" A hand shot up in
the top row. "Last night! It was *Casablanca*." In that moment
I resolved to go back to basics, explaining without any hint
of condescension the difference between Ingrid and Ingmar
Bergman, and the fact that they were not related to each other.
At the end of the six-week course, that same Texan student
came to my office and told me that he was utterly converted to
Bergman, and that he loved even the most austere of his films,
Winter Light. "One more soul…" as the missionary would
have said in darkest Africa during the 19th century.

The following year, I felt even more at ease in selecting eight
Westerns for study during the Summer course: *Little Big Man*,
High Noon, *My Darling Clementine*, *Shane*, *Winchester '73*,

Rio Bravo, The Gunfighter and *The Outlaw Josey Wales*. The programmes attracted a large audience of students and public from the Santa Barbara area, and I introduced each title and then encouraged discussion following the show.

During my annual sojourns in Santa Barbara, I rented a guest cottage from two of the loveliest people I had ever met, Howard and Jean Fenton. Howard had worked during the 1940s and '50s at 20th Century Fox, painting backdrops for films like *The Razor's Edge*. Then he had become Professor of Art at UCSB, and acquired increasing fame as a painter, whose spacious, evocative land- and seascapes were much sought after. Late in life he had built with his wife a gleaming white villa set in an acre of land which, by the time I arrived, burgeoned with all manner of exotic trees and fruits—lime, lemon, grapefruit, avocado and fig. Jean kept a shotgun handy for culling the rattlesnakes, and then hung their tails like trophies in her kitchen. More benign were the lizards of every length and pattern that lay contented on the sun-struck stone wall fringing the circular pool beside my guest cottage. Far below the treeline the Santa Barbara Channel embraced the islands of Santa Cruz and Santa Rosa, ten years before the oil derricks started dipping and rising like ancient predators searching the sea.

As we strolled through the hills in Montecito, Howard would regale me with stories of the vintage Hollywood. He had started as a driver for Gary Cooper, he had roomed with Henry Fonda in the early 1930s; he had hung out with Marlene Dietrich. His brother Leslie Fenton had made a modest name as a screen actor and married Ann Dvorak. Howard still knew so many of the Hollywood stars who lived discreetly in the Santa Barbara area. Richard Widmark would come up for a drink at the end of the day, put his booted feet up on the kitchen table, and repeat for me the sadistic giggle that made his name in *Kiss of Death*.

Another guest in the Fentons' kitchen was costume designer Dorothy Jeakins, who had won an Oscar for her work on the Ingrid Bergman version of *Joan of Arc*, as well as two other Academy Awards and a host of nominations across the years. I learned from her that bright white shirts and blouses had to be rinsed in tea so that they would not appear too dazzling on film. Dorothy knew the Huston family well, and had designed costumes for several of John's films. She mentioned a touching incident when John's daughter Anjelica Huston was caught up in a traffic accident on a Los Angeles freeway while her longtime lover Jack Nicholson was shooting *The Postman Always Lives Twice* in the Santa Barbara area. Nicholson dropped everything to charter a helicopter that airlifted Anjelica to hospital.

Most of the stars who had retired to Santa Barbara cherished their privacy, and grew accustomed to being forgotten. Dame Judith Anderson, the fearsome governess in Hitchcock's *Rebecca*, lived in a modest house on the edge of town but was delighted when one remembered her best roles. She agreed to become honorary President of a film festival in Santa Barbara should I manage to launch it. Petite, watchful, and happy to swallow a drink or two, she was then navigating her mid-eighties, with the role of a late lifetime still on the horizon, as Minx Lockridge in the soap opera *Santa Barbara*. When we were attending an alfresco party to coincide with the wedding of Prince Charles and Diana Spencer in the summer of 1981, she caught sight of me from the other side of our hosts' spacious pool. Without hesitation, Judith walked towards me and would have strolled across the very water had not another guest seized her arm in the nick of time.

One could never be sure of the identity of one's fellow guests at the dinner parties organised with such aplomb by the wealthier denizens of Montecito. One evening I found myself seated next to a tiny lady with spectacles and curly grey hair. When "Mrs. Martini" heard that I was lecturing on film, she said, rather shyly, that she had once been in the movies. The moment she mentioned *City Lights*, I realised that this was Virginia Cherrill, the blind flower-seller with whom Chaplin falls in love. Not only that, but she had married Cary Grant and retired from acting in 1933. Two marriages later, she lived in Santa Barbara with her husband Florian Martini, a Polish airman who had served in the Second World War.

Another survivor of the silent era charmed us all that night: Eleanor Boardman, former wife of King Vidor and imperishable star of that director's *The Crowd* in 1928. She had, like her friend John Gilbert, failed to make a successful transition to talking pictures, but had retained her youthful beauty into her eighties. She told me her secret: rising late, then placing slices of fresh cucumber over her face and lying still for two hours before lunch. An arcane titbit of information, but it would have been more interesting to hear about King Vidor and Eleanor's roles, and the studio grind during the 1920s.

Other luminaries of that same generation (born in the 1890s) would come up the coast to Montecito for the weekend — George Cukor and Frank Capra, for example. Mel Ferrer lived near Carpinteria, high in the hills in a discreet domain that included a long, slender "lap-pool" which Mel used to keep his tall figure in shape into his eighties. Passionately committed to theatre, he recalled how he and Gregory Peck had launched the La Jolla Playhouse far back in 1947.

Throughout the first ten years of the *International Film Guide*, I had determined to focus on good filmmakers of whatever kind or creed. I had crossed into the Russian sector of Berlin at Checkpoint Charlie, in order to view films by Konrad Wolf and Kurt Maetzig at the DEFA studios. I had included sections on such ostracised regimes as Greece (under the junta), Cuba and South Africa. As Eastern Europe under the heel of the Soviet Union had demonstrated, excellent films could emerge from even the most repressive conditions. After the Soviet invasion of Czechoslovakia in 1968, our correspondent in Prague, writing under a pseudonym, submitted an uncompromising text for the *International Film Guide*. We printed it in the 1970 edition, which appeared in late 1969. Three years later, Josef Škvorecký published his *All The Bright Young Men and Women*, about the youthful brilliance of a generation led by Miloš Forman, Věra Chytilová, Ewald Schorm, Jiří Menzel and others. I suddenly came upon a footnote stating that the minister in charge of monitoring foreign publications had seen the article in *IFG*. The journalist had been immediately dismissed from his post and was apparently working as a concierge in a provincial school. This was a stern reminder that the price of a free press can be terribly high.

On the positive side, our annual helped Polish director Krzysztof Zanussi obtain a visa for Italy prior to filming his documentary on Pope John XXIII; the bureaucrat behind the desk challenged his identity as a filmmaker, and Krzysztof produced a copy of the 1976 edition of *IFG*, featuring him on the cover as one of our "Five Directors of the Year." The visa was promptly granted.

Flashback: Dušan Makavejev

No filmmaker of his generation from Eastern Europe could match the charisma and originality of Dušan Makavejev. Forever bustling from festival to festival with his inspiring wife Bojana Marijan—who contributed to the sound and music on many of his works—he embodied all that was best in Tito's Yugoslavia. Long before the six republics descended into bitter, vicious wars of attrition with one another, Makavejev was a unifying spirit, the cynosure for all filmmakers in Yugoslavia. Serbian born and bred, he inspired contemporary directors from Croatia, Slovenia, Bosnia, Macedonia and Montenegro with his passionate discourse and his broad-minded dialectic. Over the years his voice grew huskier and his hunched back more pronounced, but his curiosity remained undiminished. He disarmed his critics with a laugh or a quip. "We in Yugoslavia are 100% Marxist," he loved to repeat, "50% Groucho and 50% Karl."

Makavejev was "First Secretary" of the Belgrade Film Archive Club in 1954 when Henri Langlois of the Cinémathèque française arrived in Belgrade with a diplomatic trunk filled with works by Clair, Feuillade, Pagnol and other classics of French cinema—all uncensored. In the years that followed, "Wajda's trilogy made a huge impression on me," he told me in 2001. "Then came *Jules and Jim, Breathless*—freedom of editing without careless editing, plus the casual treatment of the story, with casual dialogue. I liked the dancing camera in Chabrol's *À double tour*. He was for me probably more important than anyone else in the early days. Some of the images from *Les bonnes femmes* have stayed with me for forty years."

Like many aspiring directors in Eastern Europe, Makavejev had to cut his teeth on shorts and documentaries, which set the template for his love of reportage and realism in future years. "One of my 'prentice films was screened at a festival of amateur cinema in Cannes in 1957. A group of us film society members travelled with two tents to the Riviera in December, and found a place to set them up in the hills behind the railroad at the back of the town, where the Algerians lived, and for one franc a day you could erect your tent!" His maiden feature, *Man is Not a Bird*, released in 1965 and selected the following spring for the Critics' Week in Cannes, revealed a socially committed filmmaker who took risks with both form and content, flashing forward and backward in time as it tells the tale of an engineer visiting the copper-processing town of Bor and falling for a young hairdresser. The visuals are bleak, but *Man Is Not a Bird* has an irreducible humour and impudence that deftly sidesteps pessimism.

Our first meeting occurred in a smoke-filled editing room in the bowels of one of those gloomy government buildings on Belgrade's Knez Mihailova. It was March of 1967, and Dušan was editing what would become the first of his international arthouse successes. The Serbian title was "Ljubavni slucaj," and Dušan explained that this meant "Love Case" in English. I suggested he should call it "Love Dossier," and he accepted this with alacrity. However, better brains than his and mine decided in their wisdom to entitle the film *Love Affair, or The Case of the Missing Switchboard Operator*. This enigmatic, amusing, and faintly sinister production opened at the Yugoslav national festival in Pula in July 1967, and was bought by Brandon Films for the U.S. following its New York Festival premiere two months later. It inaugurated the golden years of Dušan Makavejev.

Much influenced by Godard, Makavejev created a dialectic that in each of his films opposed interludes of documentary to scenes of fantasy. At the same time he pioneered a forensic approach to cinema. In *Switchboard Operator*, an erstwhile revolutionary and civil servant who has been relegated to the status of rat-catcher, seduces and then inexplicably murders a young woman in contemporary Belgrade. The sex scenes in *Switchboard Operator* are stitched together with interviews with a sexologist, images of the autopsy on the victim's corpse, clips from Dziga Vertov's *Enthusiasm*, and laconic comments on the life of rats that roam the city sewers.

Makavejev's next work, *Innocence Unprotected*, was selected for Berlin in June 1968, and *W.R.: Mysteries of the Organism* featured in the first edition of the International Forum for Young Cinema in 1971. *Innocence Unprotected* portrayed the Serbian athlete Dragoljub Aleksić, who in 1942 had made a film about his own gymnastic feats, interspersed with stretches of wide-eyed melodrama. Makavejev virtually "re-made" this exercise in vanity, tinting some sequences, and bulking it out with a collage of wartime newsreel clips and interviews with Aleksić himself and his original cameraman.

At the Berlin Festival of 1970, Makavejev was a member of the jury and showed his mettle off-screen when Michael Verhoeven's West German entry, o.k., dealing with the rape of a Vietnamese woman by four American soldiers, aroused the wrath of jury president George Stevens. Makavejev argued forcefully that any filmmaker has the right to speak freely about world issues, and, accused by Stevens of being an agent for the East German government, he finally resigned. Rumours circulated that West German Chancellor Willy Brandt then personally intervened in the crisis, and Stevens agreed to reconcile with Makavejev and his fellow jurors.

The initials W.R. stand for Wilhelm Reich, the Austro-American psychoanalyst who claimed to have discovered "orgone" energy, which enhanced one's sexual energy. Reich's written work was still banned in the U.S. when Makavejev began his research for *W.R.: Mysteries of the Organism*—and as late as 1960 his books had been literally burned at the request of the Food and Drug Agency of the time. Looking back from the perspective of 2001, Dušan said: "My cinema is one of essays—but the essays are not always evident, they are often hidden."

To some degree *W.R.* serves as a disquisition on the life and experiments of Reich, but to an even larger degree it is a call to arms against censorship and intolerance. Makavejev offers a clear dialectic between the frustrations and stupidity of rigid ideology (read: Communism) and the freedom of a Reichian world. He then proceeds, in the manner of Magritte or Braque, to fill his canvas with a cluster of sundry clips from the 1946 Soviet film, *The Vow*, about Stalin, one of which follows a close-up shot of a plaster-cast phallus. The fictional thread of *W.R.* describes a doomed affair between Milena Dravić and a Russian skater, contrasted with the zestful copulation of Jagoda Kaloper and "Comrade Ljuba." Theory and practice, the irrational and the rational, thus meet in head-on collision, and the result is a film that mauls the sacred iconography of both the U.S. and the Soviet Union, affirming that "Politics is for those whose orgasm is incomplete." It's a classic utopian parable, in the mood of Huxley's *Brave New World* or Orwell's *Animal Farm*. Jagoda Kaloper travelled with *W.R.* to campuses across America, and I introduced her and the film at the University of Rochester. The undergraduate audience of the early 1970s revelled in Jagoda's nude scenes, even if the political references often seemed out of reach. In Yugoslavia, however, *W.R.* was banned without ceremony—for sixteen years—and in many other territories the film enraged the censors.

"At the end of 1972, the liberal leadership in Serbia was forced to resign," Makavejev recounted to me in a 2008 interview. "An ideological/fundamentalist tsunami threw the media into a kind of psychotic vertigo. Already printed books were chopped up into old paper, theatre plays were removed from the repertory, and a campaign against the 'black wave' in films treated us as foreign agents." It was time for this paradigm of the avant-garde to depart for new horizons. He acquired a charming apartment at the foot of the Rue de Seine in Paris, and pressed ahead with his next project. Entitled *Sweet Movie* (1974), it was shot in Montreal, Niagara Falls, Paris and Amsterdam, with no contribution from Yugoslavia.

A satire on everything from Communism to beauty pageants, and from chastity belts to coprophilia, *Sweet Movie* also addressed the ghastly crimes of the Stalinist era, notably the massacre of Polish officers in Katyn Forest in 1940. Scatological in the extreme, scattershot in its relentless assault on bourgeois values, *Sweet Movie* was premiered at the Cannes Festival. Meeting Makavejev in the Petit Carlton café after the press screening, I said I had reservations about the film. Makavejev turned on his heel and stalked out of the bar. We would not talk again for several years. Looking back, I think that my disappointment stemmed not so much from the flaunting of taboos in the commune scenes as from the childishness of several sequences—although there's a fine line between childishness and frivolity, or as Makavejev would say, between chocolate and excrement!

In *Montenegro*, funded by the Swedes in 1981, Makavejev used such Bergman eminences as actor Erland Josephson and editor Sylvia Ingemarsson. In Susan Anspach, he also found the perfect actress to play his bored bourgeois housewife, who kicks over the traces by setting fire to the bedclothes, and eventually poisoning her entire family. While her husband is abroad, she finds solace in an underground nightclub, where the Yugoslav immigrant known as "Montenegro" satisfies her sexual cravings. The film marked a return to Makavejev's provocative form of the 1960s and early 1970s, even as its linear narrative helped to attract a large audience in numerous countries.

In October 2006, I recorded two interviews with Makavejev for Criterion, one on *W.R.* and the other on *Sweet Movie*. There he confirmed that he liked making satirical films, because he could then "smuggle across" some ideas and information that might otherwise be boring, and that for him editing was more important than shooting. The following year, he spoke to me for a book that the European Film Academy published to mark its 20th anniversary. "Our hand-held cameras were curious and critical," he noted. "Instead of performing, our actors were asked just to be alive. Our stories on film became unpredictable, as in life." Our final conversation was at the Berlin Festival in 2008, when we talked on stage at the Berlinale Talents programme and Makavejev reiterated his desire that people should see his films more than once, that they could return to it as one returns to Mark Twain or Dostoevsky and gleans something fresh and new each time.

By the 1990s, Makavejev's cinema lay like a beached whale on the sands of time. *The Coca-Cola Kid*, *Manifesto* and *Gorilla Bathes at Noon*, made between 1985 and 1993, all failed to reach a wide audience. The antic wit was no longer so acerbic, the surrealism no longer so engaging, nor the political comment so trenchant as it had been in his heyday. Long into the future, nonetheless, Dušan Makavejev will remain a figure as emblematic of his period as Ken Kesey in literature or Velvet Underground in music. I like to think that Dziga Vertov and Salvador Dalí would have been his lifelong fans.

I knew in 1972 that I was taking a risk when I published in *IFG* an introductory survey of contemporary Iranian cinema. The author was Hajir Dariush, a witty, intelligent man who, with some fellow directors and film buffs like Freydoun Moezi-Moghaddam and Bahman Farmanara, had launched the Tehran International Film Festival in that same year. Confronted by works of such merit as Dariush Mehrjui's *The Postman* and Bahram Beizai's *Downpour*, one had to admit that despite the Shah's vice-like grip, Iranian society seemed able to live with art.

Hajir urged me to come to his country for the second edition of the film festival in November 1973. Thanks to the favour in which film was held by the Shah's second wife, Farah Diba, the event had acquired a sizeable budget. Stars and directors were to be invited in droves, all expenses paid. During the next three years, virtually every icon of Hollywood visited the Tehran Film Festival. When the Shah's sister hosted a reception one evening at her space-age villa, distinguished guests were taken by bus ("for security reasons") from the Hilton Hotel overlooking the capital. Faces I can still remember in that single bus included the dancer Ann Miller, the choreographer Hermes Pan, the directors William Wyler, Frank Capra and Rouben Mamoulian, alongside actors Gregory Peck, Goldie Hawn, Stella Stevens, James Mason and Trevor Howard. Christopher Lee came in a separate limousine. "I always have my own chariot," he boomed.

Although the Shah's militia could be glimpsed on the roof of the hotel, weapons at the ready, one was blissfully unaware of the darker reaches of the regime, and the dreaded basement torture chambers of the Evin prison, which stood not so far removed from the luxurious purlieus of the Tehran Hilton. I certainly felt a wave of remorse for having succumbed to the honeyed approaches of my intellectual Iranian friends. The best that can be said for the Shah is that within a few years he swept Iran from the 18th century into the 20th, while behaving like a despot from an even earlier age.

When Herb Lightman, the genial editor of *American Cinematographer* magazine, became detached from our party during an excursion, we were at first alarmed, until my friend Ian Jessel quipped, "There must be a Missing Persians' Bureau around here somewhere!" By the end of the festival, one became quite adventurous. Returning on my own from a screening in the city centre, I hailed a cab with difficulty. Eventually, a driver screeched to a halt beside me and urged me to get in the back. To my amazement, I found I was seated next to René Clair, while a peasant and his young goat were somehow squeezed into the front passenger seat. As the car careened around street corners, it was hardly reassuring to note that the speedometer needle was stuck at zero.

The highlight of the festival for foreign guests was a trip to the ancient site of Persepolis near Shiraz, pausing for a night in the fabled Shah Abbas caravanserai at Isfahan. The two faces of Persian culture would become manifest in the mosques of the 16th and 17th centuries and the pre-Christian splendours of Persepolis. Travelling south into the hot desert in small, claustrophobic planes, even the most urbane of stars grew tetchy. One young British actor lost his composure while our plane needed to be repaired and we were all herded into a "waiting area" with no indication of how long we might be delayed. Suddenly he cracked, screaming that he needed to return home to London immediately. Iran was, of course, one of those countries as complicated to leave as it was to enter. After much procrastination, the local guides found a battered car, and our friend was last seen heading into the dusty distance. He survived to play some of the most glamorous TV roles of the late 1970s and '80s, and to leave us with the realisation that stars also sweat.

Michael York, the handsome hero of films like Joseph Losey's *Accident* and Bob Fosse's *Cabaret*, proved altogether more sophisticated. By some miraculous legerdemain, he could change clothes in the most confined of spaces, and descended the steps of the plane in immaculate garb at each stop, to the delight of the local press photographers. He sent me a gracious, handwritten letter on the day of his departure, thanking me as "patrol leader" and extending his apologies to H.M. The British Ambassador that he could not attend luncheon the following day.

The columns of Persepolis still surged into the azure sky, but at that time the site was filled with immense quilted tents, erected by the Shah for the celebration of 2,500 years of Iranian Monarchical Rule in 1971, a lavish affair to which the world's great, good, and not so good, were invited. Our guides assured us that all manner of snakes and scorpions had been purged from a 30 sq. km area around the site. Along with Karnak, Machu Picchu, Angkor, and the Taj Mahal, Persepolis remains one of the most imposing historical sites I have ever visited.

The unfamiliarity of the surroundings, and the difficulty of making international phone calls, left some of the distinguished guests ill at ease. Even the smallest incident could unnerve them. I had, for some bizarre reason, been appointed head of the British delegation by Gwyneth Dunwoody at the Film Production Association of Great Britain, and so complaints tended to reach my ears first. One morning James Mason approached me in a foul mood, asserting that a box of ladies' lingerie had been delivered to his suite. I promised to investigate but, before I could do so, Margaret Hinxman, the delightfully civilised critic of the *Sunday Telegraph*, approached my breakfast table. "Peter," she said with a mischievous smile, "I think there's been some mistake in the laundry room because I have just received some men's underpants, all wrapped nicely in tissue paper. They're certainly not mine." When James Mason heard about the confusion, he did not laugh, but Margaret did, until the tears rolled down her cheeks.

Hajir Dariush himself would emigrate to France, where his fluency in the language earned him employment as a cultural bureaucrat, and he died all too young. Those mid-1970s film festivals remain to some degree a memorial to him. How swiftly the currents of international politics change! While we gathered in Tehran in 1973, the British Secretary for Trade and Industry was concluding arrangements at Persepolis to invest some £250 million in Iran. As I write these lines, fifty years later, the British government has effectively joined the United States in freezing Iran out of the international community of nations. Only one trend remains constant: the excellence of Iranian cinema, then and now, exemplified by such masterly works as *The Seed of the Sacred Fig*, *No Bears* and *A Hero*.

In 1977, the Indian High Commission in London invited me to the Delhi film festival, and I seized the chance to see a country that had been brought to life with such perspicuity by the films of Satyajit Ray and Mrinal Sen. Among the British contingent was the film critic of *The Observer*, Philip French, and John Gillett of the British Film Institute, who immediately noticed something wrong with the projection. "I must get this chap to change his carbons," he whispered to me before tiptoeing up to the projection booth.

At the Information Department of the BFI, John had been a godsend to me in my fledgling days as a film critic, allowing me access to files, and even letting me set up my small portable typewriter behind a bookcase at the back of the library. His commitment to cinema could, however, distract him from the everyday world. As we travelled by bus to the Indian prime minister's residence to foregather with distinguished festival visitors like Elia Kazan and Ellen Burstyn, I saw a family begging beside the road. One of the youngest children had her hand pulled back and taped behind her head, in an obvious attempt to create a handicap that would attract more money. Shocked, I nudged John, who was seated next to me with his nose in the festival programme booklet. "Mmmm, yes," he mumbled in all innocence, not looking up. "I'm just trying to check on the screening schedule of this retrospective." I still have a snapshot of John at the tomb of Mahatma Gandhi. His jacket is wound tightly around his chest and fully buttoned; his shirt and tie reinforced the impression of an Englishman well and truly abroad. An Englishman, however, with the gentlest heart imaginable. John's impish sense of humour transcended his formal image and made him the most entertaining of companions.

Flashback: Satyajit Ray

While the revolution in cinema in the late 1950s and early '60s occurred primarily in Europe, there were always two exotic Eastern names that shared the arthouse marquee: Akira Kurosawa and Satyajit Ray. Ray (pronounced "Rye," and no kin to that darling of the *Cahiers-Movie* crowd, Nicholas Ray) was, as my Indian friends pointed out with a certain condescension, a Bengali. The fact that Calcutta was a major metropolis meant little to Hindus who were accustomed to their language and cities yielding the sub-continent's most talented filmmakers as well as what was then the nascent Bollywood.

I had fallen in love with Ray's exquisite sensibility, his use of music, and his direction of (often) amateur actors. *The*

World of Apu and *The Music Room* touched me the most, although each new Ray film came as a fresh adventure, culminating in the penetrating satire of *Days and Nights in the Forest*. I was invited to meet him at the home of Marie Seton, a small, intense, chain-smoking Londoner who was held in high regard for her books on Paul Robeson and Sergei Eisenstein, and especially for her brilliant reconstruction of Eisenstein's *¡Que viva Mexico!* A friend of Jawaharlal Nehru and Krishna Menon, Marie was then at work on her biography of Ray. As I came forward to be introduced, Ray unfolded himself like a stork from a comfortable arm-chair. He was fully 6 feet 5 inches tall, with an imposing head and a sensual mouth. His rich, marsala-dark voice gave him an effortless authority, and alongside Orson Welles, he was the closest to a Renaissance man I have ever met, brilliant not just as a director and writer, but also as composer and designer. Working with modest means, he had the knack of finding exactly the right camera set-up, enabling his actors to express their innermost feelings.

At Delhi in 1977, the producer Suresh Jindal invited some of the film festival guests to his house to hear about Ray's first film in Hindustani, *The Chess Players*, which was then in production. Ray explained that this story of two noblemen preoccupied with chess served him as a metaphor for the political intrigues of 1856, during the final throes of the Moghul Empire.

A day or two later, Ray arose with the rest of us in the small hours so that we could reach Agra in time to see the Taj Mahal in the roseate light of dawn. An image I shall never forget is of Antonioni and Kurosawa accompanying him around the shrine—three of the cinema's great masters laughing and chatting informally. Ray gave off an intense self-confidence without seeming in the slightest degree arrogant or complacent. Never sentimental, he probably agreed with the king in *The Chess Players*, who says that "Nothing but poetry and music should bring tears to a man's eyes." While in Agra, he told Kurosawa about a mythical tree in India that measured almost one mile in girth. Much later, Kurosawa wrote to him, reminding him of that incident, and saying, "I have always felt from the first time I met you that you are the kind of man who is like a huge tree. A great tree in the woods in India."

In July 1990, Ray sent me an elegantly handwritten letter saying that, "Until recently, I had no opportunity to take a look at my early films—although I occasionally felt the urge to do so. Over the last couple of years my son has built up a collection of video tapes of most of my films, and at last I've had a chance to re-view my efforts of 25/30 years ago. I must say I was most agreeably surprised to see how little they show their age." Apologising for not sending a snapshot he took of me with Kurosawa and Antonioni, he noted that, "I'm hopelessly disorganised in everything except filmmaking." His Ibsen adaptation, *An Enemy of the People*, had appeared in 1989, and he would complete his wonderful swansong, *The Stranger*, in 1991. Less than a year later he died, at the same age—70—as Orson Welles.

By 1977, our publishing programme had reached its peak, with several titles each year appearing under the Tantivy imprint, and other film books that we distributed on behalf of A.S. Barnes & Co. The most ambitious and also the most foolhardy of our ventures was *World Filmography*. This was a series of books to be published over a fifteen-year period that would eventually cover, year by year, every feature film made anywhere in the world. The films would be classified by country, and would include main credits and a concise description of each title's content. Of course all this would later be achieved by the Internet Movie Database, but this was more than twenty years before the invention of the world wide web brought the internet into the homes of film buffs.

We commissioned researchers in as many countries as possible. Most were already known to me through film festivals, or as correspondents for the *IFG*. The first volume, for the calendar year 1967, took almost a decade to compile, with data on some 1,500 feature films flowing in from 45 countries. I was amused when the Canadian magazine *Take One* wrote: "Peter Cowie is positively the hardest-working person we know. How he manages to run London's prestigious Tantivy Press (and edit their annual *International Film Guide*), and still show up at as many film festivals as he does has always been something of a

GENERAL EDITOR: PETER COWIE

1967
1967
1967

WORLD
FILMOGRAPHY

mystery. Now the crazy fool has embarked on yet another project that might—all by itself—daunt weaker souls: a *World Filmography*."

Later that year, the 1968 volume was also published, but it became clear that the workload was too much for our small concern, and the operation fell slowly and inexorably into oblivion.

In the spring of 1978 I made my first trip to the Far East, thanks to an invitation to attend the fledgling Hong Kong Film Festival. Bruce Lee may have been long dead, at the tragically young age of 32, but Shaw Brothers' studio was bustling with several productions when a few of us visited the lot in Clearwater Bay. Watching the technicians at work on foley effects was irresistible. Men sat cross-legged, beating sacks of grain with flails to create the sound of everything from kickboxing to gusts of wind. Others pattered on a variety of drums to simulate horses galloping through a village.

A few months earlier, we had selected King Hu as one of the Five Directors of the Year featured on the cover of the *International Film Guide*. Hu had been born in Beijing but had been obliged to stay and work in Hong Kong in the wake of the Communist takeover in mainland China in 1949. Thanks to Derek Elley, I met Hu in London, and when I arrived in Hong Kong he and his wife escorted me happily around various parts of the (then British) enclave. Hu's *A Touch of Zen*, made in 1969, was only discovered in the West thanks to a screening in Cannes six years later. It remains an epic as sophisticated and visually dazzling as any samurai movie from Japan. Hu had expanded a ghost story into a full-scale philosophical adventure, using the CinemaScope format to full advantage.

Roger Garcia, one of the festival organisers, kindly indulged my love of ping pong by taking me to a club in Kowloon, where I was allowed to knock up with some of the younger members. After a few minutes I was exhausted, not to say bewildered by the speed and ingenuity of the Chinese players, who were using sponge-covered bats as opposed to the pimple rubber bats still common in Britain.

For a few days I flew to Japan because George Perry, then editor of the *Sunday Times* magazine had commissioned me

to interview the latest generation of Japanese directors. From
the moment of arrival, this was a startling experience. Narita
Airport, serving Tokyo, had just been opened, in the teeth of
sustained and sophisticated opposition from anti-militarist,
anti-American and left-wing groups, comprising students and
even farmers whose land had been compulsorily requisitioned
just several years earlier, when construction began.

As we left the terminal building to catch the bus into Tokyo,
I could hear the distant shouting and chanting of protesters
beyond the perimeter. The previous month, protesters had
managed to occupy the control tower, smashing equipment and
offices. When I hailed a taxi to go to my hotel, I noted that the
elderly driver wore spotless white flannel gloves and ran after
me when I left him, as a tip, the change for my yen banknote.
The unfathomable language, and the habit of bowing at every
new encounter added to the sense of deracination, but also to a
feeling of exhilaration that has stayed with me across the intervening decades.

Kazuko Kawakita, whom I had met in Cannes, proved a
lively and knowledgeable host. She also arranged for me to have
a young translator who was none other than Ian Buruma, later
to become well known for his non-fiction writing on Asian and
philosophical topics. We criss-crossed Tokyo over the next two
days, but although I recall the directors I interviewed (Yosh-
ishige Yoshida, Kazuhiko Hasegawa, Sachiko Hidari), only two
left a lasting impression: Shuji Terayama and Nagisa Oshima.

We found Terayama in a tiny building in Roppongi (the
capital's equivalent of South Kensington, although the shabby
streets belied such status — wealth, like emotions, being scru-
pulously concealed in Japan). The most idiosyncratic of the
younger generation, Terayama shone in both theatre and film.
Copies of *Cahiers du cinéma* were on sale in his cafeteria and the
obligatory Brecht posters dominated the walls. "Raising money
is hard," he told me. "But you can always find a rich widow or
an opulent store to finance a picture. But distribution is still in
the hands of the major companies." His short films were made
primarily for friends and for showing at small film societies. He
had made an impact in Europe and the States with his avant-
garde, off-the-wall cinematic experiments, *Throw Away Your
Books, Let's Go into the Streets* and *Pastoral Hide-and-Seek*.

Like Bergman, he divided his time between stage and screen, using the same crew in his films as in his theatre productions. Terayama would die at the age of just 47.

Nagisa Oshima was more durable and more influential. Tall, dignified, well-dressed, you would never think that such a gracious individual could have the courage and commitment to produce such films as *Diary of a Shinjuku Thief* and *The Empire of the Senses*. Indeed while I was in Tokyo he was being tried for obscenity because a publisher had released risqué stills from *In the Realm of the Senses*. Oshima was a smouldering volcano, whose characters often resorted to violence to express their loathing for the militarism inherent in Japanese traditions. But death for Oshima was in direct opposition to Japanese tradition, "whereas for Yukio Mishima," he said, "death is a fusion with the great tradition of the past."

"Young directors today are very mild compared with the late 1960s," Oshima remarked when we met. "The big companies are opting for spectaculars and historical subjects. A talented man like Teshigahara [*Woman of the Dunes*] has become a potter, apart from working in TV from time to time." Yoshida told me that he believed Oshima to be the only director of his generation with real integrity.

By night, Kazuko Shibata escorted me round the bars of Shinjuku, each tinier than the last, and each with its bottle of whisky marked with the name "Shibata" or "Kawakita." A couple of rounds, and it was into the taxi and on to the next watering hole. I remember reaching my hotel utterly inebriated, blundering around the minuscule room with its bathroom prefabricated from a kind of shellac and featuring an automated toilet that played music and emitted puffs of scent at judicious moments.

Returning to Japan several times in the years since 1978, first with *Variety*, then for research and sheer pleasure, I have sensed that the salient features of Japanese life have been to some degree blunted (or some might say smoothed) by the ever-mounting wave of mass tourism. Thanks to the persistence of the Shinto ideal, Japan appears the cleanest country in the world, and possibly also the politest, and most respectful of others. I finally managed to clamber up the hillside cemetery where Ozu's grave resides in the grounds of Engakuji Temple in

Kamakura. Several hundred metres away lies the family tomb-stone of Akira Kurosawa. Someone had placed a half-smoked cigar on the edge of the grave, as if in homage, but the contrast with Ozu's grave was stark. A few flowers for Kurosawa, and at least twenty bottles of sake, beer, and whisky adorning the granite slab below Ozu's headstone, on which the single char-acter "Mu" or "Nothing" is engraved. You realise that Ozu was the most beloved of all directors for his fellow Japanese; he described the detail and rhythm of their daily lives, while Kuro-sawa, majestic and inventive, found his public outside Japan. He was, if you like, Beethoven to Ozu's Chopin.

In September 1979, just one year before Lech Walesa climbed over the wire fence of the shipyards in Gdańsk and started the revolt that would change the face of Poland, I was invited to that Polish seaside city, the former Danzig in East Prussian days, for the annual festival of Polish feature films. Andrzej Wajda popped up everywhere, introducing his latest film, *The Young Girls of Wilko*, chairing the Polish Association of Film Authors. When I said how much I admired *Everything for Sale*, he smiled wryly: "I was in London in January 1967. I'd spent an evening meeting David Mercer. When I got back to my hotel, Polanski called to tell me about Cybulski's death. Ever since then I've regretted not having thought of getting Mercer to do the screenplay. It was a wonderful chance, and I missed it." He reflected that "The real weakness of the Polish school of the 1950s, and the reason for its inevitable disappearance, was that its films presented heroes who were more stupid than History. To my mind, it's wrong to stand on the side of History instead of on the side of your hero." He still resented the delay in the foreign release of *Man of Marble*, arguably his greatest work. "Many politicians from the 1950s were still around, and they didn't relish being criticised. That's why the export licence was withheld for so long."

Flashback: Andrzej Wajda

September 2013: Andrzej Wajda, 87 years young, sits quietly in an armchair overlooking the Venetian lagoon. Beside him lies a stylish cane, in his lapel the red rosette of the Légion d'Honneur. This is an hour or so before the world premiere of *Walesa, Man of Hope*, his 36th feature film. I ask him what prompted him to make it, and he says with a laugh, "I think the boy deserves a film!" After all, Walesa at 70 is, one feels, a mere stripling in the eyes of this Polish maestro. When he goes on stage to accept the Persol Award from Venice festival director Alberto Barbera, Wajda reminds us that *Ashes and Diamonds* had won two prizes at the Mostra "55 years ago this month." Wajda has marked each of the past seven decades with at least one major film.

As *Walesa* starts to unfurl, my mind flits back to September 1979 when, at the Gdańsk Festival of Polish Feature Films, I interviewed Wajda in a hotel overlooking the sea. As he entered the room, Wajda radiated an almost electrical charge of energy. He had made three films in the previous twenty months, was acting as head producer at the prestigious "X" Unit, and was dashing from one meeting to another in his capacity as chairman of the Polish Association of Film Authors.

He could grasp "the whole equation" in a twinkling, and did so with passion and humour. When seeing friends, he would throw back his head and laugh like a lusty teenager. But what I also noted was his capacity to preface each response to my questions with a thoughtful, abstract comment that set the concrete facts of his answer in a philosophical context. When, for example, I queried the end of his majestic *Man of Marble*, he leaned forward and said: "The fact that the bricklayer, Birkut, loses physically doesn't mean that his ideas are destroyed. He must die, because death at the end is vital both to Greek drama and to Communist propaganda." He added that the irony, and the dynamic camerawork of the film, sprang from his working alongside young people such as Agnieszka Holland and Krystyna Janda.

When Agnieszka came in to collect Wajda for his next engagement, I told them both I had witnessed an enthusiastic reception for *Ashes and Diamonds* at Hunter College in Manhattan a few months earlier. Wajda gave vent to a bray of delight: "God!" he exclaimed. "How talented we were in those days!"

I next sat down with Wajda in Warsaw in 2002, when I talked to him for my book, *Revolution!* He remembered

Boleslaw Michalek's book about Andrzej Wajda,
was published by Tantivy in 1970.

meeting the unforgettable hero/victim of *Ashes and Diamonds*, Zbigniew Cybulski, in Kraków, where students interested in the arts used to gather for summer camp. He could still feel the vivid sense of loss on hearing that Cybulski had been killed after slipping on the steps of a fast-moving train he was trying to board. In 1967, *Everything for Sale* became Wajda's elegy for Cybulski's brilliant career as an actor. As an enlightening aside, he told me through his translator that when Cybulski sniffed the blood on his hands at the close of *Ashes and Diamonds*, "he does so with a strange, reflexive movement. This gesture transports us from the world of symbols into reality, where biology, with its unpredictable reactions, rules."

In 2006, the Berlin Film Festival asked me to deliver the speech in honour of Wajda when he accepted a Golden Bear. In the quarter century since our previous meeting, Wajda had served in the Polish senate, made around fifteen films, and been awarded an Oscar for lifetime achievement. Afterwards, at a dinner with his wife and a few friends at the Paris Bar on Kantstrasse, he spoke about his next project, which would pay homage to his father who had been murdered by Soviet troops in the 1940 massacre at Katyn. Wajda would be over 80 when *Katyn* was nominated for the Academy Award for Best Foreign Language Film.

And so back to Venice, where *Walesa, Man of Hope* astonishes even hardened critics with its exhilarating vigour. Wajda seems by some mysterious alchemy to have retained his youthful energy, his political finesse, and his flair for pacing a story that works like *Danton* and *Man of Iron* demonstrated so vividly.

It is after midnight but as the credits roll, Wajda joins Lech Walesa in the balcony to acknowledge the cheers of the audience. Finally, as the applause goes on and on, Wajda and Walesa spontaneously raise their arms and link hands in a gesture not just of "solidarity," but also in defiance of the encroaching years.

In 1979, my agent in London, Gerald Pollinger, sold U.S. rights to my proposed Bergman biography to Scribner's. I had already been delighted that Secker and Warburg had acquired the British rights for a project that remained unwritten. But Scribner's! To visit that fabled building on Fifth Avenue was exciting; to take the elevator beside the bookstore and be escorted to a library the walls of which were panelled with bookshelves containing the names of legendary authors I had admired for so long—Ernest Hemingway, Edith Wharton, F. Scott Fitzgerald, Thomas Wolfe…

The senior editor (and later to be the company president), Jack Galazka, greeted me warmly. He asked when I felt I could deliver the manuscript. I said that I would have to do various interviews with Bergman's collaborators, as well as other research in Sweden, and that probably I could not complete the work for almost two years. Flexing his gleaming leather shoes, the avuncular Galazka responded with a comment that seemed ever so faintly complacent: "Well, we have been around since 1846, so I'm sure we shall still be here when you finish your manuscript." Little did he, or I, know that within a few years Scribner's would be absorbed by Macmillan, and, not long afterwards, even the great Scribner's bookstore would close and give way to a perfume emporium. Looking back, I was fortunate to have been published by Scribner's in the United States and later by Faber and Faber in the U.K.

Sweden has always been the aristocrat of the Nordic region. Its public buildings, its villas, evince an almost complacent grandeur. No neighbourhood in Scandinavia can rival Stockholm's Old Town for sheer picturesque, pastel-shaded beauty. Swedes enjoy an unrivalled quality of life. Cosseted from womb to tomb, in exchange for hefty taxation, these calm, slow-speaking citizens have always found it difficult to empathise with Ingmar Bergman's metaphysical perspectives on life. I remember meeting Gunnar Björnstrand (who played the Squire in *The Seventh Seal* and was the male lead in *Smiles of a Summer Night*) with his wife in the lobby of Stockholm's legendary Red Windmill cinema. I was emerging from *The Silence*, and Björnstrand gave me an indulgent smile as he doffed his fur hat: "A bit over the top, isn't it?" he said. There's no doubt that the sleek, mundane lines of Swedish society seem far removed from Bergman's often sombre world, with its harsh quarrels and its often candid sex.

Flashback: Jacques Tati in Sweden

Jacques Tati, in his mid-sixties when I encountered him, was at first intimidating. He gazed at you with an owl-like intensity. But he proved most affable, light years away from one's image of a movie director; rather, with his neatly groomed grey hair and suit and tie, he resembled a distinguished banker or diplomat on vacation (although his burly shoulders reminded you that he had played for fun a boxer, a wrestler, and a tennis player in his early short films).

I was in Stockholm in January of 1974 to catch up with new Swedish films, and staying at the Hotel Diplomat on Strandvägen. In those days, the hotel's lobby was on the second floor, and when I climbed the stairs at the end of an afternoon, there was Tati on the sofa in the lobby. Bumptious as always, I dared to introduce myself and tell him about the work I'd done to promote *PlayTime* back in 1967, producing a brochure for the Dutch premiere at the request of the local distributor.

We chatted of this and that. "At the age of 22," he said, "I decided to go into films. I used to play rugger [rugby union football] every Sunday, and afterwards I would put on a little pantomime for our team." He explained that he was in the process of making a film for Swedish TV entitled *Parade*, a tribute to the circus world he had so adored in his childhood during the Great War. I asked him how he managed to capture the characteristics of a human being in a few deft strokes. At this, he unfurled those endless legs, stood erect at six feet three inches, and drew me to a large circular window that overlooked the street. "Look," he ordered, and I looked, seeing a steady flow of people on their way home after the day's work. "Now, see him," he gestured, and I saw a man with a porkpie hat swinging his briefcase with aplomb. Tati explained how he picked such figures from the crowd ("I don't want actors you can recognise in life"), then magnified their mannerisms so as both to amuse his audience and reveal a personality. "I can wait on the corner down there for two hours," he said, "until comedy comes along." *PlayTime* remained his favourite film. "We shot it in 70 mm," he recalled, "because a man dropping his umbrella in a huge airport is more 'drastic' than it is in a tiny room."

Then someone arrived for a meeting with him. Like Monsieur Hulot, Tati stood poised on the balls of his feet as though ready to break into flight. It reminded me of what he had once said at a press conference in Cannes: "I'm the opposite of a Chaplin or a Keaton. In the old days, the comic used to come on and say, 'I'm the funnyman in this film. I know how to dance, sing, juggle, do the lot.' But Hulot—he's life. He doesn't need gags. He only has to walk." He

shook my hand formally in farewell and vanished into the
bowels of the hotel with his colleague.

I enjoyed my regular trips to Stockholm during the 1960s and
'70s. The more I explored Swedish cinema, the more I wanted
to write about it and campaign for its lesser lights, whose work
was rarely exported. In 1964, I went to the fledgling offices
of the Swedish Film Institute on Kungsgatan. Established the
previous year, this love child of engineer and film critic Harry
Schein then comprised but a handful of employees, among
them Christer Frunck as Information Officer, K-H. Lindquist
in charge of sales, and Aina Bellis as Schein's P.A. The film
archive, which came under the aegis of the Institute, remained
in the outskirts of the city. Schein received me in his attractive,
well-lit office, with a portrait of his wife Ingrid Thulin adorning
the massive desk. Smoking and laughing incessantly, he promul-
gated his vision of a Swedish film industry that would continue
to have Bergman at its head but that would, thanks to a tax on
every ticket sold at the domestic box office, possess the means
to surge ahead. He liked the first edition of the *International
Film Guide* and immediately placed a half-page advertisement
in our next issue, in which he declared the Film Institute to be
"a foundation formed by the Swedish government and the
entire Swedish film trade. The purpose of the Swedish Film
Institute is to promote the development of Swedish film art, to
increase the understanding of film as an art in general, to assist
in the distribution of foreign films of artistic importance, and to
finance technical, artistic and academic training and research in
the art of film."

   Harry Schein ignited strong feelings of love or hate. More
than one young executive, more than one filmmaker, was effectively crucified by Schein's ruthless disdain. But none could
dispute his efficiency and his passion for reform in a conservative profession like film production and exhibition. As I found
through the years, his grinning bonhomie, his incessant flow
of wit and wisdom, masked a personality at odds with the
world. A charismatic figure on television and in the media, he
seemed lonelier than anyone in Sweden. In 1978 he finally left
the Institute—to his chagrin—and I wrote to him saying that
had played an historic role in the development of Swedish film.

He responded with characteristic irony and conceit: "Who cares about history, except for those who are themselves part of history?"

A new generation did indeed emerge as a consequence of Schein's initiative, which had taken shape due to his friendship with men in high places, notably Olof Palme, the future Prime Minister. I quickly met and became familiar with neophyte directors like Bo Widerberg, Jan Troell, Vilgot Sjöman, Jonas Cornell, Jan Halldoff and especially the arrogant, charismatic Jörn Donner, who would remain a close friend for the rest of our lives. One evening in February 1965, Donner called me at my hotel, and suggested I accompany him to the laboratory where he was editing his second feature, *Adventure Starts Here*. The extracts I saw struck me as stiff and as awkward as the title of the film, but I was fascinated by Donner's laconic, assured view on life — a cynicism that, as so often, concealed a certain vulnerability, even insecurity. He talked of going to Berlin in his late teens, of novels that he had already written, and of his penetrating study of Ingmar Bergman that had come out in 1962. I found it hard to keep up with his drinking. Like many Swedish-speaking Finns, he could consume enormous quantities of beer and schnapps, vodka, or whisky.

Flashback: Vilgot Sjöman

Of all the Swedish directors caught in Bergman's shadow, Vilgot Sjöman was the least resentful. He was a good six years older than Bo Widerberg, Jonas Cornell, Kjell Grede and even Jan Troell. Deep down he regarded himself as a writer-observer more than a filmmaker. When he was just 17 years of age, Bergman told him over coffee that he was "gifted," and cast him as Theseus in his production of *A Midsummer Night's Dream* in 1942. In 1948, his maiden but very mature novel, *The Teacher*, was published to much acclaim, at a time when a restless Bergman was still struggling to find his idiom. He even beat Ingmar to the draw where Harriet Andersson was concerned, for she starred in the screen version of Vilgot's novel, *Trots*, shot a few months before she embarked on *Summer with Monika*. Despite his flying start as a novelist, and despite the avuncular support of

Bergman, Vilgot had to wait until he was almost 40 to make his first feature film.

I first met Vilgot in 1965, after his first two films, *The Mistress* and *491*, had appeared to mixed reviews. He cut a rather morose figure, with his often unsmiling gaze, his face masked with a blonde beard and hair that sprang like young corn from his skull. "A filmmaker should stick to his background," he said. "But I have to learn the profession in order to do things in a different style. That's why I did *491*; I knew that to become a good director, I had to learn how to handle violence." Breaking taboos seemed already a part of his DNA. In *491* a young woman is forced to have sex with an Alsatian dog. The film he was preparing when we met, *My Sister, My Love*, featured incest in the late 18th century. "Artists and their audience are attracted by taboos," he noted, "and this is one of the things that fascinates me."

Less than two years later, Vilgot hit the big time with *I Am Curious—Yellow*. Like Oshima's *In the Realm of the Senses* and Kechiche's *Blue is the Warmest Colour*, the film became notorious for its sex scenes. Attending a FIPRESCI seminar at Hässelby Castle outside Stockholm, I came out of a private screening into the frenzied crowd of journalists and photographers, eager to gauge the reactions of the international press. This was, after all, the first time that a penis—albeit flaccid—had been shown in close-up in a commercial Swedish film. "*I Am Curious* really reflects the experience of young people in this period," Vilgot told me. "The realisation that you're involved in political questions. Going out and doing something about it. And the inevitable clash between reality and your own emotional problems." He regarded the two films, *Yellow* and *Blue*, as not sequential so much as laid on top of each other so that a pattern of social behaviour emerges. He had somehow transmuted his own mid-life crisis into a quasi-masterpiece.

Bergman and Sjöman cherished a mutual admiration. Bergman would support him through thick and thin in the early years of the younger man's career as a director, and Sjöman reciprocated with a brilliant book, *L136, The Making of Winter Light* (1963), which revealed the Master in all his moods. When Bergman was running the Royal Dramatic

Theatre in the mid-1960s, he and Vilgot would go for long evening walks near Karlaplan, gossiping about actors and directors and debating issues of Life and Death.

My Swedish friends always offered generous hospitality—dinners at home (with those who were married) or in one of the comfortable, epicurean restaurants of the capital. Every evening during my visits was occupied in this way, dining and chatting with Bengt Forslund, the young producer who would soon be nominated for Best Picture at the Academy Awards (*The Emigrants*); Christer Frunck, who drove me around the hill towns behind Cannes during my first visit to the festival in 1965; Bo Johan Hultman, a programmer for arthouses and TV who lived with his wife and various children in a large villa in Djursholm; Nils Petter Sundgren, a laser-brained film critic who had early mastered the art of interviewing on Swedish television; and Jonas Cornell, for whose tall, elegant actress wife Agneta Ekmanner I nurtured a secret yearning. Bengt in particular shared my optimistic, impulsive and romantic view of the world and our little life.

Flashback: Bibi Andersson

Everyone changes with the years, but actors do so in the public glare. Bibi Andersson began as the innocent ingenue of Bergman films like *The Seventh Seal*, *Wild Strawberries*, and *The Magician* in the late 1950s, the archetypal Nordic blonde with a heart of gold. Her features glowed with a warmth often denied to beauty. The eyes were small, but their blueness was all. (Her portrait vied for space with those of Brigitte Bardot and Monica Vitti on the walls of my student rooms at Cambridge.) Then, in the summer of 1966, she returned in *Persona* as an altogether more mature person and actress. The peaches-and-cream innocence of Mia in *The Seventh Seal* and Sara in *Wild Strawberries* had been replaced by an empirical poise and candour that still fell well short of disenchantment.

Bibi often deplored the lack of good roles for women, but by the time she reached thirty years of age, she had demonstrated her ability to outlive the starlet's hour. Nurse Alma in *Persona* is a character in whom physical charm grows

With Bibi Andersson (right), in Cannes during the late 1960s.

subordinate to psychological strength and weakness. Charged with caring for the mute and seemingly sullen actress Elisabet Vogler (Liv Ullmann), Alma appears not to recognise that Elisabet is in fact her alter ego, the "soul image" of her personality. A tipsy Alma tells the actress about a day at the beach when she and a friend had spontaneous sex with two strangers, and Bibi releases the erotic coils of this monologue with a control and cadence so skilful that it sounds more carnal than most screen orgies look. Both she and Bergman felt embarrassed about shooting this scene, and so they dispensed with rehearsals. And it went perfectly on the first take.

A similarly demanding scene occurs outdoors, when Alma, feeling angry at Elisabet's betrayal, breaks a glass by mistake on the terrace and then leaves a single, jagged shard on the path. Elisabet emerges from the house and cuts her foot. In a few seconds of mysterious osmosis, Bibi's expression conveys to us the sense that her desire for revenge is drawing Elisabet inexorably toward the fragment of glass. Like all the best actors, she projects her thoughts from within.

The weight of *Persona* lies heavily on Bibi. She must veer instinctively from insouciance to moodiness and unpredictable explosions of anger. In her concluding monologue, in which Alma compels Elisabet to accept the truth about her loathing for an unnamed, unseen son, her concentration is affecting because it marks the limits of humankind's pitiful efforts to comprehend itself and its emotions. Alma's failure becomes Bergman's—and Bibi's—triumph.

When I was introduced to her in Stockholm in 1968, Bibi had moved on from her love affair with Bergman and expressed sympathy with the feminist movement of that period. She became friends with the actress turned director Mai Zetterling, and in Zetterling's *The Girls* (1968), Bibi could articulate her views (and those of the director) on the position of women in modern society—and did so with forthright intensity. At the close of the movie, her character sends her male counterparts spinning to the ground in the stage presentation of *Lysistrata*; in another sequence she strips before her husband in a nightclub, hurling her bra into his face in an anguished gesture that prompts a whole bevy of women to follow suit and strip.

In 1973, I was preparing a study of Swedish actors. Bibi invited me to her villa in Lidingö, with its plethora of paintings and drawings and a delicately coloured chandelier from Florence. She talked without airs and without illusion. Bibi had an inquiring mind, an independence of spirit. Beneath her assurance lay reserves, you felt, of humility and gentleness. Maj-Britt Nilsson (*Summer Interlude*) had been the idol of her youth. "She was so natural," Bibi said fiercely. She then complained that Swedish directors were reluctant to cast her in uncharacteristic roles and said how much she had enjoyed making *The Kremlin Letter* (1970) for John Huston, where the script called for her prostitute to be neurotic, beautiful, sexy, and yet utterly ravaged by life.

In the early 1980s we talked again at a small dinner hosted by Agneta Ekmanner (who later graced Bergman's *In the Presence of a Clown*), and Bibi reminded me that she had begun work in the acting pupils' group at Svensk Filmindustri on a salary of 300 kronor a month. Svensk could assign her to any kind of small role, but the compensation was really that she spent hours watching—and learning—on the studio's stages.

Good parts eluded her after the age of 50, although she did make the most of a small but elegant role in *Babette's Feast* (1987). We last met in 2006, when she was living in the South of France and came to Cannes for the launch of the Bergman Foundation. We had a little chat, and then some clips were shown from Bergman's private archive. During a change of DVDs, I saw her slip away with her friend. But then she unexpectedly peeped her head around the door as though she had forgotten something, caught my eye, and waved and smiled farewell.

Flashback: Bergman Actresses

Just as Welles had his coterie of favoured players from the Mercury Theatre, so Ingmar Bergman established a true repertory company of actors who remained loyal to him year after year, on stage and screen. Some, like Stig Olin and Birger Malmsten, he had known since his twenties. The earliest comrade in arms was Erland Josephson, who had met Ingmar at the age of just 16. Then came the "Malmö" generation—actors who worked alongside the maestro at the Municipal Theatre in Malmö, starting in 1952. Over the years I came to know several of these key personalities in Bergman's world, among them Harriet Andersson, Erland Josephson and Gunnar Björnstrand, as well as Bibi Andersson, Liv Ullmann and Max von Sydow.

Preparing my biography of Bergman in the late 1970s, I sat down with Birger Malmsten and Maj-Britt Nilsson for a cup of afternoon tea at Stockholm's Diplomat Hotel. Both were dressed with that impeccable formality associated with the generation born soon after the Great War. Maj-Britt was

as gracious and as amiable as those characters she inter-
preted in the 1940s. Films, I felt, had never been her raison
d'être. She retired from the screen in 1961 to concentrate
on the success of the Vasa Theatre in Stockholm, which she
ran with her husband Per Gerhard. She had met Bergman
at a Stockholm restaurant with Stig Olin, and he cast her in
To Joy. Then followed her finest role, as Marie, the troubled
ballerina in *Summer Interlude*.

Many of Bergman's great actresses—Harriet Andersson,
Bibi Andersson, Gunnel Lindblom, Ingrid Thulin, Liv
Ullmann—were born in the decade between 1929 and
1938. Harriet Andersson was the non-conformist of the
troupe, with a fondness for leather blousons and a tomboy
sassiness. I first interviewed her in the mid-1960s, when she
shared her life with Jörn Donner, appearing in four of his
severe, dispassionate films. She eschewed conventional
glamour ("we use much less makeup in Swedish films than
they do elsewhere") and brought a self-possessed earthi-
ness to each new part. "I keep half of my head full of feeling,
and the other half full of technical concerns," she said as
we had drinks in KB, the Artists' Bar in central Stockholm.
She found the "spider" sequence in *Through a Glass Darkly*
quite easy to do, "because I have always dreaded spiders,"
she laughed, "and I could imagine it trying to consume my
personality, consume me as a woman, and crawl over my
body, face, and hands."

Although time after time Harriet seemed to have been
cast aside by Bergman, relegated to small roles at the Royal
Dramatic Theatre, she would prove the most durable of
all his actresses. From *Summer with Monika* in 1952 to the
claustrophobic TV movie, *The Blessed Ones*, which Bergman
directed in 1986, she was regularly brought back from obscu-
rity by her Svengali. Nothing between *Smiles of a Summer
Night* (1955) and *Through a Glass Darkly* in 1961; *All These
Women* in 1964, and then eight years before she returned
to the Bergman fold in *Cries and Whispers* (1972); then yet
another decade before she played the sinister nanny in *Fanny
and Alexander*. And that suited Harriet just fine. "I like to go
to my work early in the morning like anyone else," she told
me. "Then, when it's finished, I can go home and lead my

own life. If you are a star you never have this freedom." When I interviewed her in Berlin in 2011, and then the following January for Criterion's release of *Summer with Monika*, she was still as feisty and unpretentious as she had been in youth, giggling as she recalled how Bergman had tried, clumsily, to kiss her for the first time.

And there were so many others, like Gunnel Lindblom, who joined Bergman's troupe in Malmö in 1954 and who signed my programme booklet at the London staging of Bergman's *Urfaust* in 1959. She quickly sought to escape her smouldering, carnal image in *The Silence* and forged a new career as a director, with committed feminist films like *Sally and Freedom* and *Paradise Place* that analysed the fault-lines in Sweden's squeaky-clean society.

Ingrid Thulin proved an elusive talent, tall and effortlessly imposing in *Wild Strawberries*, *Brink of Life* and *The Magician*. She married Harry Schein, founder of the Swedish Film Institute, in the 1950s, went to Hollywood briefly and in her single starring role, in Minnelli's *The Four Horsemen of the Apocalypse*, her lines were dubbed by Angela Lansbury. In *The War is Over*, however, Resnais knew how to bring out the warmth beneath her icy demeanour, and Visconti gave her the most charismatic of parts as Sophie von Essenbeck, the decadent Nazi "Mutter" in *The Damned* (1969). Like Gunnel Lindblom, she turned to directing, and in *Broken Sky* (1982) she evoked her own childhood in the far north of Sweden with a tenderness one encountered rarely in her film roles or her off-screen personality.

Nor can I forget Gudrun Brost, who sat in a small apartment in Malmö in 1979 and talked to me about her part as the clown's hapless wife in *Sawdust and Tinsel*, coping with freezing surf and a recalcitrant bear from Canada. She too I had met in 1959 at the Princes Theatre on Shaftesbury Avenue, when she stole her scenes as Martha, the lover of Mephistopheles, in Bergman's *Urfaust*. "Ingmar brought to bear the same discipline on his filmmaking as he did to the theatre," she said, "perhaps with a little more delicacy for the cinema. He was a wonderful listener, and did not talk too much. And often he would stop rehearsing at 2 p.m., instead of pressing on until 4 p.m., and the result was that we would come back with more energy the next day." You didn't need to be a wife or a lover to succeed under Bergman's guidance. As Gudrun Brost said: "I've loved him, but only with the soul!"

These talented women, whether mistresses of Bergman's or just intimate colleagues, to a certain degree mirrored the diversity of Bergman's five wives—some blonde, some brunette, some cool, some warm, some short, some tall. Like the male actors, they all expressed surprise at their fame beyond the borders of Scandinavia. United by their love of live theatre as well as the cinema, they regarded themselves as "good companions," coming to work not in limousines but by train or tram, receiving a decent living wage but never a six-figure fee. Loyal to Bergman on stage in the winter, and on camera during the fleeting Swedish summer, they were never stars, merely players—but what players!

Not all my Swedish acquaintances were filmmakers first and foremost. The painter Törbjörn Axelman made an engaging first feature with the precious title of *Well, Well, Well... Or The Song of the Blood-Red Lobster* (1966). Törbjörn much appreciated some paragraphs I devoted to the film in a report for *The Financial Times*, and invited me to a dinner at the exclusive Opera Cellar in Stockholm. He brought along his friend Lee Hazlewood, the American musician who had written the worldwide hit, "These Boots are Made for Walkin'" for Nancy Sinatra. Lee had fallen in love with a Swedish woman, and relished life in Stockholm. His lazy, Oklahoman drawl was engaging, especially when he asked the waiter to "put some more fire under these freets."

Lee and Törbjörn would collaborate on a couple of feature films, *Smoke* (1971) and *A House Safe from Tigers* (1975), but they were too self-reflexive, too self-indulgent, ever to attract either critical praise or public support. They listened politely to my comments after each private screening, sensing that I did not, or could not embrace the films as being successful. Törbjörn was sentenced to prison in his seventies for shooting a man dead outside his home on Gotland, and attempting to shoot two policemen. Yet even behind bars he continued to paint, and exhibited some of his canvases in 2011. Had he lived in

America, he would have by now been executed. Lee, on the other hand, enjoyed a full life, with his music and songs popping up in numerous films, including *Full Metal Jacket*, *Forrest Gump*, *Fargo* and *Ocean's 13*.

In 1971 Harry Schein appointed me a member of the Quality Awards Jury, which met annually to view all the films made during the previous twelve months and to divide the pot of subsidy money between them according to artistic merit. This led to certain anomalies. A film that might be quite worthy, and politically correct, would be seen by at most a few hundred spectators in Sweden but could walk away with a sizeable chunk of lucre. Many of the critics who made up a good portion of the jury found it perplexing to praise any but the finest of Swedish films. When I would speak up for a director in danger of being neglected, Harry Schein would raise a laugh around the table by joking that "Peter Cowie has an orgasm every time he sees a Swedish film!" I remained on that jury as the only non-Scandinavian citizen for eleven years.

Flashback: Jan Troell

The people of Skåne, Sweden's southernmost province, only speak when there is something sensible to say. As reserved as New Yorkers are loquacious, Jan Troell has made a virtue of silence and the laconic disposition of his fellow countrymen. In his early short film, *Interlude in the Marshland*, the railroad brakesman played by Max von Sydow asks a watchman, "Do you have many children?" There is a pause. Then the reply. "I've been here for eight years now."

I met with Troell through my close friend Bengt Forslund, who worked at Svensk Filmindustri in the 1960s and who was the co-screenwriter of Troell's greatest achievements, *Here Is Your Life*, *The Emigrants* and *The New Land*. We really bonded, however, at the Oberhausen short film festival in Germany in 1967, when *Interlude in the Marshland* was screened. All Swedes speak pretty good English, but Jan, who had trained as a schoolteacher, could draw on a rich vocabulary and, after long consideration of each question, would articulate the most thoughtful of answers.

He stood apart from the other members of the Swedish New Wave (Widerberg, Sjöman, Halldoff, Donner etc.), not just because he came from the south but also because his early stint as a cinematographer enabled him to bring to his direction a lyrical fluency unique in Swedish film. Based on Eyvind Johnson's novel, *Here is Your Life*, at 170 minutes, was the longest Swedish feature up to 1966, even though it was cut by as much as a quarter of its length for foreign release. The young Olof (Eddie Axberg) advances shyly through life in northern Sweden while the First World War takes place more than a thousand miles away. Troell caught perfectly the wry mix of wit, misfortune, idealism and discovery of Johnson's story, and marked the film unforgettably with his own warm glimpses of the countryside and its inhabitants. Griffith, Renoir, Donskoy, Ford: these are the directors whose legacy one would never have expected to find in Scandinavia.

Troell almost fell victim to his own success. I remember visiting Stockholm during the final months of the 1960s and hearing that Jan was still editing his monumental adaptation of Vilhelm Moberg's novels about the emigration of Swedish farmers to North America during the late 19th century. And still editing... Not until March 1971 did *The Emigrants* open in Stockholm. But it proved a triumph, both with critics and at the box office. In the U.S., it was nominated for five Academy Awards, including Best Picture. Troell had an eye for natural beauty (birds against a skyscape, for instance), as well as for impressionistic effect. He discovered moments of tranquillity and humour to leaven the harrowing ordeal of these indebted farmers, and he gives plastic form to the primitive sense of purpose that draws the emigrants together.

Jan could never quite come to terms with Hollywood. He suffered during the shoot of *Zandy's Bride* for Warner Bros., notably because union rules in the United States prevented him from being the cinematographer as well as director. And when I visited him in an editing suite in London's Mayfair in the spring of 1979, he was grumbling about the producer Dino De Laurentiis' watching over his shoulder as he cut *Hurricane*, the misbegotten remake of John Ford's 1937 film about racism in Polynesia.

Two years later, however, Jan could once more film in his native land. *The New York Times* commissioned me to write a piece about the shoot of *The Flight of the Eagle*, the story of a Swedish engineer's ill-fated attempt to reach the North Pole in a balloon in 1897. I flew to Kalix, almost nudging the Arctic Circle, and then transferred to a snowmobile that took me at speed over the ice in the Gulf of Bothnia. "Sub-zero temperatures tear through one's parka," I wrote, "and the persistent crashing of the runners against ridges of pack-ice drives to the bone. Just when the journey seems most interminable, a huge black puddle appears on the ice, like the arbitrary remnant of some doomed expedition. This is the balloon casing that five hours later will bloom and lift Max von Sydow, two other actors, and two concealed balloonists, into the Arctic sky." Jan, with his beloved Arriflex snugly on his shoulder, had to wait for hour after hour before the wind was right and the balloon could be hoisted into the air.

The gentle Jan Troell never acquired such eminence as Bergman, but his films are intense, sensitive, and above all humane. One of his most underrated achievements is *Everlasting Moments*, made in 2008. It pays tribute to the early days of photography, and to Maria Larsson, a working-class Swedish woman whose talent in the field rendered her images poignant and evocative of her time at the turn of the 20th century. Troell's abiding gift is to observe the faces of individual people, so that we're persuaded that they are in the same room—the same frame—as us. These faces address us, like the self-portraits of Rembrandt, saying, "You too are a human creature, with all its faults and virtues; you, too, will understand…"

When Criterion decided to publish *The Emigrants* and *The New Land* on Blu-ray, a producer flew from New York to meet me in Malmö. Together we went to Jan's house on the seashore a few kilometres outside the city. There we recorded two days of conversation, in which Jan offered lucid memories of the shoot of both films. Between takes, as it were, we visited his work cabin alongside the house, where he was hard at work on a new film. When I left, he gave me a copy of Kurt Mälarstedt's book about him, writing on the title page: "Dear Peter, Thank you for turning the nightmare of an interview into a lovely conversation!"

A non-conformist, I could never have settled in the ultimate conformist paradise that Sweden prides itself upon being. I admired the standard of living, the quality of food and commercial goods. I marvelled at the esteem in which culture was held by the state. You could go to the Royal Dramatic Theatre in Stockholm and see a production by Bergman or Sjöberg, and pay only a handful of crowns for your seat. You could secure financial support for a film project however ill-conceived and ponderous in execution, such as Susan Sontag's *Brother Carl* or Peter Watkins' *The Gladiators*.

The price for this utopian liberty has always been high, if acceptable to a majority of Swedes, who have sometimes paid taxes of more than 50% without demur. Sweden is a wonderful place in which to fall ill. The hospitals have superb facilities, and you are accepted for surgery and treatment irrespective of either means, nationality, creed or colour. Most of my friends have retired on pensions that enable them to travel abroad and to eat out regularly at restaurants, as well as maintaining a cottage in the archipelago or deep in the idyllic countryside. But you must be careful to toe the line in everyday matters. If you walk across a pedestrian crossing when the sign is red, you may be accosted by a well-meaning Swede who will tell you that even though no traffic is approaching for hundreds of yards on either side, "Here in Sweden, we obey the law." If your child is invited to a birthday party at 4 p.m., and you ring the doorbell at six minutes past the hour, a mother will appear with a reproachful look and remind you that her party indeed began at 4 p.m.

Flashback: Sven Nykvist and Gunnar Fischer

Or should it be Gunnar Fischer and Sven Nykvist? Nykvist may have acquired a much wider renown and won two Academy Awards in Bergman's service, but Fischer created the rich, humanistic black-and-white imagery of Bergman's heyday, in films like *The Seventh Seal*, *Wild Strawberries* and *The Magician*. Nykvist was twelve years younger than Fischer, but died five years before him (Fischer could still chat to friends at the age of 100). Both men studied under the great Julius Jaenzon at the studios of Svensk Filmindustri. Each in his own way was the archetypal Swede: talking only when it made sense to talk, fiercely loyal, and manifesting a deep love of seascape and countryside. Both had an under-rated, slow-burning sense of humour.

Gunnar had joined the Swedish merchant navy as a chef, dabbled with painting, and then fell for the movies. He was already in his sixties when I met him, living modestly in the Stockholm suburb of Bromma. Long discarded by Bergman, he seemed nonetheless encouraged that the maestro had allowed him to film the credit sequence for *The Touch*— a series of views of the town of Visby on Gotland. He said he had learned a lot from Dreyer while shooting *Two People* in 1945—just to try to make it very simple and avoid cheap effects. Throughout the 1950s he relied on a trusty Mitchell camera and his canny eye for improvisation. On *Summer with Monika* (shot for just a few thousand dollars), for example, he used a bath full of water out of shot to create the reflection of sea-water inside the small boat as Monika awakes on her first morning in the archipelago.

If Gunnar could never match the stereoscopic quality of Sven Nykvist's photography, he knew instinctively how to achieve the chiaroscuro effects so beloved by Bergman, who was a devotee of German expressionist cinema. Two of the best examples are in *Wild Strawberries*, as Isak Borg observes his wife committing adultery in a forest glade (all constructed in the studio), and the climax of *The Magician*, with Vogler pursuing Dr. Vergérus through a cluttered attic.

The son of Lutheran missionaries, Sven Nykvist was inspired by his father's skill at photographing African wild-life, and in 1941 joined Sandrews (the great rival studio to Svensk Filmindustri). In 1953 he applied to shoot *Sawdust and Tinsel*, and shared the task with Hilding Bladh, who filmed the exteriors. Bergman had been sceptical at first, but was stunned when Sven contrived a 180° pan around the actor Åke Grönberg clutching a pistol. Conflicting schedules prevented the two men working together again until 1959, when Gunnar Fischer was on loan to Walt Disney Produc-tions, and Bergman turned to Sven for *The Virgin Spring*.

Dawn and dusk were the saving phases of the day for Nykvist, who used a Debrie camera for his classic Bergman films. Dawn as Max von Sydow uproots the birch-tree in *The Virgin Spring*; dusk as Gunnar Björnstrand watches his family stage the "play-within-the film" in *Through a Glass Darkly*. "We have long summer evenings here in Sweden," Sven told me, "so we don't use night shots with filters." He said that the landscape of Fårö contained very little colour, and that made it better for shooting. "In Nordic cinema," he emphasised, "the rhythm is slower, but every camera movement has significance." He was keenly aware that Bergman's interest in human beings had intensified with each passing year, and so close-ups of faces had become more vital to him.

Sven rather enjoyed the fact that his nickname among the crew was "two faces and a teacup." *Persona* marked the apogee in the collaboration between Sven and Ingmar. "One of the more difficult tasks for me on *Persona*," he said later, "was to light the close-ups because they involved such incredible nuance." He aimed to catch the light in an actor's eyes, since for him they represented "the mirror of the soul."

Sven even travelled to Munich to work with the exiled Bergman on *From the Life of the Marionettes* in 1980. He could not locate anyone in Bavaria to process the black-and-white stock. "Finally, I found a man I had worked with twenty years before, and he processed it for us," he recalled with a grin.

Working in Hollywood gave Nykvist the experience needed to deal with Bergman's most complex production, *Fanny and Alexander*, where the camera dollies through room after room and a bevy of actors throng the sets. He received his detailed shooting script from Bergman three months prior to filming. During the shoot, the two men met each morning and wandered through the sets together, discussing the lights to be used. When I visited the studio to watch a day's filming in 1982, Sven and Ingmar hardly talked to each other—a nod here, a muttered word there, and the complicity could not have been closer. Complicity, indeed, sustained the extraordinary team spirit at the heart of all Bergman's films.

In 1991, I was asked to present Sven with the Silver Medallion of the Telluride Festival. He seemed extremely happy, and yet rather apprehensive of the ceremony. When I arrived at the Ice House Lodge to collect him about half an hour before the event, I knocked at his door without success. After pounding away for a minute or two, I thought I heard a suppressed groan coming from the room. Knowing of Sven's fragile health, I asked the porter to open the door with a master key. When we entered, there was Sven, seated in an arm-chair, smiling benignly at us. He had committed the error of swallowing a couple of beers (or more...) which, at the rarefied height of 8,750 feet, is not recommended. Together, the porter and I managed to get Sven upright and manoeuvre him down the stairs. By the time we reached the street, he had recovered his faculties and was joking about the Scandinavian weakness for any free alcohol. On stage at the Sheridan Theatre, he regaled an affectionate audience with stories about Bergman. He flew out of Telluride early the next day, and I doubt he ever ventured to such a high altitude again.

In the ensuing years, Sven would manage to shoot Richard Attenborough's *Chaplin*, Lasse Hallström's *What's Eating Gilbert Grape?*, as well as two films by Liv Ullmann, *Kristin Lavransdatter* and *Private Confessions*. But he never worked with Bergman again. Tragically, he fell victim to aphasia in 1998, and for the last few years of his life could scarcely recognise friends or make himself understood. But his finest work will speak eloquently for him long into the future.

Flashback: Erik Nordgren

While researching my biography of Ingmar Bergman, I became intrigued by the fact that friends and fellow critics in Sweden never mentioned the composer Erik Nordgren. Yet he had written the music for so many of the acclaimed Bergman films. Certain other composers, like Dag Wirén, Erland von Koch, and Lars-Johan Werle, had on occasion scored movies for Bergman, but under the old studio system in Stockholm, where Svensk Filmindustri reigned supreme and Nordgren was the resident music director, he was the turn-to man for veterans like Gustaf Molander, as well as for younger filmmakers like Hasse Ekman, Lars-Eric Kjellgren and, even later, Jan Troell.

Bergman's "troupe" always stuck close by his side, on and off the set. During the typical shooting day, the Master would be surrounded by Gunnar Fischer or Sven Nykvist behind the camera; P.A. Lundgren, the set designer; Mago or Cecilia Drott checking the costumes; Börje Lundh attending to makeup; and Katinka Faragó, his faithful script assistant. Nordgren, though, never spent downtime with the director, as did the crew and actors like Gunnar Björnstrand or Erland Josephson. He kept to himself, in the manner of most fine composers. Tall, grave, well-groomed, with rather severe dark-framed glasses, he could have been taken for a notary or a civil servant. He had studied the violin and viola as well as conducting and composition at the Stockholm Royal Academy of Music, and as the Second World War came to an end, he composed the music for his first feature film, Hampe Faustman's *Crime and Punishment*. In 1947 he met Bergman, who had written the screenplay for Molander's *Woman Without a Face*. He scored his first film for Bergman, *Thirst*, two years later.

Nordgren is credited with the music for eleven films by Bergman—among them *Smiles of a Summer Night* (1955), *Wild Strawberries* (1957) and *The Magician* (1958), and the last being *The Virgin Spring* (1960), with its evocative use of medieval instruments. For Nordgren, less was more. As early as 1952, he and Bergman were using a kind of musique concrète for a passage in *Summer with Monika*. Nordgren could endow certain scenes with considerable suspense by introducing a single guitar or a harp or a solo drum, as in the brilliant sequence in *The Magician* when Dr. Vergérus stumbles frantically around the attic to escape from Vogler's clutches.

Although he worked uncredited on the odd film in the early 1960s, Nordgren resurfaced with a bang in 1965, when he wrote a folk melody for Troell's short subject *Interlude in the Marshland* (now restored and included on Criterion's release of Troell's magnificent 1966 debut feature, *Here Is Your Life*). Max von Sydow, as the itinerant brakesman, whistles the tune as he walks and then dances along a single railroad track in the far north of Sweden. Gradually, the accordion takes over, and the waltz rhythm suggested by Nordgren during the shoot seems to express the character's repressed energy. When I visited Jan Troell in 2015, he brought out his harmonica to play what he calls Nordgren's "Marshland Waltz." When one hears it in a slightly more sophisticated form behind the opening shots of *Here Is Your Life*, the melody immediately sets the mood of the film—the dance of life, punctuated by setbacks but always pressing forward in eager anticipation of the next turn in the road.

On a winter's morning in November 1979, I took a train out to the maritime community of Saltsjö-Boo, about half an hour from Stockholm. There, in a leafy street filled with discreet villas, Nordgren lived in retirement, after decades as head of the orchestra department at the Swedish Radio Symphony Orchestra. We talked of Bergman and Troell, and he took me downstairs to his studio, with a battery of electronic equipment impressive for the period. He recalled his first meeting with Bergman, in the late 1940s: "It was quite an experience, because I felt he had some psychic probes that he sent into me, looking everywhere at once. In a way, it was rather frightening, although very nice, and after thirty seconds, I felt that he knew everything he wanted to know about me."

He noted that Bergman would always send him the script at the outset. "But then nothing would happen until the film was cut. At the beginning, I would try and work out a score from the script, but I realised Ingmar knew exactly what kind of music he wanted. He wrote his screenplay with music within it, as it were." So once the film was well under way, the two men would discuss the music, Bergman would signal the ideas he wanted in the score, then leave the composer to his own devices. When editing commenced, Bergman took over, applying the appropriate music to passages throughout the film.

Nordgren was impressed by Bergman's musical awareness. "In *The Seventh Seal*, there's a place where the double basses go down to their lowest tone, which is a C, and Ingmar, who was at the recording, reacted immediately and said, 'What was that?' It was a very unusual tone, even in a normal symphony orchestra, but Ingmar heard it immediately. It's really quite remarkable, because he was not a musician and not a composer. And, of course, you can't hear it in the film, because it won't work in optical sound!"

For *The Emigrants* (1971), Troell again turned to Nordgren. "I like it very much when he describes the way the four seasons run into one another. [Erik] wrote four smaller pieces in which the music is, so to speak, immobile, and not a narrative that one has to follow. He wrote them in keys that harmonised with each other so that, at the editing stage, you could fade one into the next one."

Perhaps the most disquieting bars of music Nordgren ever wrote are heard off- and on-screen in *Here Is Your Life*, during Allan Edwall's memory of his wife's death—at first, a delicate, high keening on the organ, then a rustic dance tune heard on an old 78 r.p.m. disc, played out until the end to rhyme with the woman's untimely death, the record left revolving, sounding like a buzzing fly. Nordgren had studied Swedish folk music for many years, and both this and the waltz tune that he first wrote for *Interlude in the Marshland* reflect his love for the Swedish countryside and its traditions.

As we said goodbye, Nordgren confided with a wistful smile that he was surprised that I was still interested in his music. "It happens all the time in Sweden that a composer suddenly is no longer *the* composer. After all, I wrote music for films regularly for around twenty-five years, and I always expected people to 'retire' me." But now, with *Here Is Your Life* at last restored to its original glory, a new generation of film buffs will discover the talent of Erik Nordgren.

I had first visited Finland in March of 1971, to serve as a member of the jury at the Tampere Short Film Festival. My host on arrival in Helsinki was Kari Uusitalo, a middle-aged man who had launched the embryonic Finnish Film Foundation, a kind of mini-clone of Harry Schein's SFI. Kari took me to a late lunch, liberally doused with drinks of various kinds, and culminating in an excellent local liqueur. I began to realise that for Finns, alcohol is as essential as air and water.

Tampere, an industrial city in southern Finland, about two hours north of the capital Helsinki, has a flourishing cultural scene. With the Cold War continuing at that time, and Finland still in the shadow of the "Big Bear" to the east, the film festival had a political edge, and we jury members watched our obligatory Russian colleague with wariness. A bureaucrat, he seemed easy-going—until the final round of deliberations. When it became clear that no Russian film would win an award, our colleague began to sob. If he did not return to Moscow with a prize, he explained, he might lose his job and even possibly be "punished." Jörn Donner, as President of the jury, suggested we create an "additional award." It would be entitled the "Great Golden Kiss," implying eternal friendship between nations, and that this would be given to the least mediocre of the Russian entries. The man from Moscow wrung his hands with joy and embraced each of us moistly on both cheeks. The festival, caught unawares, presented him with a wooden sculpture that lay conveniently to hand, as tangible evidence of the prize.

That evening, all foreign guests were invited to one of the best sauna facilities in the city. Stripping naked, we plunged into showers and then into the warm dry embrace of the large sauna cabins. One of our hosts told us that the tradition was to open the large picture windows and wallow, nude, in the snow for some seconds before lurching back inside for beer and schnapps. The second-string critic from one of Britain's largest daily newspapers, a shy individual who wore his glasses (if nothing else) in the sauna, ran eagerly out into the night and flung himself into the snow. Almost as soon as he came back, however, he collapsed on the marble floor, his face deathly pale. Without hesitation, a Finnish critic who had struck up a close friendship with my colleague during the festival, now straddled the unfortunate Brit and—still nude, of course—applied a passionate "kiss of life." Fortunately, it worked.

For many in Finland, the logical reward of drinking is to get drunk, rather than to bathe in bonhomie. Only then can one escape the relentless cold and the encroaching darkness (which in winter can prevail for up to twenty hours a day). Whenever I took the plane back to London at 9 a.m. on a Monday morning, I noticed how the Finns around me ordered drinks as soon as the seat-belt sign was turned off. They continued drinking until, at Heathrow, they staggered towards passport control in a state of inebriation and had to be helped through the formalities by their group guide.

Flashback: Jörn Donner

Had Jörn Donner been born anywhere other than Finland, he would have been world-famous. As it was, he dominated the Finnish cultural scene for several decades. Prolific writer, film critic, director and producer, as well as a politician and the cofounder of the Finnish Film Archive (at the age of 24), Jörn stayed a close and cherished friend for more than fifty years.

We first met in Stockholm in the autumn of 1964, when I interviewed him about his early features as a director, made in Sweden—notably *To Love*, a romantic comedy with the Polish heartthrob Zbigniew Cybulski. Jörn was a Swedish-speaking Finn, one of a minority of some 6% in Finland. He wrote in Swedish and had been appointed film critic at the Stockholm morning newspaper *Dagens Nyheter* in 1961. He had made an auspicious debut behind the camera for Sandrew studios in Stockholm with *A Sunday in September*, which won the Best First Film prize at the Venice Festival in 1963, and I knew of his reputation as one of the first in-depth interpreters of Bergman's work. Throughout his life he remained fascinated by Bergman, and we called on his expertise at Criterion on numerous occasions, for example when he and I discussed *Smiles of a Summer Night* for a supplement for Bergman's classic comedy. He also contributed a ninety-minute documentary on Bergman for the Criterion edition of *Wild Strawberries*.

A year after our first meeting, when I was back in Stockholm writing about new Swedish cinema for *The Financial Times*, he called me one evening at my hotel and suggested he show me some clips from his film in progress, *Adventure Starts Here* (1965). The chain-smoking young man of 32 who drove me at breakneck speed out to the laboratory that night was charisma incarnate. Sardonic, egotistical and remarkably knowledgeable about world affairs, Jörn obliged you to take him on his terms or not at all. Some of his works, like *Adventure Starts Here* and *Rooftree* (1967), were austere and humourless to such a degree that they flopped at the box office, even though they starred Harriet Andersson, by then Jörn's partner. She would dominate perhaps his most thoughtful film, *Anna* (1970), about a doctor, recently divorced, going out to an island to reflect on her situation.

Dispirited by his failure to win critical or public praise in Sweden, Donner returned to Finland, which proved a smart move, because he could now show a more ironical and salacious side of his personality. *Black on White* (1968) brought him at last the recognition he craved as a director, even running on London's Oxford Street for several weeks. A tart satire on the "perfect modern Scandinavian family," it starred none other than Donner himself as the philandering refrigerator salesman who gleefully indulges in erotic antics with a woman he meets on the road. *Portraits of Women* (1970), *Tenderness* (1972) and *Hangover* (1973) confirmed his competence, if also his facetiousness, as a director, and he achieved even more notoriety with a corrosive documentary on his native land, *Fuck Off! Images of Finland* (1971).

Donner was a true loner, a writer who published dozens of books and hundreds of film reviews and provocative articles. His style owed something to Hemingway, with its spare, rugged prose and a clinical approach to the emotions of life. In 1985 he won the Finlandia Prize, his country's most prestigious literary award, for *Father and Son*, one of a suite of novels featuring the bourgeois Anders family. I translated another, *Angela and Love*, into English, so that a German producer could consider making a screen version of it (which never happened). It was a joy to read Jörn's lapidary Swedish, all adverbs pared away, the punctuation sparse and the paragraphs terse. He could drink deep into the night, but his unquenched rage to create enabled him to rise at dawn and head for his desk with monastic regularity.

In 1986, we were both on the jury of the Vevey Comedy Film Festival in Switzerland. Midway through, Jörn announced gruffly that he was flying to Budapest for a business meeting. He would only return, if at all, on the final day. It was characteristic of Jörn's spoiled-child approach to certain obligations (I know, because I had to step into the role of the president at short notice). Yet despite his often surly, laconic exterior, he manifested a tenderness—especially with women.

Most of my memories of Jörn remain engaging. Sitting together for hours in a small office in Richmond in Southwest London, subtitling into English a 16mm print of Jörn's documentary *Three Scenes with Ingmar Bergman*. Sharing premises with him in Helsinki, and learning how to use a fax machine for the first time (Jörn loved all forms of techno-logical advance, providing they helped him to write faster). Planning the first front cover of my new annual *Scandinavian Guide* in 1985, a project to which Jörn gave wholehearted encouragement and practical help. Making the driest of martinis together, after a sauna. Or playing incredibly incom-petent tennis at the massive residence he occupied in Bel-Air while acting as Consul General for Finland in Los Angeles in the mid-1990s.

Jörn enjoyed traveling in the U.S., although for several years his fleeting membership of the Communist Party in Finland caused him problems with the immigration author-ities. Not so, fortunately, when he received the Academy Award for Best Foreign Language Film in 1984, as producer of *Fanny and Alexander*, making him the first and thus far only Finn to have won an Oscar. "Thanks, the members of the Academy," he declared when accepting the award with Bergman's wife, Ingrid, "for having very good taste. I think so." That same year he had also produced one of Bergman's most valued TV movies, *After the Rehearsal.*

His accomplishments were many, and in many fields. He was a member of the Finnish Parliament, and then of the European Parliament in Strasbourg. He was on the board of Marimekko, Finland's textile giant; managing director of the Swedish Film Institute from 1978 to 1982; and then chairman of the Finnish Film Foundation (1981–1983). He proved a successful sales agent for Rauni Mollberg's masterly *The Earth Is Our Sinful Song* in 1973, and encouraged a youthful Aki Kaurismäki, helping behind the scenes to produce *Hamlet Goes Business*. As if that were not enough, I was with him in Helsinki when a popular evening newspaper voted him "Finland's sexiest man" on its front page—for the third succes-sive year.

Our final meeting was in 2010, when he came to Montreux to celebrate my birthday, combining it, of course, with making yet another film—a TV documentary on the life of Finland's renowned President Gustaf Mannerheim, who had ended his days by the shores of Lake Geneva. Jörn was writing books and involved in film production almost until the year of his death. The last of his fifty-five films as a producer and thirty-five as director was *The Memory of Ingmar Bergman*, a documentary about the cultural figure who had marked his life more than any other. In November 2019, he wrote to me that he was "still ill, not much being done. But I survive, so far. In six weeks the days will be longer..." So when Jörn Johan Donner finally passed away on January 30, 2020, it was as though a storm had abated or a comet had streaked out of sight.

Since 1980 I had been contributing occasional, long articles to the Arts & Leisure section of *The New York Times*. The paper paid its freelancers somewhat less than its rivals, but it was widely read and respected. I interviewed Ingmar Bergman in Munich for *The New York Times*. Other subjects included Jan Troell, Laurence Olivier, Tom Luddy and Sir Denis Forman.

Flashback: Laurence Olivier

While still at high school, I saw Laurence Olivier on stage in *The Entertainer* at the Palace Theatre in London. Even when viewed from the gods, his performance as Archie Rice was super-charged with energy and bitterness. With his extravagant make-up and trashy clothing, he made of this obsolescent music-hall performer more than just a figure of fun. His was the tragedy of the clown who yearns to play Hamlet.

In the 1964 *Othello* at London's National Theatre, Olivier re-minted so many of the great speeches. He filled out the text with smiles, chuckles and gestures until Othello could be seen not as the magnificent warrior of tradition but as a gullible outsider in the Venetian army, delighted as a sand-man to have landed such a fair prize as Desdemona, and grovelling and whining when he feels her to be false. Purists cried shame at Olivier's Al Jolson-style black-face, and yet the intensity of the performance on stage seemed to transcend such criticism—an intensity diminished in the rather awkward filmed version.

David Plowright, head of Granada TV, during the 1970s and '80s, was the brother-in-law to Olivier, and at a family gathering at Christmas 1981, he noted "a stubble of beard and a gleam in Larry's eye" that suggested the time was ripe to mount a television version of *King Lear*. Olivier had played Lear only once previously, at the Old Vic in 1946. "When you're 39, you're full of spunk and vinegar and the toughness of the role doesn't upset you very much," he told me. "But the age comes naturally now. If you're 75, which I am, it's damned hard to find roles, and Lear—well, it sounds terribly boastful, but there's nothing to it. He's just a selfish, irascible old bastard—so am I. It's a straight part for me. Absolutely straight. My family would agree with that: no wonder he's all right, they would say, he's just himself, he's got just that sort of ridiculous temper, those sulks. Absolutely mad as a hatter sometimes."

Television, however, never attracted Olivier in quite the same way as the theatre or the cinema. "I must be a director's notion of hell where TV's concerned," he confessed with a sly, sidelong look, "for I cannot do anything the same way twice." On set at the Granada Studios in Manchester in 1983, Olivier seemed gentle, tall with a trim white beard, and full of piteous disbelief, his mouth agape as though gasping for salvation. When he blew his lines he put his hand to his head in frustration and apology to all and sundry. The crew called him "Sir."

I met him subsequently in a nondescript, barely-furnished room at Granada's London offices. Suited and groomed, he seemed wary of my presence until the moment I mentioned the vivid memory I had of his final Bosworth Field speech in the *Richard III* he directed in 1955. Without prompting, he proclaimed, with a force that made the windows tremble, "A horse! A horse! My kingdom for a horse!" It was as though he had flown back across the decades to the scene of Richard's ruin, and to his own apogee as an actor.

The consumption of vodka, more Russian than European in its sternness, had, I believe, a debilitating effect on culture in Finland. You could not find a people more appreciative of the arts, and for a country with a population of, until recently, less than 5 million they have produced such giants as Sibelius in music, Aalto in architecture, Gallen-Kallela in painting, and Linna and Waltari in literature. To which can be added a prodigious skill in textiles, glass, and woodwork. During the 1980s, numerous filmmakers of merit were at work, Rauni Mollberg above all, but also Mikko Niskanen and the young Kaurismäki brothers. I arranged an interview with Niskanen for a Monday morning. When my interpreter rang the bell of his apartment, the director's wife came to the door. She informed us that Mikko was rather the worse for wear after a weekend of drinking with friends. Could we come back on Wednesday? We did, but the answer was, sadly, the same, "Mikko still has a hangover."

One winter, my partner and I were invited to spend the weekend with Rauni Mollberg and his partner on his island not far from Vesilahti, in the Finnish lake district. Rauni had been shooting his masterpiece, *The Unknown Soldier* (1984). He led us across a frozen lake to the island. The silence was ghostly, broken only by the chink of the bottles in Rauni's back-pack as he trudged over the snow-shrouded ice. By Sunday afternoon, having enjoyed the wood-fired sauna, and meals of reindeer meat and freshly-caught fish, we found that poor Rauni could no longer rise from his arm-chair. The last of the vodka had been consumed, and even Rauni's mighty, stentorian voice was muted. Almost the same scenario played out when I spent a couple of days with my second wife Françoise on Rauni's island in the early 1990s.

Flashback: Rauni Mollberg

Unlike the younger talents in Finnish cinema, Rauni Mollberg arrived late on the international scene. He was 43 when *Earth is Our Sinful Song* smashed all box-office records in Finland and began a triumphant march around the world's film festivals. But before that, Rauni had acted in around two hundred plays on stage and directed more than a hundred hours of drama on television.

As the Range Rover charged along the snow-capped roads near Toijala, in central Finland, the burly, voluble Mollberg lifted a hand from the wheel at every turn to greet a friend or neighbour. In his local community of Vesilahti, Mollberg was not so much a celebrity as an institution. He was after all the quintessential poet of the ordinary people, the everyday, the universal experience.

Hard to believe, as we drew up before a large but simple school-house, painted in that terra-cotta hue so characteristic of the Nordic countryside, that Mollberg had been able to produce in these modest circumstances a series of masterly films—*Earth is Our Sinful Song, Pretty Good for a Human Being, Milka* and *The Unknown Soldier.* For the school-house was his studio, his "Hollywood." On the walls of Mollberg's spartan living quarters were mementoes of the past: pictures of him posing with Muhammad Ali and playing Claudius in a stage production of *Hamlet,* and some of the numerous awards bestowed on *Earth is Our Sinful Song.* The main room was crowded with army tunics from the Second World War. Here the youngsters would don their gear before going out, in Mollberg's movie, to meet their destiny amid the horrors of the Karelian Isthmus in 1940-44.

Over the next eighteen months, Mollberg would confront his greatest challenge. Väinö Linna's classic war novel, *The Unknown Soldier,* had been filmed by Edvin Laine in 1955, and overnight assumed the dimensions of a national epic. Remaking it may have seemed an invitation to disaster, like cloning *The Big Sleep* or *Stagecoach.* Mollberg, however, radiated an awesome, cheerful confidence about his project. For starters, he adopted a different tack to the story. Where Laine's production hailed the patriotic heroism of young soldiers flung into the maelstrom of the struggle against the Russians, perpetuating the Churchillian image of "tiny Finland" defending its heritage against terrible odds, Mollberg's new film demonstrated the brutalising impact of war on the individuals of an entire generation. No heroes, only victims.

Mollberg recalled with a smile how his own father used to get drunk during every furlough, and then depart for the battlefront with a suitcase of bottles—only to have it stolen, without fail, on every occasion. An autodidact where film is concerned, Mollberg was proud of his proletarian back-ground. It made him a profound humanist, a director for whom the relationship between Nature and humanity was vital. As a schoolboy he adored poetry and recited it well, and if any one quality elevated Mollberg to the ranks of the major Scandinavian filmmakers, it was his uncanny gift for rendering in lyrical sounds and images the love-hate kinship between his characters and the wilderness beauty of their surroundings.

Earth is Our Sinful Song came as a revelation in the meagre landscape of the Finnish film, in 1973. Its description of life and frustrated love in a remote Lapp village during the 1940s touched the authentic pulse of a rural community. These Lapps may wear traditional costumes, but their passions—sexual and religious—throb with a frightening strength and desperation. *Earth is Our Sinful Song* demonstrated the truth of the adage that the best films are the most national in character.

With *Milka* (1980), Mollberg returned to Lappland. In his own words, "it strives for more poetry than *Earth is Our Sinful Song*. It is not such an earthbound film." At its centre stands the tremulous, vulnerable figure of Milka, the girl on the threshold of womanhood. Yet more beautiful than this heroine is the naked forest, among whose trees Mollberg's camera lurks and prowls. Nature and people merge in a mysterious symbiosis.

For all his restless energy, Mollberg found time to contemplate life's fundamental dilemmas and to enjoy the good things of the Finnish countryside—a fresh fish, for example, skin drawn carefully off from head to tail-tip as Mollberg loudly proclaimed his dislike of *Apocalypse Now*. During the meal, on his private island near Vesilahti, he dreamed up a striking shot for *The Unknown Soldier*: a mother, searching for her boy in a mound of corpses, recognises him by the stiff, upflung finger that had resulted from a civilian accident. Out came the briefcase, and Mollberg jotted down the idea before pursuing our conversation.

For years, he yearned to embark on a remake of *The Egyptian*, Mika Waltari's epic novel about ancient Egypt, which had been brought to the screen by Michael Curtiz in 1954. 20th Century Fox owned the property, and Rauni asked me to write to them ("in polished English") to see if he could purchase the remake rights. The studio refused, pointing out that it had bought the rights for every conceivable audiovisual use "in the known universe." Rauni was dashed, but he did go on to make at least one more major film—*Friends*,

Comrades—about a ruthless and corrupt nickel baron in the far north of Finland.

The Finnish summer, excruciatingly brief, contrasted with the winter months and offered my local friends an escape which they seized with relief. Nothing can match the beauty of Finland in early June, with the birch-tree trunks gleaming white, and the forests and fields seem clad in a green that has a tinge of yellow in it. As summer advances, this green darkens, until by late August it gives a sombre impression, ceding the environment to autumn. Even the rites of drinking seem more cheerful in June and July; the nights are short, and the myriad lakes invite the naked swimmer to shed his inhibitions.

In January 1983, I served as Director of the biannual Nordic Film Festival, which moved from country to country according to which capital felt able to stage the event. There was a modest quota of films screened from each of the five Nordic nations ("Scandinavia" being a term that excludes Finland and Iceland), and so my task was very difficult when it came to choosing the films from Finland, the host country. Filmmakers in small nations tend to observe each other warily and with ill-disguised envy should one of their ilk attract praise from abroad or succeed in finding distribution in the major territories of Europe and America. Mika and Aki Kaurismäki showed me their maiden feature, *The Worthless*, and without hesitation I selected it for the festival. It struck me as quirky and witty in every way. Not a great film, but an original one.

A few days later I had a visit from the Finnish Film Chamber. Their managing director urged me to withdraw the invitation to *The Worthless*. "You don't understand, Peter," he said with a faintly condescending smile, "but this film doesn't show Finland in an accurate way. For example, you cannot order alcohol in a roadside café, you have to go to a state-rec-ognised liquor store. And besides, people don't behave like the characters in this film." I felt constrained, all the more so because I knew this man socially and liked his sardonic sense of humour—a quality that I perceived in *The Worthless*, but that clearly eluded my friend in his official capacity. I decided to keep the film in the festival. And the rest, as they say, is history. The Kaurismäki brothers soon established an international

Finnish Cinema

PETER COWIE

following, and Aki would have his features selected for the competition at Cannes, and distributed throughout the world.

During the festival, I arranged a seminar at the Swedish-Finnish Cultural Centre on the theme of "The Challenges and Responsibilities Facing the Film Critic in the Nordic Countries." My guests included the legendary French critic of *Le Monde*, Louis Marcorelles, the British film historian John Gillett, and journalists from West Germany, Sweden, Norway, Denmark and Finland. I questioned whether a critic based in a small language area runs the risk of both over-rating and under-rating his or her national product. Spread over two days, this seminar was typical of many such gatherings I attended during my years based in Finland, and was generously supported by the various cultural institutions in the region.

Although he appreciated my foresight in taking *The Worthless* for the Nordic Festival, Aki Kaurismäki, like so many filmmakers I have known, took umbrage if I expressed anything less than passionate enthusiasm for his work. During the mid-1980s, a new feature of his was screened at Hanasaari Cultural Center outside Helsinki. I must have let my reservations appear too sharply to him, because Aki sent one of his lieutenants to deliver a message. "Aki says you should meet him outside the building—this matter can be settled with knives." Granted, the messenger himself seemed drunk, and the snow was falling steadily outside the windows, but I refused the invitation. Mika, always the more mature of the brothers, apologised to me later. In subsequent years, I moderated post-screening sessions with Aki, and on one occasion, at the Barbican Centre in London, this most unpredictable of auteurs demanded that the carafe of water beside us on stage should be exchanged for a carafe of Scotch.

When one is tarred with the critic's brush, as I was in my twenties and thirties, most filmmakers regard one with a blend of wariness and condescension. They feel that whatever they may say runs the risk of being distorted or misinterpreted. A handful of directors, however, have expressed a genuine interest in my work and my life. When I was first introduced to Kenneth Branagh, he immediately told me that he had found my biography of Coppola invaluable when preparing to make *Frankenstein* under the American Zoetrope banner. Jodie Foster, featuring on a panel with me at the Telluride Festival in 1991, said she had enjoyed my book on Orson Welles while studying at Yale. And Henning Carlsen, that most delightful of Danish directors, repeatedly presented me with a bottle of Gammal Dansk Bitter Dram after I had praised the tipple during a late-night meeting at some festival or other.

Flashback: Henning Carlsen

Henning Carlsen had many talents. He was a writer, a filmmaker, activist, and even a cinema owner in his native Denmark. His masterpiece, a screen adaptation of Knut Hamsun's novel, *Hunger*, won the Best Actor Prize for Per Oscarsson at the Cannes Festival in 1966, and his many other feature films were shown at festivals around the world, from Berlin to Venice.

Carlsen's best films display a singular plastic beauty, and are characterised by a profound warmth of feeling for individual human beings, whose faces loom out imploringly from

the anonymous mass like those frantic sufferers in the wood-
cuts of another Scandinavian artist, Edvard Munch. Henning's
early film *Dilemma*, based on a novel by Nadine Gordimer
about the injustices of South African society in the 1960s,
exemplified his sensitivity and commitment.

His facility for observing people in their everyday habitat
helped Henning immensely when he came to make *Hunger*,
but his talent enabled him to transcend the mere recording
of reality and thus achieve a heightened realism worthy of
Knut Hamsun's autobiographical novel about a starving
writer. As Pontus, Per Oscarsson staggers like a scarecrow
through the autumnal streets of Kristiania (later to become
Oslo), reduced to gobbling dust from cupboard shelves,
chewing paper, begging a bone from a local meat market,
and is soon at the mercy of his hallucinations.

I met Henning and his zestful wife Else Heidary on
several occasions during the last thirty years of his life. He
was teeming with ideas, forever planning his next project
with quiet conviction. But he needed reassurance, and would
wait anxiously to hear one's response to his latest film. With
his flowing white hair and beard, he cut an imposing figure at
festivals and film seminars, and appeared on stage with me
at London's National Film Theatre for a conversation about
his career.

Henning juggled a number of passions. He accumulated
a collection of early cinema toys, zoetropes and kineto-
scopes, and I facilitated a meeting between him and Francis
Coppola, who had a collection himself. The two men were
instantly on the same wavelength, and Henning would talk
with affection of the welcome he was given by Coppola at
his vineyard in the Napa Valley. In 1968, Henning began
managing the fabled Dagmar Cinema in Copenhagen for a
number of years, following the death of Carl Th. Dreyer, who
had programmed the movie theatre since 1952.

Not every film that Henning directed would prove
successful. *The Wolf at the Door*, his 1986 film about Paul
Gauguin, failed to ignite, despite the contribution of Jean-
Claude Carrière to the screenplay and the presence of Max
von Sydow and Donald Sutherland in the cast. *Un divorce
heureux*, made in France, may have been too reflective

of Henning's own marriage travails and did not attract an audience.

I wrote enthusiastically about his last major work, *Did Somebody Laugh?* To some degree, it was a remake of *Hunger*, and dealt with unemployment in Denmark during the 1930s. The young protagonist is naïve and diffident, tossed aimlessly about like a boat cut free of its moorings. Like Pontus in *Hunger*, he walks through the dismal streets and sleeps on park benches. "*Hunger* deals with the dissolution of an intellectual," said Henning, "whereas this new film describes the resignation of a working man. I don't want to be a prophet; I want to address the subconscious. In the 1930s, people felt that nobody was to blame for their being unemployed. Today, they believe that society has rejected them." Looking back, it was a privilege to have known a filmmaker of such consummate wisdom, tolerance, and fantasy.

In my twenties and thirties, I had visited Eastern Europe on a number of occasions, always for gatherings concerned with film. Long nights of drinking with new-found friends and creative talents, in rooms thick with cigarette smoke, gave me a perspective on life very different to what I had acquired in England. Conversation was more serious, opinions were more ambivalent, and ideals, although held in check, brimmed to the surface on so many occasions. Film industry people in Hungary, Poland and Yugoslavia all welcomed what I had done with the *International Film Guide*, and felt that it opened a window on the world of cinema. And so Finland, poised between East and West, offered me accommodation, reconciling my need for independence with a yearning to ply my trade as a writer beyond the confines of England. It was also a country where athletics took pride of place among summer sports...

While a passion for films has governed all my adult life, an even greater passion—sport—possessed me from my very early teens. Many sports, however, just do not excite me: rugby, horse-racing, golf, basketball, baseball and American football. I have always followed at least four sports very closely: athletics, tennis, soccer and cycling. I discovered all of them around the age of 13 to 14. I embraced Arsenal and all its players—Jack Kelsey in goal, Cliff Holton up front. I visited Highbury to see Arsenal play, and stood on the terraces with my father in 1954. One year earlier I had thrilled to the news of Louison Bobet's triumph in the Tour de France. In May 1954, I listened on my school radio to Roger Bannister's breaking the mythic 4-minute mile barrier at Oxford, and immediately began following every aspect of athletics, from the Olympics to cross-country running.

Thanks to my parents' kindness, I subscribed to the late lamented monthly magazine, *World Sports*. By the time of the Melbourne Olympics in 1956, I was ready to compile the most elaborate scrapbook, in which I wrote down every result of every event. I could as easily have become a sports statistician as I did a film historian. Listening to sports events on the radio seemed just as exciting then as watching on high-definition TV does today.

Although I represented Charterhouse a few times at 880 yards and at cross-country, my performances never impressed anyone except my parents, and my athletics aspirations came to an abrupt halt in 1960 when I entered for the half-mile trials at Cambridge. When I saw the name "H. Elliott" on the list of runners in the second heat, I quietly walked away. Herb Elliott was the hero of the hour, unbeaten at 1,500m, then taking a degree at the university.

While I have had the privilege of attending the football World Cup at Wembley in 1966, the Olympic Games in Sydney in 2000, the inaugural World Athletics Championships in Helsinki in 1983, soccer matches at Highbury and the Emirates Stadium, and even Test cricket at Lord's, I have never managed to make friends with sports personalities in the way I have with filmmakers. Through the years I have enjoyed a brief frisson in shaking hands with racing driver Stirling Moss, sprinter Carl Lewis, Arsenal soccer hero Thierry Henry, and tennis maestro Ilie Năstase. The cyclist I most admired, Eddy Merckx, once pushed past me roughly to gain a place in a self-service cafeteria at the New York Bicycle Show, but that was about as close as I ever got to encountering a true champion of the road. Even in my fifties I was thrilled to meet Roger Bannister in the flesh after a screening at the NFT of the official documentary on the 1948 Olympics. He asked me if I had been a runner myself. "800 metres,"

I replied. "Hmm," he said, appraising me with a doctor's jovial eye. "You seem a bit too tall for that."

This love of certain sports has never diminished. When Arsenal are playing (which means almost twice a week), I keep my internet connection open so that I can check the score every few minutes. During July I watch the Tour de France every day.

Since my youth, following certain sports has been a passion as abiding as films or literature. From an early age, I attended athletics meetings in London, and queued to gain access to the outside courts at Wimbledon during the first week of the tournament. I have always watched the occasional big event in golf, and have retained a more than passing interest in cricket.

The individual achievement in sport beguiled me more than team spirit. I, who at school had failed to make an impression in the "major" games like cricket, soccer, and even rugby, could only admire the feats of others. I, who throughout my youth and adult years struggled to play tennis, to ski, or to do better than the average in athletics, drew vicarious pleasure in watching others soar to greatness. I have a tendency to identify with a certain player or athlete in my favourite sports, and this loyalty has provoked many a broken night as I await the results of games across the globe. Early idols included Tony Trabert, the only man to win Wimbledon and then the U.S. Open without losing a set; Emil Zátopek, the Czech who dominated distance running in his time; Jack Kelsey, Arsenal's goalkeeper; and Neil Harvey, the Australian batsman. In recent times, I have found Roger Federer and Lance Armstrong to be the most consistent and outstanding sportsmen (Armstrong may have emerged as a cheat and a liar, but his strategic skill and his climbing talents were quite simply without equal).

By launching two annuals on sport during the early 1980s, I was able to earn money from my hobby. *International Cycling Guide* (under the editorship of Nicholas Crane) covered all aspects of cycling, from touring to commuting, to racing on the track and on the road. *International Running Guide* took courage from the burgeoning, worldwide fitness obsession which nascent companies like Nike, Reebok, and Sub 4 were busily encouraging.

Thanks to my contacts in Finland and to our editor, Cliff Temple, I could negotiate the perfect launch platform for the

Running Guide. Every member of the international press received a copy of the book in their goody bag at the inaugural World Championships in Athletics in Helsinki in August 1983. The organisers offered me press credentials, and so each day I would take the bus to the stadium in time for the start of the track and field programme. After all, the Finnish tradition in athletics was immense and out of all proportion with the size of the population. A statue of the immortal Paavo Nurmi stood at the entrance to the Olympic stadium in Helsinki. I felt immensely and unreasonably proud as I sat behind my little TV screen, and gazed down at the finishing straight, where world records were set in the women's 400m and the men's 4 x 100m relay.

In and around the press room I met some of those men I admired—Chris Brasher, whose triumph in the 1956 Olympic steeplechase I had heard over the radio during the night at Charterhouse school; the robust and cocky Steve Ovett, then entering the late afternoon of his career; Brendan Foster, the British distance runner who had been appointed head of Nike's U.K. branch and who supported our *Running Guide* with several pages of advertising; and Jamaican sprinter Don Quarrie, who had won four Olympic medals, including gold at 200m in Montreal in 1976. A few months later, I was introduced to another hero of mine, Lasse Viren, who won both the 5,000m and 10,000m at consecutive Olympic Games. Pencil-thin, self-deprecating like so many Finns, Viren was in professional life a policeman in a provincial town.

My twin passions, film and sport, came together in 2017 when Criterion worked with the International Olympic Committee to produce a massive box-set of all the official Olympic films from 1912 to 2012. No fewer than 53 documentaries were painstakingly restored, and I had the privilege of writing essays on all of them—essays that were collected in a handsome book accompanying the DVD and Blu-ray editions. A handful of the Olympic films have become classics in their own right—Kon Ichikawa's *Tokyo Olympiad*, for example, Leni Riefenstahl's brilliant if notorious *Olympia,* and Claude Lelouch's engaging, informal study of the 1968 Winter Games in Grenoble. Carlos Saura directed the Barcelona 1992 documentary, and Miloš Forman, John Schlesinger, Mai Zetterling and Arthur Penn all contributed segments to *Visions of Eight*, a record of the Munich 1972 Summer Games.

I was living only half an hour away from the IOC head-quarters in Lausanne, and grew to respect the films department, headed by Robert Jaquier, and also his colleague Jean-Louis Strangis, who could edit together all manner of archival clips even under the tightest of deadlines. Television coverage may be all-encompassing, but by its very nature it is evanescent. Thanks to the Olympic films, one can recapture the magic of legendary performances such as Paavo Nurmi's five gold medals at the Paris 1924 Summer Games, Jesse Owens' triumphant sprinting at Berlin in 1936, or Joan Benoit's landmark victory in the inaugural women's Marathon in Los Angeles in 1984.

Like films about composers, films about sporting heroes are not often convincing. The actors involved do not have the same prowess as the famous names they are trying to portray. Team sports are easier to convey on screen—baseball (*Bill Durham*, *Field of Dreams*, *The Natural*), ice hockey (*Slap Shot*), basketball (*Hoop Dreams*) and American football (*Any Given Sunday*). Twenty-first century movies on the subject of tennis, track & field and cycling have tried hard to present an authentic picture of their sport. But *Race*, *The Program*, *Challengers*, *Borg vs McEnroe* and even *Battle of the Sexes* are frustrating because one yearns to see the real athletes in action, rather than an impersonation. I've been more engrossed by films that build a fictional story against a sporting background, like *Rocky*, *Breaking Away*, *Bang the Drum Slowly* or *Bend It Like Beckham*. However, nothing in this field can surpass a well-written documentary like *When We Were Kings* (on boxing) or the peerless *Tokyo Olympiad*.

Flashback: Iceland

In the early 1980s I met Ágúst Guðmundsson, a young Icelandic director who showed me his maiden feature, *Land and Sons*. Ágúst had studied at the National Film and Television School in Britain. *Land and Sons* was based on a novel by Indriði G. Thorsteinsson, and Ágúst brought it in on a budget of just $130,000. An instant success, it attracted 110,000 Icelanders to the cinema (equivalent to 90 million Americans going to see a single new release).

I was captivated by the landscape as well as by the lyricism and lucidity with which Ágúst tells his tale of young Einar, truculent and introspective, who wants to move to the island's capital, Reykjavik, abandoning the family smallholding. Ágúst himself struck me as more English than the English, with his courteous demeanour and his sense of irony. Almost his polar opposite, Hrafn Gunnlaugsson was the other flag-bearer of a new generation of filmmaking in Iceland. Hrafn would charm you into eating mortified shark and washing it down with plenty of schnapps; his work was from the outset fierce and courageous, dealing with the Viking themes familiar from the "sagas," notably in his breakthrough, *When the Raven Flies*, in 1984. Both *When the Raven Flies* and Ágúst's less ambitious *Outlaw* found cinematic means to evoke the Middle Ages that were more convincing than Hollywood's epics, including Richard Fleischer's impressive *The Vikings*.

My first trip to Iceland took place in 1984. I was invited to the Nordic Film Festival in Reykjavík, following my work as head of the event when it was held in Helsinki in 1983. I learned that bathing in the hot, sulphurous pools could be accomplished nude, and with members of both sexes, as the heat had a negative effect on libido. I watched in a crowded bar as one man dared to approach another's female companion, and was struck down with a single terrible blow by his rival. Nobody reacted, and it was explained to me that this was quite normal, and that any hard feelings would be drowned in liquor. I travelled over rough terrain in the interior of the country, admiring lunar landscapes and the volcanic black of the earth—topographical features that had already appeared in *Star Wars*, and would be used in the future by productions as diverse as *Prometheus*, *The Tree of Life*, *Interstellar* and *Game of Thrones*.

Step by step, year by year, the Icelandic cinema, like some glacier descending from the mountains, made its mark on the world scene. Hrafn's *When the Raven Flies* was screened in Berlin in 1984, and three months later Thorsteinn Jónsson's *Atomic Station* attracted crowded houses and warm applause at the Director's Fortnight in Cannes. Filmmakers in Reykjavík were happy to mortgage hearth and home in order to complete their dreams, and audiences cheerfully paid up more for a ticket to a domestic film than for routine foreign fare from Hollywood or Europe. At that stage the Icelandic government, although sympathetic to film, could not provide more than about 20% of a new production's funding. Most of the budget had to be covered by private investment, and fortunately banks at the time were keen on investing in the cinema. There were only about two hundred actors and actresses in the local union, and no studios as such existed.

By 1995, having visited Iceland on other occasions, I felt impelled to write a slim book about the country's film history, and it appeared under the auspices of the Icelandic Film Fund. The cover featured an image from Friðrik Thor Friðriksson's *Children of Nature*, which in 1992 was among the final five nominees for an Academy Award in the Best Foreign Language Film category. Icelandic cinema had come of age.

Flashback: Norway

Although I had studied Swedish film history in relative depth, I knew literally nothing about cinema in Norway. I had heard vaguely of Tancred Ibsen and Arne Skouen, but nobody else. Then in 1970 I was contacted by a young man named Jan Erik Holst, who regretted the sketchiness of the Norwegian section in the *International Film Guide* and asked if he could meet me. He was about to study at the University of Stockholm at the time, and came to see me in Hotel Diplomat. I was immediately impressed by this tall, fair-haired film buff wearing a green velvet suit. He was a decade younger than I, but we were on the same wavelength from the start. I agreed that he could write an article in the next edition of the *Guide*.

At almost the same time, another youthful Norwegian, Lasse Henriksen, wrote to me and said I should visit Oslo to discover the "new" Norwegian cinema for myself. He was completing his debut feature film, and would introduce me to other cineastes. I accepted and stayed with Lasse and his friend, Chris Boger, who was also at work on a film, entitled *Butterfly Autumn*. Lasse had a smooth and articulate manner, easing himself into your good graces as to the manner born. He came to see me at home in London, accompanied by the actress Cherina Schaer, who had just appeared in Sam Peckinpah's *Straw Dogs*. Lasse explained that he was a Mormon, and that Cherena was but one of his various wives, as permitted by that church. He startled my own wife by asking why the space under our stairs was empty. "You need stores," he said seriously, "for the coming storm..." I later learned that the polygamy of which he spoke so glibly had been banned by the Mormon movement as far back as 1902.

During that fleeting interlude in Oslo, I met Pål Løkke-berg and his ex-wife Vibeke Løkkeberg, as well as Anja Breien, whose proto-feminist debut, *Rape*, was wet from the labs and eagerly anticipated. Jan Erik Holst and the head of the Norwegian Film Institute, Jon Stenklev, arranged a private viewing of *Rape* for me, and it was clear that Anja Brein had a bright future ahead of her. Vibeke, a charismatic actress, fancied herself as a director, but I found her work too abstract and spaced-out to be convincing. *Love is War* went on to win a Silver Bear for Best Cinematography at the Berlin Festival, and *Rape* was selected for the Director's Fortnight in Cannes. I had the impression that all these new Norwegian movies were rough-hewn, well-meaning and experimental in form. Almost every production depended on state aid, but the system of subsidies for domestic production was not so well-entrenched as in neighbouring Sweden or Denmark, and budgets were pared to the limit.

A quarter of a century later, Jan Erik Holst, by then director of the Norwegian Film Institute, invited me to write a book about the country's filmmakers, past and present. He himself had written the definitive history—in Norwegian—and so we both saw my endeavour as a concise, non-academic study that would prove useful to distributors, exhibitors, journalists and film buffs. As I had done with Iceland, I covered the historical aspect quite tersely, and concentrated the body of my text on the latest wave of Norwegian auteurs.

In the first edition, which appeared in 1999 under the title of *Straight from the Heart*, I discussed some eighty feature films, selected from around three hundred produced by Norway since the spring of 1971. "Norwegian cinema," I wrote, "does not have the Swedish urge to improve the world. Nor do Norwegian directors suffer from the cosy, somewhat self-satisfied approach of their counterparts in Denmark. [...] The fierce natural beauty of Norway, so familiar from tourist brochures and fjord cruises, figures on the screen only as required for dramatic or historic purposes. Urban life provides the grist of Norwegian cinema. Small-town existence does not appeal." I was intrigued by the wide variety of viewpoints expressed by directors like Berit Nesheim (films about children and young people), Bent Hamer (slow-burning comedy), Nils Gaup (spectacular historical epics), Anja Breien (women's issues) and Unni Straume (experimental, dramatic abstraction).

I used to believe that my history degree at Cambridge would have little or no effect on my career as a writer. In retrospect, however, I realise that my university studies had taught me the value of research. I would even go so far as to say that research constitutes as much as three quarters of the work underpinning a book. You cannot commence the writing phase until you have completed the research, and once you have completed the research, the writing will flow smoothly.

Like every writer of my generation, I progressed from working in long-hand, to composing my text on a typewriter (manual, and then electric), and then on a word processor. I suspect that tapping away on a computer screen is more satisfying to the non-fiction author than it is to the writer of fiction. You can bring all your sources up on the screen easily, and cut and paste into your main text much more swiftly than in the past.

Some of my books have depended almost wholly on research. When I embarked on *The Godfather Book* for Faber and Faber in 1995, I was lucky enough to have the trust of Francis Ford Coppola, who encouraged me to visit his library in Rutherford, California, where all his files, letters, as well as his own research into the subject, were guarded with diligence by his librarian, Anahid Nazarian. Four years later, I had access to the files for *Apocalypse Now*, and could trace the gestation of that unruly masterpiece from start to finish.

I followed a similar path when researching my more recent biography of Ingmar Bergman. The Bergman Foundation allowed me to work at peace in an office within the Swedish Film Institute Library, and every day the curator Hélène Dahl would bring me Bergman's workbooks, and private photo boxes. She would school me in the intranet that enabled me to view the many thousands of letters Bergman exchanged with people over the years, from Stanley Kubrick to Laurence Olivier. At Stockholm's Royal Dramatic Theatre, the same routine functioned well: Dag Kronlund, the resident archivist, gave me access to the files of correspondence that Bergman had undertaken during his years at the head of the theatre. Fortunately, I can read Swedish, and this enabled me to penetrate the archives more efficiently than, for example, I could when preparing my book on Kurosawa while not reading or speaking Japanese.

Not all research is completed within the confines of a library or archive. Interviewing as many individuals as possible adds depth to any serious study. For my Bergman biography, I had managed to record conversations with a majority of his colleagues and relations. Coppola also permitted me to reach out to everyone who had been involved in the *Godfather* movies, and on *Apocalypse Now*. Some of the great names (Brando, Pacino) declined to be interviewed. But it is a curious truism that you often hear the most revealing memories from the lesser lights, such as cameramen, production assistants, even "script girls" like Katinka Faragó and Teruyo Nogami, who worked with Bergman and Kurosawa respectively, for more than fifty years.

Like Hemingway, I prefer to write in the morning and finish the session in mid-sentence, thus enabling me the next day to pick up where I paused. The process starts while I am still half-asleep, around 6 a.m. I find that phrases, and sometimes whole sentences and ideas, come into my mind as I lie in the darkness. The trick is to recall these elements two hours later, having eaten breakfast, scanned the headlines on the net, and showered and shaved.

In defiance of the computer, I often print out the first version of a book or an article. I read the text carefully, cut certain passages, move paragraphs around to suit the narrative flow, and correct irregularities of spelling or fact. Then back to the iMac, to implement such changes and amendments.

Until the mid-1980s, my focus of attention had been on filmmaking in Scandinavia. In 1984, that began to change, even though I was then living part of each month in Finland and thus absorbed by Nordic society. During my final summer of teaching at UC Santa Barbara, *The New York Times* commissioned me to write a profile of Tom Luddy. I knew Tom as the programme director at the Pacific Film Archive in Berkeley, as the former partner and masculine muse, as it were, of the pioneering chef Alice Waters, and as a co-founder of the Telluride Film Festival.

Tom swore by the *International Film Guide*, and we shared an interest in Eastern European filmmakers. My days in San Francisco with Tom coincided with the Democratic Convention in the summer of 1984. He swept me along in his wake to parties, to jazz clubs, and to friends who recounted anecdotes about this human Rolodex who seemed to know everyone of importance in the film world—including their phone numbers, which he could recite from memory.

I also happened to arrive in North Beach when Tom was in the last stages of pre-production on *Mishima: A Life in Four Chapters*, to be directed by Paul Schrader. Francis Coppola and George Lucas served as executive producers on the project, which helped to cement Japanese participation in the financing of the film. Meeting Tom each day in his office high up in the sea-green Sentinel Building on the corner of Kearny and Columbus Streets brought home to me how significant Coppola's influence was, not just in the Bay Area but on a global scale.

In 1972, I had lined up around the block with hundreds of others to see *The Godfather* during its first run in Times Square. The film had exerted a seismic effect on my notions of auteurism. This was the first time in film history that a masterpiece by any measure had also become a smash hit at the box office. I recalled seeing and liking Francis Ford Coppola's maiden studio film, *You're a Big Boy Now*, in Cannes in 1967. I had experienced the almost transcendental press screening of *Apocalypse Now* at Cannes in 1979 and was convinced that Coppola had established himself as a major figure in movie history. Despite his relative failures (*One from the Heart*, *The Cotton Club*), I felt the urge to write at length about his work. Tom arranged for us to meet, in Francis' eyrie at the top of the Sentinel Building, where Dean Tavoularis had painted a fresco in the domed ceiling—"Coppola's cupola," quipped Francis. Great of girth and fierce of beard, he exuded an amiable authority. He said he thought it was rather early for a book to be

written about him, but a rapport seemed to develop between us, and not just one of age (we were both born in 1939).

Back in London and Helsinki, I plunged headlong into a book-length study of Coppola's life and films. Two years later, I visited San Francisco again, and showed the typescript to Tom

Luddy. He said he would read it over the coming days. When I entered the office on Monday, however, he told me that Francis had come into his office late on the Friday, seized the manuscript and driven up to his home in Rutherford for the weekend. The next day he had called Tom and told him that he liked my book, but that there were gaps as well as factual errors that required attention, and that Tom should arrange for me to return to the Bay Area for interviews with him.

Francis and his wife Eleanor welcomed me to their period home in Rutherford, with its wrap-around veranda and its white wood facings. Vines stretched out as far as the eye could see, across the floor of the Napa valley. A short stroll from the house stood a bungalow. You went up a few steps, and inside were desks and all manner of objects, from Francis' trusty portable typewriter to a refrigerator for cold drinks, reference books, and piles of screenplays. There I taped our conversations, ranging over his childhood, his youth, his career, but never his private life, which has always been, as it should be, guarded with discretion.

At the end of the day, Francis wandered into the kitchen and started preparing pasta and other Italian dishes for the evening meal. Guests were offered wine and could enjoy slivers from an immense block of Parmesan cheese. Lunches and dinners were family affairs; Francis loved being around children, and he would often burst out into song to amuse them. One evening his uncle Anton, an opera conductor, regaled us with anecdotes; film-makers would arrive en passant, as well as colleagues like casting director Fred Roos or costume designer Milena Canonero. I found myself intrigued by the personality of Francis' brother, August who, with his patrician manner, lived up to his name. "Augie" was then Dean of Creative Arts at San Francisco State University and was, by Francis' own admission, the model for the Motorcycle Boy in *Rumble Fish* and, I suspect, for the similar figure of Flamingo in *Twixt*. With black hair swept back over his head, and a gaze that exuded authority and self-confidence, "Augie" remained the antithesis of his younger brother, and yet the two men were linked by an unshakable loyalty.

In early 1988, I visited Francis on the set of *Tucker: The Man and his Dream*. The vast Ford plant at the Richmond Marina had been dressed to serve as Tucker's auto warehouse. Seated in a canvas chair, Francis directed quietly, while Jeff Bridges, Martin Landau and other cast members hovered close to him for instructions. He had directed *One from the Heart* from an Airstream trailer, but here he was more approachable, watching each take on a newfangled portable view-finder.

On my honeymoon in 1989, I took my wife Françoise to visit Francis in Rutherford, where he was rehearsing actors for *The Godfather Part III*. It was a hot and inauspicious day, because Al Pacino and Diane Keaton were on the verge of breaking up, and Pacino wanted Francis to re-write his scenes. We witnessed much significant door-slamming, and were consoled by brief meetings with Dean Tavoularis, the set designer, and Eli Wallach, who was to play Don Altobello. My appointment with Francis was postponed, and postponed... until in the end we gave up and went back to San Francisco.

Francis liked my biography, which had just appeared, and felt bad about our missed appointment. Two months later, he was in Rome, shooting *The Godfather Part III*. Peter Bart commissioned me to do a front-page article for Variety on this most anticipated of sequels. I met Francis at Cinecittà, and then at "Ciak," a diminutive restaurant in the heart of Trastevere. As the meal progressed Francis went through a copy of the book page by page, occasionally scribbling a correction; to his credit, he never attempted to alter any of my opinions or judgments on his films.

From then on, he seemed to trust me, and throughout the 1990s, I would see Francis on my visits to the West Coast. He asked me to write the texts to appear alongside the objects in his small museum at the winery in Napa, and when I suggested a book on the making of *The Godfather* trilogy, he agreed to open his archives to me. *The Godfather Book* was bought for the United States by Chronicle Books in San Francisco, only for them to cancel publication when Marlon Brando refused to let his image be used on the cover. This was followed in 2001 by *The Apocalypse Now Book*, in which I strove to recapture the dizzy fervour of that project. Fortunately, Francis owned the negative of *Apocalypse Now* and provided all the images we needed. When this title appeared to coincide with the re-release of the expanded version, *Apocalypse Now Redux*, at the Cannes Festival of 2001, Pathé in France purchased three thousand copies of the French edition to distribute to the French and international press.

During that same year I received an invitation from Kim Aubry, a DVD producer involved with Francis' Zoetrope operation. Paramount were about to issue *The Godfather* on DVD for the first time, and Francis had insisted that the authoring and editorial work be done out of his San Francisco offices. Kim, who liked *The Godfather Book*, felt that I could make a significant contribution to the project. I was assigned an office in the Sentinel Building and worked alongside some talented technicians, including film editor Serena Warner and the DVD author and compressionist Anthony Ruffo. I compiled a "family tree" for the Corleone family and wrote "biographies" of the major characters, then a timeline of events, so that viewers could grasp the chronology of the *Godfather* saga, and a glossary of "Mafia Slang."

When most of the material was ready, Kim and I flew down to Los Angeles to unveil the content of the DVD to a room full of Paramount executives and attorneys. An amusing moment occurred when a still came up on the screen of Al Ruddy receiving the Academy Award for Best Picture. "Who's this guy?" asked one of the lawyers as he sat complacently at the table in his trademark black tee-shirt, dark blazer, and shades. I pointed out that it was Ruddy, and that he had produced probably the greatest motion picture ever to emerge from Paramount Studios!

Francis confided to me during the late 1990s that he had made much more money from the success of his wineries than he had from his films, even if that very day Zoetrope had received a payment of several million dollars from Columbia Pictures for *Bram Stoker's Dracula*, which had appeared some years earlier and continued to generate considerable revenues. Along with Gerry Byrne and others from *Variety*, I attended a memorable evening in October 1997 at Coppola's freshly-restored Inglenook château, with Abel Gance's *Napoléon* projected on a giant outdoor screen while guests sipped Francis' best wine, Rubicon, and inhaled Cuban cigars.

The success of Francis' wine estates served as comfort and compensation for the fact that few critics, and even fewer audiences, applauded his films of the past twenty years. *The Rainmaker* could not be faulted, but lacked the originality and driving force of his best work. I liked both *Tetro* and *Twixt*, modest of aim and enjoyable on their own terms. In some ways Francis seemed to have been hoist with his own petard. Forever attuned to the small, intimate project, he achieved his greatest acclaim for the large-scale epics like *The Godfather* and *Apocalypse Now*, to which he brought a panache and an operatic grandeur that he failed to replicate in his low-budget movies—with the glorious exception of *The Conversation*. The project he had cherished for more than forty years, *Megalopolis*, at last appeared in 2024. The mixed reviews and poor box-office reception were due in part to the absence of Francis' legendary colleagues Vittorio Storaro, Dean Tavoularis and Walter Murch, but also to the absence of a strong producer who might have kept the project on the straight and narrow both aesthetically and financially. When firing on all cylinders, however, Francis Coppola possesses a breadth of vision and a command of technique akin to that of Orson Welles or Luchino Visconti.

3.
A New Age

By the spring of 1988, my life and career had reached a turning point. The various annuals I had launched during the 1980s had begun to wither on the vine, despite my personal enthusiasm and almost desperate commitment to their cause. *The International TV & Video Guide*, the brainchild of my Finnish friend, Olli Tuomela, never gathered momentum, and appeared only for four years. The *International Running Guide* (soon re-named *International Athletics Guide*) also stumbled after a promising start; apart from the major equipment manufacturers, advertisers were few and far between. We published *International Cycling Guide* for seven years, and then sold the title for next to nothing. My editor, Nicholas Crane, could not have been more passionate and meticulous in his approach to a project that sought to unite the racing, tourist, and casual cyclist in a single, illustrated almanac. I accompanied him to the New York Bicycle Show, and to British gatherings where we would follow races and encounter those in the trade. *The International Music Guide* proved the most enduring of all these annuals apart from *IFG*, but by 1987, in its eleventh year, its time seemed to have expired in the light of a catastrophic fall in record sales for classical music.

During a decade in which Thatcherism eroded official support for the arts (as did the Reagan years for culture in America), we struggled to find a discriminating public for our books. In 1985, however, I had developed possibly the most successful idea of my career. *The Scandinavian Guide* was built on a simple premise: an annual book offering information about the Nordic area that would make it indispensable for the business community. The articles covered politics, the economy, the arts, sports, and of course a guide to the finest hotels, restaurants, and tourist sites. Having lost faith in traditional book distribution channels, I decided to approach a handful of major companies in Scandinavia and sell an exclusive edition of the book for use as a corporate gift to their clients around the world. The response was amazing. Working with enterprises like SAS Scandinavian Airlines, Neste Oil in Finland, and the various national tourist boards, we were able to sell as many as 15,000 copies, avoiding the book trade altogether, and receiving payment from our clients in less than a month after delivery of books. It was manna from heaven, and for five years the book proved a money-spinner, making up for the sluggish performance of the other annuals.

Flashback: Emir Kusturica

Six republics constituted the former Yugoslavia, and of these Serbia and Croatia were the most predominant. During my visits to Belgrade, Zagreb and Pula, I noticed the rivalry between directors from the various regions, but not yet the hostility that the death of Tito would unleash. Almost every film director in the six republics could be described as a maverick, none more so than Emir Kusturica. His long, candid face, framed with a luxuriant growth of hair, retained the look of youth. Kusturica dominated every room he entered with an easy bonhomie and a wit as dry as a martini. Born in Bosnia Sarajevo, he had earned international acclaim for his first two features, *Do You Remember Dolly Bell?* (Best First Film prize in Venice in 1981) and *When Father Was Away on Business* (Palme d'Or in Cannes in 1985).

In the late winter of 1988, he invited me to visit the shoot of his third feature, under the working title of *Home for Hanging*, and which would emerge as *Time of the Gypsies*. High above the northern slopes of Belgrade, and enveloped in woodland, stood Avala Studios, for forty years the HQ of Serbian moviemaking. On the fringe of this rather decrepit lot, I found a huddle of small trucks and personnel preparing to shoot a scene in a cramped wooden shell that would appear on screen as a gypsy trailer, lumbering along the highway by night. Two technicians pushed some arc-lights back and forth on rails beyond the trailer window to simulate traffic. Another rocked the entire structure by hand to give the impression of a bumpy ride.

The unit was small and amiable. There was no sign of a script as such. Kusturica had scribbled out the details of the scene on two close-packed pages ripped from an exercise book. After each take he would call "Stop!" and study these sheets carefully. As the afternoon wore on, the building grew chilly. No heating, no sound-proofing. Everyone smoked to keep warm and to keep calm. As one young Serbian quipped, "It's the cheapest pleasure!" In Yugoslavia, where inflation was raging at around 120% and counting, such gallows humour kept body and soul together.

Later, over espresso in a Belgrade hotel, Kusturica reminisced about the early days of shooting on the film, in the heart of a 50,000-strong gypsy encampment near Skopje, when the rains came and the cold was so fierce that everyone clustered for warmth around the biggest bonfire they had ever seen. At least the production was bolstered by American money—a co-production between Columbia Pictures and Forum Film Studios of Sarajevo, with Columbia paying half the budget upfront and retaining world rights outside Eastern Europe. "This is the first time in our movie history," declared Kusturica proudly, "that the Americans have paid for a film being shot in our language [Serbian]."

Both *Dolly Bell* and *When Father was Away on Business* dealt with youngsters. "At the end of the day," smiles Kusturica, "every film is about the process of growing up." *Time of the Gypsies*, like all Kusturica's early work, is a rites-of-passage movie that tracks the destiny of Perhan, a teenage gypsy boy. He crosses the Italian border and slips under the fey and fiendish influence of an older gypsy named Ahmed. He soon becomes a "slave," stealing as to the manner born and enriching the faceless criminals who treat the boys as a pimp treats his hookers. The story was closer to reality than to Kusturica's fantasy. When the director tried to take his young gypsy cast to locations in Italy, the border police three times turned him back, claiming that some of these "actors" were wanted in connection with robberies on the Italian side.

Kusturica told me that he loves the Romany life. "Gypsies are integrated into our society," he said. "They go to the same schools, they share the same interests. Gypsies are extroverts, they like soccer, and movies on TV, just like the rest of us."

I asked him if he would be tempted to work abroad. "I've always disliked the orthodox Hollywood studio type of movie," he reflected. "But when I saw the work of Jim Jarmusch I realised that you could have independence of vision and make a film in America. And what I am sure of is that I must do a movie under conditions different to those I've experienced thus far in Yugoslavia." He said this with a hint of weariness. It was 10 p.m., and since early morning Kusturica had been coaching and coaxing his cast of non-professionals. "They can make mistakes on camera, but they can't lie, and when you see the rushes, you appreciate the feeling they radiate."

Vilko Filac, his cinematographer, arrived to discuss the next day's shoot. He and Kusturica chatted awhile about the colour scheme, and about the lights-at-night motif that would distinguish the movie. As Kusturica, looking incongruous in the hotel lounge in his faded no-name sweatsuit and sneakers, prepared to leave, he quoted a remark by his friend Miloš Forman: "In the States you make films with money. In Europe, you must make them with friends."

In May of 1988, my world was suddenly shaken. During a visit to the Nordic Film Festival in Rouen, in Normandy, I was much charmed by the co-organiser of that event, Françoise Buquet. One fateful day during the Cannes Festival of 1988, while standing outside the Star Cinema in the Rue d'Antibes, waiting for a screening, I heard my name called softly, and then more loudly. I turned to see Françoise in the queue behind me, and so we chatted and agreed to have dinner the following day. When I returned to my hotel that evening, there was a message from Roger Watkins, editor of *Variety*. Could I meet with him and the publisher of the paper, Syd Silverman, the next day at around 5 p.m? I was puzzled, and intrigued, all the more so as Roger stipulated that I should rendezvous with them in the back of the Carlton Hotel bar, and not on the terrace where such meetings usually took place.

When I arrived in the rather shadowy area of the bar lounge, I was greeted by Roger and Syd, and also by Bob Hawkins, the paper's vice-president and a familiar figure on the festival circuit. The Silverman family had recently sold *Variety* to Cahners, a division of Reed International, the multi-national media giant. Roger explained that they had often noted, and been exasperated by, my ability to get advertisements for the *International Film Guide* that *Variety* itself failed to secure. They offered to acquire the *Guide* and to appoint me as Business Manager for *Variety*'s European operations. "You'll never have to sell another ad for the *Guide*," said Roger reassuringly, "our reps will do all that." Alas, this proved not to be true, but I was amazed that at my age (48) someone could seek me out and make me an offer I couldn't refuse.

Intoxicated by the meeting, I met Françoise in my favourite fish restaurant in Cannes, La Coquille. We were seated at a tiny table against the wall, but from the first moments we were entranced with each other. By the end of that memorable evening, I was well and truly in love, and when I said a shy goodnight to Françoise outside the flat she was sharing with her team from the Nordic Film Festival, she looked up at me, smiled, and said quietly but firmly, "Don't worry, Peter."

My sales manager, Anne Richardson, came to my room the next morning for the daily meeting to discuss the clients who should be approached at the festival. I confided in her, and told her about the offer from *Variety* and the possible new relationship with Françoise. She said without any hesitation, "I should accept both!" I kept reminding myself of one of my most esteemed Shakespearian quotations, "There is a tide in the affairs of men which, taken at the flood, leads on to fortune." I have never regretted accepting both the proposal from *Variety* and the opportunity for happiness afforded by Françoise.

Returning from Cannes, I visited the *Variety* offices, then in St. James' Street. It was a bright, sunlit day, and I recall how impressed I was by meeting staffers Elizabeth Guider, who wrote with authority about TV issues, and Don Groves, the European editor with whom I struck up what would become a lifelong friendship. The soon-to-be President of Cahners was an imposing, cigar-smoking man named Bob Krakoff. His manifest admiration for what we had accomplished at Tantivy set him apart from other executives. Bob ensured that I was taken seriously by his peers at Reed International, the parent company of Cahners, and he invited Françoise and me to dinners and exhibitions.

My official title at *Variety* was European Manager, and in January 1989 the paper's editor, Roger Watkins, sent a letter to all staff announcing my appointment. He said that I would have "overall responsibility for editorial, business and administration in this important and developing geographical area." In practice, I had little influence over editorial issues. The journalists looked somewhat warily at their business colleagues, and asserted, quite rightly, their independence and integrity when it came to criticising, for example, the product of a major advertiser in *Variety*.

My first challenge involved Church and State. In other words, some of the most important *Variety* bureaux in Europe were run like fiefdoms by individuals who both solicited ads from clients, and reviewed new films from those same clients. Purging any hint of corruption from our offices was not easy, and involved the loss of one or two colleagues who had devoted many a long year to the cause of the paper.

The second challenge was to establish a daily paper during the Cannes Festival. The first "Daily Screening Guide" appeared on May 11, 1989, in a modest A5 format running to 32 pages, in full colour. My title of "Editor" involved my sitting virtually all day in a cramped, crowded room in the Carlton Hotel, typing out screening times and gathering material from the journalists. This was passed to our designers, Graffiti Productions, who sent it to the printers near Nice. By about 6 a.m. each day, the magazines were ready to be delivered by truck to Cannes, where sleepy-eyed volunteers trekked to hotels, leaving piles of *Variety* in the lobbies and public rooms.

All too often, however, the printing ran late, meaning that the magazines only reached the hotels at about 9 a.m. I would then field phone calls from irate advertisers, who quite rightly complained that most executives had left their hotels for the morning screenings or to meet with colleagues. However, we were blazing a trail, and within a few years *Variety* and its rival trade papers all published "dailies" at Cannes, Berlin, and various other markets like MIFED and the AFM.

During the autumn of 1989, I flew to Berlin to meet with a potential printer for a daily to be issued during the next Berlinale. I had to rise at dawn to catch an early plane (flights to Berlin in those days were slow because aircraft were obliged to reduce speed when flying over East German territory). The meeting with the printer went well, and I was in bed by about 9 p.m that night. Suddenly I was awakened by lights flashing on the wall of my room overlooking Nürnbergerstrasse, near the Zoo. When I went to the window, I could see scores of cars with headlights flashing, and honking as though in some wedding procession. I switched on the TV and saw that the first stones in the Berlin Wall were being broken off and thrown to the ground. It was the evening of November 9, 1989. I threw on some clothes and started walking eastwards towards the East German border. When I arrived at the Wall, people were cheering, weeping, shouting, trying to grab pieces, even fragments of the detested concrete that had destroyed so many lives, so many families, since its erection in 1961. It was a heady experience.

Roger Watkins' successor as editor of *Variety,* Peter Bart, also fresh in the saddle, rather liked my track record as an author, and in particular because of my relationship with Francis Coppola, whom he himself had sought out to direct *The Godfather* at Paramount eighteen years earlier. So I did file some stories for *Variety*, including coverage of the Moscow Film Festival of 1989 and the shooting of *The Godfather Part III* in Rome. I spent almost ten days at the monstrous Hotel Rossiya near Moscow's Red Square, marching down 100 metre corridors to my cockroach-infested room. I would spend hours in search of a fax office to despatch my copy to New York, finally bribing my official guide with some lipstick purchased in a foreigners-only store. Even then, the connection was broken in mid-transmission on various occasions, and I was relieved to climb aboard my British Airways plane at Sheremetyevo Airport. As we took off, passengers broke into sustained applause. One did not imagine that the Berlin Wall would be breached less than four months later, nor that Gorbachev's courageous programme of glasnost would end in the collapse of the U.S.S.R.

At *Variety*, I was happy to discover that there was a triple-glazed wall between editorial and publishing. Neither could tell the other what to do. An Eastern European government film bureau might be offering to pay for a supplement on its production, but we could not accept it unless our journalists were given a free rein with their copy. This separation worked well so long as a mutual respect existed between Editor and Publisher. We were fortunate that Peter Bart and Gerry Byrne, although cut from very different cloth, did indeed respect each other, and this added to the reputation of the paper at the expense of other trade periodicals where such probity was lacking.

Under the guidance of Bart and Byrne (to whom I had the pleasure of reporting for almost a dozen years), *Variety* surged to editorial and economic heights. By the mid-1990s, the movie and TV industry read every word in the paper, and our advertising and subscription revenue stream broke all records. We had to fend off the misguided efforts of various Harvard MBAs who would be assigned by the parent company to keep *Variety* on the straight and narrow. One such manager demanded to know why we ran film reviews in the weekly paper. When I said it was the section most eagerly read by international readers, he asked, with a bewildered concern, why there were no advertisements in that section. I told him that such advertisers all wanted to be up at the front of the paper, a truism in all magazine publishing. His eyes glazed with misapprehension and he switched to the favourite topic of such "suits": could I obtain a pass for him and his wife to the black-tie screenings at Cannes?

In my new role at *Variety*, I was obliged to speak more often in public. Having never relished this in the first four decades of my life, I suddenly found myself more at ease on the podium. My interventions varied from moderating one-on-one conversations with producers, directors, actors and technicians to serving as master of ceremonies at conventions such as Cinema Expo in Brussels or Amsterdam, and CineAsia in Singapore and Hong Kong. Gazing out at more than one thousand delegates at a lunch or dinner seemed at first daunting, but I soon learned to introduce jokes and puns throughout the event, and within ten years I felt quite at home when asked to make even an impromptu speech. Among the personalities to whom I presented awards in London during my tenure were Andrew Lloyd Webber (a devoted fan of the paper) and Judi Dench.

Variety in its heyday was known as "the bible of show-business." The industry read it for two reasons. First, for its essential flow of breaking news stories concerning the state of the studios, who was taking over whom, and which films and shows

were making the most at the box office. Second, for its film
reviews and, to a lesser extent, its stage and concert reviews. The
film reviews were consulted daily and weekly by sales agents,
distributors and exhibitors as eagerly as oracles were followed
in ancient times. They gave a speculative snapshot of the fate of
each film at the box office, whether domestic or international. If
a new film by a much touted European director was "panned"
by *Variety*, then within minutes, and certainly hours, the sales
agent would find that buyers were demanding a reduction in the
acquisition price. If, on the other hand, the paper raved about an
offbeat production from Sweden or Switzerland, then the sales
agent's phone would be busy with calls from potential buyers,
and even from Hollywood studios eager to snap up the remake
rights.

Of course there were those happy to see *Variety* make a
gaffe in "calling" the film at the box office, as happened with
various glamorous productions, from James Bond to *Croco-
dile Dundee*. But these industry pundits often forgot that the
Variety reviewer was the first to see the film, sometimes wet
from the labs, in a small viewing theatre and with no audience,
either public or professional, to serve as a sounding-board. Our
critics had to file their copy within a short time of seeing the
picture and, as the internet assumed more and more significance, within hours and even minutes.

Since the earliest days of Hollywood, producers have tried
to woo trade journalists, some with junkets to exotic locations,
where they could mix with the stars and the creatives behind
the film, some on a one-to-one basis. Directors like Robert
Altman and Warren Beatty were happy to develop friendships
with critics such as Pauline Kael, in the hope of securing a better
notice. With a movie costing so much more to produce than a
book or a painting, there was relentless pressure from on high
to get the production off to a fast start.

The publishing side of *Variety* also felt this pressure.
I remember having lunch with a much-respected producer in
Madrid. As we sipped our coffee and brandy, he slyly asked if
and when his new film would be reviewed, as it was going to be
submitted to the Cannes Festival. He went on to suggest that if
the review was favourable, he would reserve a hefty amount of
advertising in a forthcoming issue of the paper. I replied as cour-

teously as I could that we had no influence over our reviewers, and that editorial integrity was a crucial element in sustaining *Variety*'s reputation. The meeting concluded on a frosty note, and no advertising was placed by that particular producer.

In 1995, William Friedkin made a thriller called *Jade* for Paramount. Sherry Lansing, then chairwoman of Paramount Pictures and husband of Friedkin, asked our editor, Peter Bart, if he could see that the film was properly reviewed. Bart rendered a judgment worthy of Solomon as he placed the initial negative review on one side, while the studio prepared a re-edited version of *Jade*. Alas, when our definitive notice appeared, it was not exactly complimentary and in the event, the much-touted film flopped at the box office.

Another feature that I followed with great interest were the *Variety* obituaries of anyone involved in show-business. Considerable research went into compiling this "necrology." One of the distinguishing marks of a *Variety* obituary was the cause of death, stated unflinchingly, whether it be a heart attack, cancer or AIDS. Jack Pitman, a veteran journalist from Chicago, worked in our London office. He had become the London drama reviewer and displayed a hard-bitten exterior worthy of Park Row or the pages of Damon Runyon. He would arrive in the office well down the morning, descending the stairs and saying with a growl that penetrated into the surrounding office: "Be of good cheer, the Pit is here." Obituaries were also his bailiwick, and I well remember his talking to Laurence Olivier's widow on the morning after her husband's demise. "Yeah, ma'am, I understand your state of mind, but I gotta have the cause of death."

Flashback: MIFED

The Indian Summer Film and TV Market in Milan, known to everyone in the movie trade as MIFED, attracted vast numbers of exhibitors and sales agents to the Fiera di Milano grounds on the edge of the city—cavernous buildings without natural light, where at the *Variety* stand I would greet our clients throughout the day alongside my esteemed colleague Bob Hawkins, who had been with the paper for half a century. At the 60th edition of MIFED in 1993, I moderated a panel entitled "The Buying Game" on some long-forgotten issue affecting the industry, where I was supported by my good friend of the time, Ian Jessel, then President of Miramax International. One of the themes that emerged from the afternoon's discussions was the clash between the Americans' belief that global markets should be paying ever more money for Hollywood product, and the international buyers protesting that this trend was squeezing their margins unmercifully.

MIFED ran annually from 1960 to 2004. Trekking through the sombre corridors at the convention centre (built, appropriately, by Mussolini back in the 1930s) was not recommended after an ample lunch. You were likely to throw up. Posters proudly proclaimed the new pornography—the physical violence, degradation and sexual humiliation offered to audiences in the dingier theatres of the period. The majority of these "films" were screened only on video. Some would never even be made; the poster showing a photograph of Marlon Brando, announcing "Brando—Brought Back to Kill a Man," merely signified that some entrepreneur was seeking to "package" a deal involving Brando. Certain veterans of MIFED told me they recalled seeing the same posters, announcing the same films, for several years. Instead of a studio system, you had in the 1990s an industry teeming with independent producers of every shape and size imaginable—hence the irresistible comparison with the bazaar or the soukh. Films cost a lot to make. They attract the gambler's temperament. At MIFED I would hear bankers say that it was much easier to raise finance for ten pictures than for one.

After three days incarcerated in Mussolini's commercial labyrinth, I escaped to the centre of Milan to see the celebrated Duomo. If you climb 150 steps to the roof, you can relive that poignant scene in Visconti's *Rocco and His Brothers* where Alain Delon and Annie Girardot have a lovers' tiff, and the music of Nino Rota soars and quivers with the passion of it all.

Our team at the *Variety* offices in London was a blend of ages and nationalities. Lee Simkins, the office manager, ensured that everything from light fixtures to box-office statistics was dealt with promptly. Eric Mika, my sales manager for many years, became a good friend with whom I had many an outrageous evening, fuelled by dry martinis and strong espresso. His natural good looks and Italianate respect for *la bella figura* brought him numerous female admirers. But he could also persuade a top executive to commit to the paper several thousands of dollars in advertising. Eric would leave the company at the turn of the millennium, but returned to Los Angeles as Publisher of *The Hollywood Reporter* for a spell. His website, *The Film Verdict*, fills a vacuum for distributors and exhibitors eager to have quick reviews of new releases around the world. Sandrine Bentata joined *Variety* at the age of 24, and immediately showed herself to be a diligent sales-person. Ebullient, French, and always in a good humour, she built up our Paris client base and also handled our business in Scandinavia.

While I was managing *Variety*'s affairs in London and abroad, Françoise had fallen on her feet in London. She launched a Scandinavian Film Society in 1991. The U.K. had an extremely active federation of film societies, but Françoise conceived the novel idea of showing only features from the Nordic region that had not yet been shown in Britain, and of asking their directors to come to the screening (held in the Museum of London's theatre) to introduce their work. One of her guests at the Festival du Cinéma Nordique in Rouen had been Max von Sydow, and now she persuaded him to become the Honorary President of the Scandinavian Film Society. With a brochure designed by my old friend Stefan Dreja, and with programme notes contributed by the loyal Derek Elley or myself, the SFS quickly attracted an enthusiastic membership base. Some two hundred film buffs would gather once a month at the Museum of London for coffee and cakes prior to each screening. Within a year, Françoise had been deservedly presented with the Best New Film Society of the Year award at the National Film Theatre.

The success of the SFS encouraged Françoise to organise tours of Scandinavian films throughout the length and breadth of the British isles. The embassies of the five Nordic countries helped considerably. They would pay for a director's accommodation in London and often arrange a small reception, or even dinner, at the embassy after the screening. Bengt Forslund, by then head of the Nordic Film & TV Fund, joined with the various film institutes in Scandinavia to pay for the airfares involved.

During the mid-1980s, I had written and delivered some of the earliest audio commentaries for classic films, thanks to a partnership between Janus Films and the Voyager Company, which soon led to the formation of the Criterion Collection. The advent of laser disc enabled a commentary to be added on the analogue track of the disc, so that the soundtrack of the film would be turned off and the commentary was audible over the imagery. All too few film buffs invested in laser discs, although for almost fifteen years I accumulated a collection of these heavy, 12 inch "records" with their attractive covers and copious sleeve notes.

I soon discovered that writing and speaking commentaries was not as straightforward as I had expected. The best commentaries on DVD and Blu-ray are often by directors, if only because they never run out of things to say about a particular scene or actor. But when I started in the 1980s (in the wake of Ronald Haver, who had recorded the first commentary for Criterion's release of *King Kong*), the studios had not yet requested their directors to participate in a commentary track as their films came up for release on disc.

In the early days, I committed the cardinal error of describing what the viewer was watching on screen. It's a practice that soon renders one's comments redundant. Instead, viewers were eager to learn about the background to the making of a film. They wanted one to talk about the director, the actors and the technicians, the budget, the locations and so on. I'm proud that Criterion continue to use my commentary for *The Seventh Seal*, even though it is now close to forty years old. I cherish a telegram from William Becker, sent after he and Jonathan Turell listened to my commentary: "Who would have thought that beneath so august a British exterior there could reside this gloriously gifted ham. Congratulations!"

When I recorded a commentary for Renoir's *Grand Illusion* in October of 1987, I found myself in the aftermath of a major earthquake in the Los Angeles region. The sound studio was in a basement in Santa Monica, and every so often the producer would interrupt my speaking because an after-shock had shown up on the screens.

Hitting one's marks, as it were, proved one of the biggest challenges when recording a commentary. One tries to write a text that will arrive at its climax at exactly the same moment that, say, an unexpected incident occurs on-screen. As a result, our recording sessions usually occupied a full day, and for three-hour features like *The Leopard* or *Fanny and Alexander*, a day and a half.

My method changed little through the years. I would first watch the entire film on my own at home. Then I would watch a second time, taking notes. Finally, I would start to speak into a small recording device, pausing the film when I ran out of breath (or ideas). I would then transcribe what I had recorded and start to polish the text. After that, I ran through the film again, filling any gaps that seemed longer than fifteen seconds ("if the viewers hear nothing for a long interval, they start adjusting their equipment," I was told by one engineer). The final stage would be to type up the script, as it were, print it out, and prepare for the recording session in New York or Los Angeles.

I often wondered if the entire exercise was worth the work involved. But every so often I would meet a film buff who would tell me how much he or she had learned from my commentary on such and such a film. Criterion commissioned me to talk on half a dozen Bergman films and for several other European masterpieces: *The Leopard, Z, Grand Illusion, Diary of a Country Priest, Salvatore Giuliano, Hiroshima mon amour* and *Casque d'or.* Perhaps the most taxing of all my commentaries was for *Tokyo Olympiad*, Kon Ichikawa's compelling documentary record of the 1964 Olympic Summer Games. Ichikawa in many phases of the film cuts sharply from one sport to another, and I had almost to gabble in order to include the basic facts of the discipline or the names of the athletes who excelled.

Oddly enough, the short "extras" I occasionally produced for Criterion were even more demanding. One usually had to select extracts from specific films to illustrate an argument, and this meant precise timing of clips, and talking over a series of still images (portraits of actors or directors etc.) But the excellent system created by Criterion meant that I worked on each occasion with a dedicated producer, who would take care of the technical issues, and who would, like an editor at a publishing house, gently coax more focused comment from me, or remind me to cover certain topics.

William Becker, who with his partner Saul J. Turell, ran Janus Films, encouraged me to do more and more work for Criterion. At one point, in the mid-1990s, he even suggested that I move to Santa Monica and join the company. I was momentarily tempted, but at that juncture I was so fulfilled at *Variety* that I demurred. Besides, Bill's son Peter Becker had entered the family business and soon proved his mettle. He and I also liked each other very much, and over the next two decades I would contribute visual essays or liner notes to some thirty DVDs, and the commentary for a dozen foreign-language films.

Flashback: William Becker

William Becker enjoyed success in any field to which he turned his amiable intelligence. Following a brilliant career at Harvard, he was one of the first Rhodes Scholars to attend the University of Oxford after the Second World War (and where a library bearing his name stands in Wadham College). A talented actor, a gifted and perspicacious writer (not least about Bertolt Brecht), he adored both theatre and cinema. He turned his business acumen to working with Roger L. Stevens, a leading producer of Broadway plays, and energising *Playbill* magazine. Not many are aware that Bill helped to finance independent films like Shirley Clarke's *The Connection*. And then in 1965, in partnership with Turell, he acquired Janus.

Theirs was an extraordinary alliance. Saul teemed with ideas for the company, while Bill remained the sober observer, swiftly dismissing a majority of Saul's visions and focusing with relentless acuity on those that really could take Janus forward (the sale of classic foreign movies to U.S. television, for example). Bill compiled an immense dossier, listing every foreign-language film within possible reach, along with numerous beloved British titles that Janus proceeded to re-present to the American public. And how proud he was when Saul won an Academy Award for his documentary on Paul Robeson.

Bill was the incarnation of Ingmar Bergman's dictum, that "only the truly efficient can be truly lazy." Even in the headiest periods of his career, he found time to complete *The New York Times* crossword after breakfast ("They make them more difficult as the week goes by!" he would say with a grin as he dismantled the Saturday puzzle at his home on Long Island). He could devote hours to his collection of incunabula (some of it more than risqué) and would not desist until he had tracked down the missing volume in a particular series of yearbooks.

I first met Bill in about 1970, when he and Saul asked me to write a brochure about the films of Ingmar Bergman. He sat at his elegant desk at the Janus offices on Fifth Avenue, the shelves behind him crammed with books on every aspect of the movies. "How much should we pay you for this?" he enquired. Plucking up courage, I muttered something about a thousand dollars. "Nonsense, dear boy," he said, "You should be paid at least $3,000." In my short happy life I had never encountered someone who offered to pay me a larger fee than I had asked for. Yet this generosity was a fundamental tenet of the way in which Bill and Saul conducted their business. Moreover, unlike most magazines and newspapers, Janus paid their contributors with a "bonded check" within days rather than weeks.

Bill's letters, dictated over decades to his loyal secretary Diane Ellis, were models of gracious composition and lucidity. Only the most watertight of contracts could survive Bill's scrutiny. He remained throughout his life a man who brought logic and pragmatism to business affairs, and who was also an aesthete in the best sense of that term. He adored the recondite and the arcane.

Over four decades we shared many a convivial lunch or dinner, in New York and often in Europe, where Bill loved to travel, combining the acquisition of rights with seeing close friends like the producer and sales agent Alain Vannier in Paris. When Bill entered a room he would, without any conscious effort, immediately become its epicentre, his blonde good looks and patrician demeanour towering over most people. I saw his innate self-confidence waver on only one occasion. It was during the Cannes Festival. Bill and I, a little mellow after a good meal, joined a reception at the Carlton Hotel. Bill was introduced to the Canadian actress, Alexandra Stewart, for whom we both had, shall we say, a certain admiration. But, inveterate smoker that he was, Bill forgot that his cigarette was still between his fingers as he shook hands with Ms. Stewart. She recoiled with a muffled scream!

When I stayed with Bill and his tireless wife Patricia Birch in Manhattan, I relished two times of day. The first was at breakfast, when Bill would enjoy toast with his much-loved Keiller's coarse-cut marmalade from Scotland, in its trademark pottery jar, and we would discuss plans for the day. And then at dusk, when Bill would serve excellent cocktails—a mint julep if you were out in the country, or usually a crystal glass of Maker's Mark bourbon in the city. Then he would regale you with stories of directors and writers he had met at a formative stage in his career—Tony Richardson (a contemporary at Oxford), François Truffaut, George Plimpton, Truman Capote, the theatre critics Ken Tynan and Alan Brien, and the film critic John Simon. His taste in movies ranged from the discreet and sensitive (*The Spirit of the Beehive*, for example) to the offbeat (the animated shorts of Bob Godfrey). He lobbied hard for Criterion—which had developed like some glorious butterfly from the chrysalis of Janus—to release titles he felt were unjustly neglected, and I appreciated my sessions with him in 2005, when together we created a list of fifty cherished titles in the Janus library, which would then be published in a spectacular box to celebrate the company's Golden Jubilee. How we rubbed our hands when we managed to include a mutual favourite, Sjöberg's *Miss Julie*, which appeared on DVD in the Criterion Collection the following year.

Re-reading some of Bill's letters over the years, I realise that behind the elegant formality, even hauteur, of his language shielded a warmth that extended to a worldwide network of friends and acquaintances. In 2006, nine years before his death, I dedicated my book on Louise Brooks to Bill, calling him "mentor, host, and friend." A. William J. Becker III was all of those things, and so much more.

Flashback: Saul J. Turell

If Bill Becker was the intellectual backbone of Janus, Saul was its beating heart. While Bill would dictate eloquent letters, Saul would bustle around his own office, the unpretentious desk replete with numerous notes on all manner of subjects.

He would scrawl his thoughts with a pencil, the lead of which often snapped under the urgent intensity of the gesture. Evelyn Walker, his assistant, would remind him of each and every appointment, calling out a final instruction as Saul, always in haste, donned his overcoat and made ready to leave for lunch at the Sherry-Netherland, or perhaps just to devour a good old pastrami sandwich on the go. His burly silhouette and rugged good looks could have brought him stardom in Hollywood's Golden Age.

Saul's trading savvy had been honed in his early twenties at Sterling Films, the company he founded in 1946. Sterling merged with the Walter Reade Organization in the early 1960s, and so by 1965, when Saul joined Bill Becker in acquiring Janus Films, he was an expert in producing and marketing films. Unlike Bill, he relished the challenge of film-making itself, and at Janus he was always surrounded by youthful editors, writers and even directors, who regarded him as their mentor. Early in 1965, he had directed, produced and co-written (with Graeme Ferguson) *The Love Goddesses*, a history of changing perceptions towards sex in Hollywood's heyday. Saul adored the silent era, and had scripted two studies of Rudolph Valentino.

During the late 1960s, he and Bill built Janus into a successful distributor, with theatrical releases of a host of European and Japanese titles, including Truffaut's *Two English Girls*, Olivier's *Richard III*, Bellocchio's *Fists in the Pocket* and Ozu's *Floating Weeds*. By 1976, despite also still working with Bill to run Janus, Saul found time to co-write, co-produce and co-edit a twelve-part series entitled *The Art of Film*. This programme drew on the rich resources of the Janus library, with segments dealing with distinctive aspects of filmmaking—cinematography, editing, music, sound, screenwriting—or an individual genius such as Hitchcock and Chaplin. This was the heyday of 16mm, with Janus both selling and renting prints to colleges and institutions across the land. *The Art of Film* series, accompanied by an attractive brochure, promoted this business. And in 1984, I helped to compile "The Programmers Guide to The Classic Collection" for Janus and its distribution partner, Films Inc. Both Bill and

Saul oversaw the production with passionate commitment and inscribed my copy of the book with kind words.

In the early spring of 1980, Saul enjoyed his finest hour, when *Paul Robeson: Tribute to an Artist*, on which he had lavished such careful research and preparation, won the Academy Award for Best Short Documentary. Saul admired Robeson's social courage and commitment. On his return to New York, he left the Oscar in the back of a taxi, only to be saved by the honesty and efficiency of the cab driver, who handed the precious statuette in to the police.

Saul's vision empowered Janus at two crucial stages in its development. Like his partner, he saw the potential for selling foreign classic films to television (this at a time—the late 1960s and early 1970s—when black-and-white movies were anathema to TV stations, let alone subtitled ones!), and he and Bill later made lucrative deals with cable channels like Bravo and CBS cable. Then, as video entered the scene, also in the early 1980s, he recognised a rich new market for the catalogue that he and Bill had built up. Saul's son Jonathan proved a conscientious and successful salesman, learning to travel across the United States to negotiate with dozens of TV stations.

For all his bulldog bluster, Saul was a generous and affectionate man. He was always ready to embrace new projects, especially from young people. "It's a great idea—let's go with it," he would say, almost before you had finished your opening sentence, because his quicksilver mind raced at such a high rate that he was always ahead of the pack. This trait led him often to truncate his speech, leaping from one partly complete phrase to another, so eager was he to communicate his enthusiasm. Saul of all people could heed Kipling's dictum, to "fill the unforgiving minute/With sixty seconds' worth of distance run." He was driven by an impulsive energy throughout the day. In the early 1980s, I flew into New York on the red-eye from L.A., and there was Saul awaiting me at the gate. He drove me to the family home in New Rochelle, and within an hour I was on the tennis court, struggling to track down Saul's powerful backhands. His wife, Renée, an aficionado of pre-Columbian art, made us lunch while Saul told stories about his mentor Walter Reade, who had been killed in a freak skiing accident in the Alps.

A few months before he was struck down by cancer at the early age of 65, Saul sent me a handwritten card: "I just wanted to take a moment to wish you a wonderful and healthy New Year, from Jon, Renée and Saul." He saw the advent of laserdiscs but not DVD, Blu-ray or streaming. A true romantic, Saul's spirit has endured across these past three decades, and is surely one of the "faces" on the Janus coin. He would chuckle and say, "Both."

The most unusual book I ever worked on was *World Cinema, Diary of a Day*. The British Film Institute began gearing up for the centenary of the cinema in 1995, and two years prior to that approached me to edit a book that seemed, at first glance, an impracticable project. It was certainly herculean. Two staff members at the BFI, Tana Wollen and Janet Willis, shouldered the bulk of the administrative work. They despatched forms, mostly by post, to more than a thousand individuals in the film world. A majority of those contacted noted down, usually in long-hand, their activity on the day of June 10, 1993. They came from all professions imaginable—producers, directors, cinematographers, production designers, editors, sound engineers, composers, documentarists, animators, distributors, exhibitors, archivists, journalists, critics, festival directors and so on. Often the submissions had to be translated into English—from Farsi, Gujerati, Dutch, Japanese, Greek, Polish, Punjabi, Turkish, Russian, Spanish, Hungarian, Hebrew or Italian.

My task was to whittle down these "diaries" into manageable and often abridged form. Some had submitted as many as ten closely-typed pages, others merely a few lines. The final tally came to around 420 entries. This literary kaleidoscope offered a snapshot of what the world of cinema was doing at a particular moment in time. "For some," I wrote in my introduction, "the day begins in an airport, or in a foreign land. Many rise at dawn, others work into the small hours, While most diary entries express the enthusiasm associated with teamwork in film-making, several lament the lack of an assignment, or ruminate on the gulf between the artifice of the cinema and the realities of everyday life. A majority of the correspondents however, is united by an abiding commitment to cinema as a medium for expression, as a team effort in the face of technical and financial challenges. People somehow survive the day as such, bobbing and weaving while the phones ring, the faxes unfurl, and the weather deteriorates on some distant location."

So many celebrated names responded to the BFI's invitation. Among the hundreds, I remember with affection the notes of Akira Kurosawa, Agnieszka Holland, Monte Hellman, King Hu, Suso Cecchi d'Amico, Terry Gilliam, Aparna Sen, Anja Breien, Dean Tavoularis, Mai Zetterling, Abbas Kiarostami, Martin Scorsese, Krzysztof Kieślowski, Sally Potter, Jeremy Thomas, Vittorio Storaro and Roger Corman.

Flashback: Sam Fuller

By the late 1950s, Sam Fuller had been elevated to auteur status by the critics of *Cahiers du cinéma*. Watching films like *China Gate* (1957) and *The Crimson Kimono* (1959) as a university undergraduate proved a refreshing contrast to my arthouse diet of Bergman, Fellini and Kurosawa. Fuller revelled in pulp fiction, carving his stories out in bold strokes, and to hell with the studios. Prolific and controversial, he was a Mickey Spillane of the movies. *Pickup on South Street* (1953) showed his experience as a reporter on Park Row, where he had basked in the mentorship of Walter Winchell and Gene Fowler. *Shock Corridor* (1963) and *The Naked Kiss* (1964) appeared sensational, and yet resonated with genuine anguish and frustration.

I never met him or wrote much about him, until *The Big Red One*, at Cannes in 1980 (albeit in an abridged version), suddenly brought him into focus as much more than a "king of the Bs," indeed as one of the most thoughtful directors of his generation. *The Steel Helmet*, made almost thirty years earlier, had dealt with the Korean War but was really a dry run for *The Big Red One*.

In person, Sam was a blunt-nosed non-conformist, small of stature but forever leading with his Cuban cigar. (Although Sam boasted that he'd had a cigar in his mouth since his early teens, he claimed never to have inhaled, which might explain how he lived until the age of 85.) He fixed you with a gimlet eye and decided instantly whether he liked you or loathed you. Gruff he seemed, humane he was. By the time I finally sat down with him, he was in his eighties, and still bursting with energy. We met through Murray Grigor, who at the turn of the 1970s had mustered a posse of film commandos at the Edinburgh Film Society in defence of mavericks like Douglas Sirk and Nicholas Ray, and then later, as director of the Edinburgh Film Festival, he had resurrected Sam. It was August 1992. I was then head of *Variety*'s international operations, and I hosted a lunch each year at the festival, bringing together filmmakers, critics, and other guests. Sam accepted our invitation, and from the head of his table regaled us with anecdotes and wisecracks about Vincent Price, Darryl F. Zanuck, Louis B. Mayer and other Hollywood myth-makers.

As coffee and brandies were served, Murray suggested that he introduce Sam to Hans-Jürgen Syberberg, the egghead director of *Hitler: A Film from Germany* (1977), a seven-hour mixed-media dissertation that the festival was reviving that summer. Syberberg was the inverse of Sam: tall, lordly of gaze, and an intellectual to his fingertips. He was in Edinburgh with the actress Edith Clever, staging one in a series of dramatic monologues, and when confronted by Sam Fuller, he turned away and refused to shake his hand. Syberberg treated him like a Z director. Sam, always proud of being a mere B, chomped on his cigar and muttered, "I've known guys like that all my life."

Sam had that effect on many snobs. His work eschewed pretension. He simply wanted to show men under fire, in war or in private life, because he'd lived through more than three years on the front lines of the Second World War in Europe. *The Big Red One* is almost an autobiography of that period, from the landings in North Africa to Omaha Beach and on to the Battle of the Bulge. Sam had seen it all, and survived, just as, back in 1930, he had kept his head down when Al Capone strode into a billiard hall in Cicero, just outside Chicago, and asked him what he was writing. When Sam replied that he was preparing a story about the homeless, the gangster grinned and quipped, "I'm homeless too, kid! Look me up, and I'll give you an interview."

As we came out into the afternoon sunshine, I asked Sam if he would pose for a photo with a copy of *Variety*. He at once agreed, and we used the image, with his permission, as our season's greetings card in December 1992. The following Saturday, I went with Murray to a BBC Scotland studio, where Sam, relaxed in a cluttered "writer's den" of a set, talked about how screenplays were fashioned and how neophyte scriptwriters should avoid the usual pitfalls of their profession. I never saw him again, so I can't pretend to have really known Sam Fuller. But his personality, his integrity, and his commitment to young filmmakers set him apart from those I've known better.

In 2000, I was offered early retirement by *Variety*. Gerry Byrne had left the company the previous year, as had Eric Mika, my sales manager, and so I felt a diminishing loyalty to the paper. My father, completely blind and a widower for the previous four years, needed care as he approached his ninetieth birthday. My wife Françoise had never felt at ease in London, with its coded society, and was attracted by the fact that the Vaud, where my parents had lived since 1964, was French-speaking. Suddenly, all these factors justified our determination to sell our house in Fulham and to move to Montreux-Vevey, where we could see my father on a regular basis. In the early 1960s, my father had suffered repeated bouts of bronchitis, and when specks of blood began to appear on his handkerchief, the family doctor recommended him to transfer to either somewhere like the Canary Islands, or an Alpine country, to prevent the risk of pneumonia and other lung infections. I was surprised when my parents chose Switzerland, although they did speak rudimentary French, so the Vaud seemed like a good destination for a man who yearned to abandon publishing and just write what he wanted, when he wanted.

I continued to write and to consult for various organisations, among them the film festivals in Berlin and Venice. I accepted three new challenges: as a consultant to Dolby Laboratories; as an interviewer for the Berlinale Talent Campus; and at the request of Marco Müller, as moderator of an annual panel discussion at the Venice Film Festival.

Throughout the 1990s, I had spent many a convivial evening with Dieter Kosslick, who was then galvanising the film support programme of the Filmstiftung NRW. As a result,

North Rhine-Westphalia became the engine room for European cinema, and Dieter ensured that his foundation was involved in a majority of adventurous new productions. Dieter did not boast a deep knowledge of world cinema history, but his fierce enthusiasm and commitment to political ideals brought him friends at all levels of the film world. His effervescent sense of humour compensated for his frequent gaffes in public, and his loyalty to friends and colleagues was legendary.

When, in 2001, Dieter took over the reins of the Berlin Film Festival from the long-serving Moritz de Hadeln, he gave the Berlinale a fresh lease on life. For him, and for most of the festival's guests, Berlin in darkest February became a time of fun and celebration. He asked me to be a member of his inaugural Jury, under the presidency of Mira Nair. All went well until, a few days after the festival began, I developed what seemed like severe bronchitis. When I found flecks of blood in my handkerchief, I called the hotel doctor, who diagnosed pneumonia. I had to remain in bed for a couple of days until the antibiotic kicked in, and then caught up with screenings as best I could. During our final deliberations, I helped to persuade the jury to give not just the usual one, but two Golden Bears for Best Film, to Paul Greengrass' *Bloody Sunday* and to Hayao Miyazaki's *Spirited Away*. Miyazaki thus earned his first major award outside Japan, which heralded international acclaim for his unique style of animation. *Spirited Away*, like *Alice in Wonderland*, defies logic in its narrative form and delights with its brightly-spangled colour scheme and lovingly-drawn images.

Dieter had conceived the notion of the Berlinale Talent Campus and secured funding for it in 2003. He asked me to give help and advice to Christine Dorn and Thomas Struck as they developed the project almost from scratch. Some four hundred neophyte filmmakers were invited from all over the world to attend a week-long Campus during the Berlinale. In the early years they would gather in the Pregnant Oyster, the name given by Berliners to the House of World Cultures in the Tiergarten. The first Talent Campus met with a hugely enthusiastic response, although technical glitches bedevilled the ticketing system. Wim Wenders was there, and I gave the opening lecture. The principle of the Campus was to bring together talented young people with established names in the industry. Famous names came willingly

With Meryl Streep and Florian Weghorn of the
Berlinale Talents team in 2016. Photo by Peter Himsel.

to be interviewed on stage by yours truly and others. The two great "Walters"—Walter Murch and Walter Salles—were among the first guests. So was Kieślowski's composer of choice, Zbigniew Preisner. Andrew Lesnie talked about his cinematography on *The Lord of the Rings* trilogy, while Charlotte Rampling made the first of three appearances, as did Agnieszka Holland.

Over the next fifteen years I had the privilege of interviewing gifted figures from across the whole spectrum of filmmaking. Composers like Alexandre Desplat, Gustavo Santoallala, Ryuichi Sakamoto, Michael Nyman and Howard Shore. The discreet and modest Max Richter, who had just won the European Film Award for his music for *Waltz with Bashir,* came to the Campus in 2009 to adjudge the Volkswagen Score Competition. This was long before he achieved global fame with his 8 hours-plus composition, *Sleep.*

Then there were production designers like Academy Award winner Sandy Powell, and Adam Stockhausen, who spoke of his work with Wes Anderson. A flow of major actors, from legends like Anita Ekberg, Meryl Streep and Isabella Rossellini, to heart-throbs of the moment such as Gael García Bernal and Keanu Reeves, as well as character actors like Willem Dafoe and Timothy Spall. And so many excellent directors—Volker Schlöndorff, Jane Campion, Paul Schrader, Bertrand Tavernier, alongside free spirits like Mark Cousins, Guy Maddin and Raoul Peck.

Flashback: Anita Ekberg

In January 2013, Anita Ekberg visited the Berlinale Talent Campus. Asked by the festival to moderate an onstage interview, I visited her in her hotel. She certainly was not treated like a glittering star. The room was modest, and so crowded with assistants and carers, not to mention baggage, that it was like the Marx Brothers' cabin in *A Night at the Opera*. Anita had broken her hip and was slumped in a wheelchair. But she accepted my small-talk, and when an assistant began wheeling her away for a meeting, she glared up at me with her fierce blue eyes, and growled, "I like you. You're my kind of man!"

That evening, dressed in black, leaning on a white cane, she came on to the stage of the Hebbel Theatre with great dignity, her long blonde hair still flowing to her shoulders, the face still full, almost leonine. Her first recollection was of working as a fashion model in her home city of Malmö at the age of 17.

Of course the conversation turned to Fellini. Her voluptuous stature had beguiled the director into presenting her as the giantess who haunts the dreams of Doctor Antonio in *Boccaccio '70*. Fellini often came to her home in Rome for lunch and petted her dogs—"but not me! He wasn't my type." Once he brought her a houseplant, but it was already dead. "He probably got it in the sale," she commented with a sarcasm that raised one of many laughs from her Berlin audience.

She regaled us with memories from *La dolce vita*. The scene when she calls Marcello Mastroianni into the Trevi Fountain by night caused him—and her—great discomfort. Mastroianni was so afraid to go into the ice-cold water that he drank most of a bottle of vodka to pluck up courage. Urged by Fellini, finally he stumbled into the fountain, soaking his suit and shirt. His clothes were hurriedly replaced, but

Mastroianni again fell into the water. Anita said that he did this three times, and all the while she was standing in the Trevi herself, her legs going numb.

It was difficult to keep the garrulous Anita on track. She complained about the dangers of walking the streets in Italy and about the cold she had caught in the German capital, which added to her woes. I asked her about working with Frank Sinatra on *Four for Texas*. "I don't want to say anything about him. We flirted. He even wanted to marry me." Victor Mature, her co-star in *Zarak*, got even shorter shrift: "We called him Victor Manure," she sneered. I sensed an intrinsic bitterness, as though life had effaced her voluptuous beauty without compensating her with fulfilment.

Still, she seemed reluctant to leave the stage, and held out her hand in farewell. "Shall I see you later tonight?" she asked. But it was a rhetorical question, of course. Two years later, Anita Ekberg was dead, at the age of 83.

Some years ago, the Berlinale Talent Campus became Berlinale Talents, but the formula remained the same, and was successfully launched in cities as far apart as Tokyo, Durban and Buenos Aires. The element I am most proud of having conceived was the Talent Press programme. We hosted a handful of aspiring young film journalists from various countries and asked them to write articles about films in the festival and events at the Campus—pieces that were then read and edited on the spot by distinguished mentors such as Derek Malcolm of Britain and Stephanie Zacharek of the United States.

Europe, since the 1930s, has been the cradle of film music. The pre-eminent Hollywood composers came from a continent overshadowed by the Nazi menace: Alfred Newman, Franz Waxman, Erich Wolfgang Korngold, Dimitri Tiomkin, Miklós Rózsa, and many more. During the Second World War and in the ensuing decades, the best film scores were the work of such émigrés, or of French, German, and Italian composers whose talent illuminated my youth: Nino Rota, Georges Delerue, Michel Legrand, Francis Lai, Ennio Morricone, Hans Zimmer and Rachel Portman. Not forgetting Bernard Herrmann, who stemmed from Russian and Ukrainian stock.

Flashback: Howard Shore

Once in a generation comes a film score that captures the hearts and minds of a public far beyond the sphere of regular moviegoers: Max Steiner's lush, romantic music for *Gone with the Wind*, the plangent, melancholy strains of Michel Legrand's *Umbrellas of Cherbourg*, or John Williams' rousing fanfares for *Star Wars*. In December of 2001, with the release of *The Lord of the Rings: The Fellowship of the Ring*, Howard Shore's richly-developed score acquired instant immortality. By the time that *The Two Towers* and *The Return of the King* had appeared, audiences and critics alike recognised that this was a soaring achievement, a "music drama" to rank with Wagner's *The Ring of the Nibelungs*. A decade later, in 2014, it was voted the greatest movie soundtrack music of all time in a poll conducted by Classic FM radio. The symphonic version of the score continues to be played live by orchestras around the world, and to overflowing audiences.

Howard Shore came from Canada, not Europe. I met him at the Stockholm Film Festival in 2007, and we found we had a lot in common. A few years later, we invited him to the Berlinale Talent Campus, and over dinner one night I persuaded him that we should do an interview book about his career, which had included collaboration with directors as diverse as Martin Scorsese, David Fincher, Jonathan Demme and David Cronenberg.

Between 2015 and 2018, I visited Howard on different occasions at his home in Tuxedo, in Upstate New York. We would meet in my guest cottage after breakfast, and record until lunchtime. Howard had begun his career on tour playing more than one thousand concerts with the rock group The Lighthouse before he became music director of *Saturday Night Live*, from its inception. During the late 1970s and '80s, he composed the soundtrack music for all of David Cronenberg's films. His scores were as experimental, even off-the-wall, as Cronenberg's films, from *The Brood* to *Dead Ringers*, from *Videodrome* to *Naked Lunch*. Each score seemed to lead to the next, and Howard's music for *The Fly* in 1986 would give birth to a full-fledged opera in 2008.

Howard has explored the darker recesses of the human mind in films like *The Silence of the Lambs* and *Se7en*; he

With Howard Shore.

has experimented from the outset of his career with electronic music; and he has enjoyed himself in creating scores to accompany comedies like *After Hours*, *Mrs. Doubtfire* and *Ed Wood*. Even films that may not have won awards for artistic excellence, such as *The Cell*, *Cop Land* and *Spider*, have attracted praise for Howard's music. No genre is beyond the reach of his versatile musical mind, from drama to documentary, from thrillers to experimental literary works like *Naked Lunch* and *Crash*, and from the romantic fantasy world of *The Twilight Saga* to controversial social inquiries like *Doubt* and *Spotlight*.

Whether I was interviewing Howard on stage in Berlin and Locarno, or attending concerts with him in New York, or just hanging out with him on his travels to Europe, I felt an affinity with this quiet, modest, articulate composer, and I hope that the interview book we eventually completed will one day be published.

I find it much more satisfying to discover a classic of world cinema through the miracle of Blu-ray (and now 4K) than to keep up with every new release that opens in cinemas. Mikhail Kalatozov's *I am Cuba*, dating from 1964, is a perfect example. To watch this masterpiece unfold in 4K is to re-live the heyday of film in the 1960s, when the aesthetic dimension of cinema meant so much. The four vignettes that make up the film, describing the desperation and the resolve of everyone from artists to peasants to bring about revolution in Cuba, are photographed by Sergei Urusevskiy in black-and-white with a fluency so miraculous that you might think the camera was dancing. Faces and landscapes have an hallucinatory quality and seem inspired by the work of Eisenstein and Dovzhenko. Even if we know that Castro's revolution turned sour, to witness on screen the idealism of the characters in *I am Cuba* remains exhilarating.

The films closest to my heart and mind are wonderful to look at and wonderful to hear. That doesn't exclude silent cinema, because live screenings of the silent classics prove that the music accompaniment played a crucial role in their success or failure.

During my involvement with the Berlinale, in the early 2000s, I came into closer contact with the European Film Academy and its energetic, enthusiastic director, Marion Döring. The EFA sponsored a panel during each edition of the Berlinale Talent Campus, and I was often the moderator. Marion seemed to like my approach to such events and asked me if I would preside over similar symposia and master classes during the Academy's awards weekend in early December.

The European Film Academy was founded in 1988 in the hope that bringing together talent from across the continent would reinvigorate the cinema both culturally and commercially. Many countries had for years loved to host an event like the Academy Awards in Hollywood. The BAFTAs in Britain, the Césars in France and the Bodils in Denmark marked an attempt to mimic the success of the Oscar broadcast. But it never quite happened — and still has not. Possibly because "Europe" is not so coherent a "republic" as the United States, and does not have continent-wide broadcasters who can be tempted to support the venture. Possibly because the timing of the awards in the final month of the year means that certain excellent films opening in the fourth quarter cannot be considered by the voters and must wait for the following year. And possibly because the babel of languages (twenty-four in the European Parliament) makes it hard for any single title to generate buzz across the entire region.

Awards are not everything, however. I found myself participating in activities that the EFA performed very well. Producers, directors, technicians and actors are regularly in touch with young talents entering the profession, whether at intimate gatherings in the countryside arranged by the EFA, or at sidebar events during the awards weekend. In December 2003, I chaired a panel entitled "Let's Talk about Content!" One of the participants, the great French stage and screen director Patrice Chéreau, confronted the difficulty of shooting in another language, as he did when making *Intimacy* in England. "I had to accept it when somebody told me 'that would never be said by English people.' I'm interested in learning something, I'm doing a film in order to learn how to make it better, in order to learn more about how to tell a story, and the English actors helped me."

The following year, when the Awards were held in Barcelona, I again interviewed a variety of talent, including Stellan Skarsgård from Sweden, Jean-Marc Barr from France, and Franke Potente from Germany. One of the perils of moderating a large panel is that not everyone has time to speak, and during an afternoon session in Barcelona the Italian star and director Michele Placido actually nodded off while the discussion was in full flow. I awakened him with a direct question, to which he grunted a negative response before returning to his slumber.

The Awards took place in Warsaw in 2006, and an even more difficult challenge awaited me. Mika Kaurismäki, the less misanthropic of the famous Finnish brothers, mounted the stage to give a speech. But he had enjoyed a liquid lunch, and started to ramble in his argument. His speech was slurred and he was swaying slightly on his feet. His allotted time came and went, and Marion Döring, seated beside me, was becoming more agitated by the minute. We tried to signal Mika to stop talking, but he seemed oblivious to such entreaties. Finally, he had to be gently but forcibly removed from the stage. In short, post-prandial panels are always tricky to manage.

My final moderating assignment for the European Film Academy was in June of 2009, when the Academy hosted a conference entitled "The Image of Europe." Numerous European filmmakers attended, among them Volker Schlöndorff, Wim Wenders, Costa-Gavras and Marjane Satrapi, whose animated film *Persepolis* had won the Jury Prize at Cannes two years earlier. We were all isolated in a castle outside Düsseldorf, where the president of the European Union, José Manuel Barroso, agreed with Wenders and Schlöndorff that film should be taught in schools throughout the EU. Once again, fine words around the dinner table, but little positive action thereafter.

At least the printed word endures. In 2007, I co-edited (with Pascal Edelmann) a special edition of the Faber annual, *Projections*, celebrating the twentieth anniversary of the EFA. The core of the book consisted of interviews with directors, producers and actors. I recorded conversations, either in person or over the telephone, with Agnieszka Holland, Ademir Kenovic, Danis Tanović, François Ozon, Irène Jacob, Paprika Steen, Margaret Ménégoz, Dieter Kosslick, Bernardo Bertolucci, Constantine Giannaris, Ventura Pons, Ken Loach, Laurent Cantet, Dušan Makavejev, Jeremy Thomas, Michael Winterbottom, Marco Müller, Jean-Marc Barr, Baltasar Kormakur and... Jeanne Moreau.

Flashback: Jeanne Moreau

Few actors have worked in cinema across eight decades. Jeanne Moreau began her career as an ingenue in 1949, and for my generation she was the icon of the French New Wave. Jean-Pierre Léaud may have been equally recognisable, but only as the exclusive alter ego of François Truffaut, while Anna Karina's fame stemmed from her involvement in the work of Jean-Luc Godard. Moreau, however, brought to the screen a singular, inimitable verve, a petulance, and a shameless gaze reminiscent of Bette Davis. Her range was extraordinary: she could play a nun in *The Carmelites*, the eccentric Miss Burstner in Welles' *The Trial*, the peroxide-blonde gambler in Demy's *Bay of Angels*, and the moody heroine of Peter Brook's *Moderato Cantabile*. She soon became a favourite of masters like Antonioni, Buñuel and Truffaut. Half-English, half-French, with a touch of Irish blood in her mother's family, she illuminated such classics as *Jules and Jim*, *The Lovers*, *Diary of a Chambermaid* and *The Bride Wore Black*.

In December of 2006, I interviewed her in Paris for the European Film Academy. Looking back, the appointment seemed doomed. My express train from Lausanne to Paris suffered an inordinate delay. I arrived barely on time at her apartment off the Rue du Faubourg Saint-Honoré. Then, during the return journey that night, I accidentally dropped my micro-cassette recorder as the train entered a tunnel. The tape unravelled amid the feet of passengers and was badly scratched. Fortunately, I had a friend at Dolby in London who was able to restore it.

As I emerged breathless from the elegant but cramped elevator, Jeanne Moreau was there to greet me—petite, gracious, and just a little nervous. But once we began sharing stories about Orson Welles, she relaxed, reached for one of her slender, extra-long cigarettes that stood in a bowl on her coffee table, and reminisced about the films she had made and the men she had known and loved.

"To me, acting is a calling, a way of life more than a career," she emphasised. "My life feeds my art, and my art feeds my life. I didn't want the destiny of a regular girl." She could not meet the usual standards of beauty in French cinema of the 1950s. "It was the period of Martine Carol, Françoise Arnoul, Dany Robin—blonde girls, big eyes, big tits." Her often soulful mien was so very different from the carnal insolence of a Bardot. Her decision to enter the theatre provoked a rupture with her father. "Even now," she said to me, more than half a century after her debut, "when I receive an award or a tribute, I think to myself, 'Yes, I was right, and my father was wrong.'" In 1950, Orson Welles attempted to cast her in his stage presentation of *An Unthinking Lobster* at the Théâtre Edouard VII, but Moreau was under contract to the Comédie-Française. Antonioni tried to sign her for *I vinti*, but again she felt bound to her contract.

When the New Wave began sweeping ashore at the close of the 1950s, Moreau was in demand here, there and every-where. If François Truffaut and Louis Malle were not quite the equivalent of Jules and Jim in Moreau's life, there is no doubt that she felt profoundly attached to both men, in particular to

Malle. "Meeting Louis was like a rebirth for me. He was never accepted by the New Wave because he was independently wealthy, thanks to his family fortune. Louis was a loner; he didn't want to be part of a group. He didn't like sitting in cafés discussing films, as did Chabrol, Truffaut, Godard and Rivette." In 1957, Malle's *Elevator to the Gallows* afforded Moreau the first truly demanding role of her screen career. "Everyone used to go out in the evenings in Saint-Germain-des-Prés," she told me. "Boris Vian was always there, and he introduced me to his close friend Miles Davis." Moreau mentioned *Elevator to the Gallows* to Davis and suggested he watch just a couple of reels, and it turned out that he already knew of the project and had met with Malle. "Let's go to the studio now," he said, "and we'll record something." By dawn, he and his sidemen had completed what would become an iconic score. Through the night, Davis stood and played his trumpet, looking like the quintessence of cool with his white shirt and tie, black blazer, and flawless grooming, while Moreau served drinks to him and the crew.

She became a muse for Welles, as for so many other creative talents. She introduced him to Romy Schneider, whom Welles promptly cast as Leni in *The Trial*. In *Chimes at Midnight*, Moreau played the delicious Doll Tearsheet, and three years later, in 1968, she luxuriated in seducing the young sailor in Welles' *The Immortal Story*. We reminisced about the great man, and as I left her apartment, she signed my copy of the Criterion edition of Malle's *Elevator to the Gallows* with the words: "For Peter Cowie, my 'link' to Orson and his beautiful films. Gratefully, Jeanne Moreau."

Am I justified in devoting a "Flashback" to this greatest of French actresses after just one long meeting? If I am, it is because her personality runs like a watermark through so many of the significant films of my youth. She was always there. After more than 140 films, her curiosity remained unquenched, her look imperturbable: the lustrous hair, the resolute eyes, the sensual, sulky mouth, the slightly rasping voice. "This is what I am," these features seem to say. "Take me or leave me." And we accept her, happily, on those terms.

From the very first month after my retirement from *Variety*, I was appointed a consultant for Dolby Laboratories. Over many years at Cinema Expo, CineAsia and other conventions, I had struck up a warm relationship with the senior executives at Dolby, including Bill Jasper, the President, and one of Ray Dolby's oldest collaborators, Ioan Allen. I had met the Dolby team at CinemaExpo and CineAsia, the two conventions I attended on behalf of *Variety*, and appreciated their respect for my knowledge of world cinema. For Dolby, I interviewed film-makers and sound engineers like the eloquent Walter Murch, and moderated panels at the Cannes Festival on topics such as "Are Movies Too Loud?"

Bill Jasper loomed over his colleagues physically and author-itatively. We became friends, and in San Francisco he would invite me to music rehearsals where he played the clarinet, and to the Bohemian Club in Nob Hill, where artists, musicians, politicians, and business chiefs mingled in a men-only environ-ment. Ioan Allen, who against all odds, persuaded the Holly-wood studios to embrace Dolby technology, was proud of his English lineage. He would take me to lunches at Le Central, the quintessential French bistro on the edge of Chinatown, where the martinis were dryer than dry and the Filet Mignon au Poivre cooked to perfection. Ioan was a technician par excellence: he knew the exact location of the "sweet spot" in any theatre or auditorium, and he accompanied many a director to film festi-vals to ensure that his movie would be projected properly.

When I met Ray Dolby himself, I liked the congenial, modest, and quiet intelligence of the man, who was one of the greatest inventors of the 20th century. In 2010, I embarked on an assignment that would take some two years of interviewing Ray about his career and compiling the outlines of his life from the myriad documents he had kept in his archives in San Fran-cisco.

Flashback: Ray Dolby

Ray Dolby did not match the conventional image of an eccentric "inventor," nor that of a business mogul. Tall, hand-some, a keen pilot and downhill skier, he eschewed the lime-light, and yet he fought with tenacity to protect his name and brand. The history of motion pictures has been marked by such innovators as Lee de Forest (sound-on-film) and Herbert T. Kalmus (Technicolor), but only Ray Dolby has become a household name umbilically linked to the fields of music and cinema in the way that Gillette and Hoover gave their names to excellence in other domains of everyday life. "Dolby" represents a benchmark by which the recording of sound and its playback on disc and in movie theatres is judged.

Not many people are aware that Ray was also one of the inventors of the original video tape recorder. The VTR was a kind of Holy Grail for the fledgling television industry during the late 1940s and early 1950s. If a way could be found of recording a live programme on tape, then it could be re-broadcast some hours later for a different time zone in the United States. Ray was only a teenager when he began research into this at the Ampex Corporation, but by 1956, at the age of just 23, he was able to preside over a press conference in California when the first video tape recorder was unveiled—to wild acclaim. Television would never be the same again.

During the mid-1960s, Ray's noise-reduction system revolutionised the record industry, eliminating the hiss that had plagued both classical and popular music recordings. Next in line was the movie industry. Ray's interest in movies dated back to his early childhood, when he saw Walt Disney's *Fantasia*. In 2010, he told me, "Whenever I went to the movies, I thought, 'This sound is really terrible. How can that industry not be paying attention to what's going on here?'" He was shocked during a visit to London's Elstree Studios to see the appalling state of the design, manufacture and maintenance of sound equipment. "Nobody cared about the sound on motion pictures in those days," he lamented. "I went to a Vice-President of Marketing at Universal who started shouting at me, saying 'You're crazy! There's only two things that sell movies: good stories and comfortable seats. Get out of here!'"

Stanley Kubrick, however, admired the work that Dolby had accomplished in the music field, and *A Clockwork Orange* would become the first feature film to use Dolby noise reduction on all premixes and masters, although it was released with a conventional optical soundtrack.

With Ray Dolby.

Star Wars would never have enjoyed such a massive success in 1977 had it not been for Dolby Stereo. If someone alighted from a cab, wearing a Dolby tee-shirt, the lines of people waiting to enter the theatre for *Star Wars* would burst into spontaneous applause and cheering. Suddenly, all the studios wanted to use Dolby, and an industry that had seemed doomed by the advent of home video entered a new phase, with "the theatrical experience" coming to the fore once again.

Ray and his engineers Ioan Allen and David Robinson sought to improve this system with each passing year. Dolby Stereo was bolstered by Dolby SR, which in 1992 gave way to Dolby Digital and then to Dolby Digital Surround EX, and, most recently, to Dolby Atmos, with its speaker channels in the theatre ceiling ("The voice of God" quipped Ray).

I was fortunate to know Ray during the final years of his life, working with him on his archives in San Francisco. He was a man who kept every receipt, every letter, let alone the innumerable patents he had developed. I waded through box-files filled with documents from his time as a Marshall Scholar at Cambridge University, from his years working for UNESCO in India, and from the time in South London where he and his tireless wife Dagmar founded Dolby Laboratories in 1965.

After a morning's interview session, Ray would take me to a light lunch in Pacific Heights, or further afield in one of his cars—the BMW, the Jaguar, or the brand-new Tesla that he loved so much. You could go anywhere with Ray and not feel in the public eye. His diffidence and self-effacing approach to the media meant that he was rarely recognised as a celebrity except by friends and business colleagues.

He could not have accomplished so much without two manifest characteristics—curiosity, and passion. His Finnish roots may have given Ray his calm, matter-of-fact attitude to issues, as well as a fondness for classical music. To his American lineage, however, he owed his technical skills and his sturdy, controlled ambition through the years.

Ray would listen to you intently and then respond to a question in comparatively few words, revealing his Nordic genes. He talked with assurance and discretion, and never with such discretion as on the subject of wealth. After Dolby became a publicly-quoted company, Ray's fortune was estimated at anything between $3 and $4 billion. "I honestly don't know how much I'm worth," he would tell me. "I never really wanted to make a lot of money, but just enough to enjoy life as I wanted. And I've done that."

During my visits, Ray and I would conduct some of our interviews at his house in Sonoma. One day, after a lengthy conversation, he strolled outside and we sat down facing the valley fringed with numerous olive trees. "Listen," he said, and we could hear the soughing of the wind in the high grass. It reminded me of certain scenes in Terrence Malick's *Days of Heaven*, which remains a glorious example of Dolby Stereo recording and re-recording. "Exactly," purred Ray. For him, on a music recording or a movie soundtrack, the silence between the sounds mattered even more than the sounds themselves.

Ray passed on in September 2013, at the age of 80. The following January, a celebration of his life was held in San Francisco. Some two thousand guests crowded into Symphony Hall to hear tributes from all sides of the film and music worlds—from Michael Tilson Thomas, Walter Murch, Mickey Hart, drummer of The Grateful Dead and George Lucas among many others. A joyous occasion, reminding the audience that almost everything we "hear," today, in shopping malls, in our own home, in movie theatres, has been improved by what Ray Dolby achieved as an inventor.

Some directors come across in person as misanthropic, vain or patronising. Others are timid in the flesh and yet exhibit on screen a personality seething with rage and violence. Ingmar Bergman and Orson Welles both assured me that they never saw their films in public once the final cut had been achieved. Of course they did, from time to time, and in the age of DVD and Blu-ray, many directors revisit their work in order to comment upon it, or at least to re-view it for technical reasons. By the same token, directors often claim not to read the critics. Bergman said that he forgot the good notices, but that the murderous review worried him for ages like an aching tooth.

So I believe that the most rewarding way of writing about films is not under the relentless pressure of deadlines, but over a long period, mulling until a work takes its place in the canon of a director's career and one can seek to illuminate it in some detail for the reader. Perhaps that's film history and not film criticism. But I've always fought to get across in some form of print my passion for those films that left an indelible mark on my consciousness, so vividly that I can recall the precise circumstances in which I first saw them, rather as one always remembers what one was doing when Monroe died or Kennedy was shot.

My response to cinema has been emotional rather than analytical. My most treasured films feature individuals with whom I can, if not identify, at least empathise. The personality of the actor exerts a great influence over that response. *Five Easy Pieces* engages me every time I see it because of Jack Nicholson's charismatic and heart-felt performance. Humphrey Bogart captivates one with his laconic, world-weary presence. Then there is the erotic undercurrent. Most critics have difficulty in admitting to it, but one's judgement of fictional films may often be coloured by one's response to the actors on a sexual level. What, in my canon, do *L'avventura*, *The Double Life of Veronique*, *Basic Instinct* and *Mulholland Drive* have in common? Of course, it's the appeal of Monica Vitti, Irène Jacob, Sharon Stone and Naomi Watts.

Flashback: Francesco Rosi

In December 2001, through the good offices of my friend Lorenzo Codelli, I arranged an interview with Francesco Rosi for my book *Revolution!*, about cinema in the 1960s. Rosi lived for decades in the fashionable Via Gregoriana, above the Spanish Steps in Rome. His hushed apartment gazed out over the city, and his sitting room was crowded with books, magazines and memorabilia. A servant brought tea as we talked, Rosi developing his complex arguments and unerring dialectic in a French that was so forceful and clearly articulated that even I could understand it. "I am a passionate man," he said, "but with the ambition to be rational at the same time—and my passion is typically Neapolitan. There's a conflict between the passion and rationality. I live situations with passion, but I try to deal with them in a rational manner."

Rosi could certainly smile at life's little ironies, but he rarely laughed aloud. He was a serious man, analysing each and every situation with admirable lucidity. He would have been at home in the Agora in Athens, verbally jousting with Socrates and Plato. Tall, burly, with his leonine head thrust forward in search of truth, he nonetheless revealed occasional moments of vanity, which made him reassuringly human. He was convinced, for example, that his 1981 movie *Three Brothers* had lost the Academy Award for Best Foreign Language Film to István Szabó's *Mephisto* by only a handful of votes, and books on his work were left discreetly within reach of a visitor.

He had established his reputation as "the Italian Eisenstein" in 1962 with *Salvatore Giuliano*, a Silver Bear winner at the Berlinale, followed immediately by the equally searing *Hands over the City* (1963), which earned him the Golden Lion at Venice. *The Mattei Affair* (1972) and *Cadaveri eccellenti* (1976) solidified his status as the most assured and socially committed Italian filmmaker of his generation. And yet, over the course of his career, this Neapolitan master could not be easily pigeonholed as merely a "political" cineaste. *The Moment of Truth* (1965), filmed in the bullrings of Spain, showed Rosi's gift for operatic suspense, as did his much later screen version of *Carmen* (1984), with Julia Migenes and Placido Domingo. *Christ Stopped at Eboli* (1979) and *Three Brothers* could have been made only by a profound humanist; set far from the corrupt whirl of the big city, they celebrate family values and the desperate poverty of the Mezzogiorno.

In 2004, Rosi was accompanied by his brother to a tribute at the Swiss Cinémathèque in Lausanne. Afterwards, Hervé and Jacqueline Dumont hosted a dinner at their home, and Rosi reminisced about shooting *Salvatore Giuliano*. In response to my rather naive question, "How did you deal with the local Mafia?" Rosi rose to his feet and, clutching his crotch with one hand, stared at me intently across the table, waited a beat, and then growled, "Like this!"

Dramatic tension, which in Hollywood films is so artificially generated, emerges almost organically from Rosi's respect for his material, and from the urgency of his inquiry. He was not preoccupied with the chronological order of events. In my commentary for the Criterion DVD of *Salvatore Giuliano* in 2004, I quoted his words to me from our earlier conversation in Rome: "I make dialectical films, and not films as theses. The term political film is improper, imprecise. I make films about reality, films in order to reveal what reality conceals. Let's say 'films of denunciation' rather than 'political films.'"

In 2008, some of us had succeeded in persuading Berlinale director Dieter Kosslick to give Rosi an honorary

Golden Bear in recognition of his career. I think that meant a great deal to him, because *Salvatore Giuliano*'s Silver Bear had been awarded after the film was rejected by other festivals. Delivering the speech in his honour, I asserted that Rosi had spent his entire career confronting issues of power and society. "Like Lindsay Anderson, he has never compromised with his material," I said, "nor has he accepted 'the way of the world.' Corruption is his lodestone, and he has brought an analytical mind to bear on scandals and outrages both real and fictional." Aged 86, Rosi mounted the stage to accept the award and delivered a ringing, if protracted, defence of political commitment in cinema. "He's the greatest living director in Europe," whispered Michel Ciment at my side, a statement hard to dispute given that Antonioni and Bergman had both died the previous July.

Flashback: Michel Ciment

We had met during the late 1960s, at Cannes, and as a result Michel wrote the French report for my *International Film Guide* for more than forty years, starting in 1970. His copy was invariably handwritten, which meant that I had to both decipher and translate his always incisive prose. Michel and I were almost contemporaries, and had started our writing careers around the same time, in the early 1960s. He would become the Pope of French film criticism, guiding the magazine *Positif* to remarkable heights, and rendering it an altogether more coherent monthly than the much-vaunted *Cahiers du Cinéma*.

Michel would say to me, only partly tongue in cheek: "I'm a man of the 19th century." He loved the written word and the spoken word, and excelled in both disciplines. However, he resisted the acquisition of a mobile phone until very late in life, and only acquired an email address a year or two before he died. He did not own a typewriter, so far as I know, and abhorred the social networks. Richard Branson once said that he had never met a man who liked wearing a tie—but clearly he had not encountered Michel who, like me, felt more comfortable with a tie than without. That, plus a V-necked pullover and jacket, completed the unpretentious image of a college professor of the 1940s and '50s.

In 1986 we spent some quality time together at the Comedy Film Festival in Vevey, where I was on the jury. We agreed on so many essential issues. We both loved the films of Francesco Rosi, Alain Resnais and Dušan Makavejev, for example. Neither of us relished writing about directors we disliked such as Jean-Marie Straub or Chantal Akerman. Of course our tastes diverged on some points. Despite protestations to the contrary, Michel was a dyed-in-the-wool auteurist, and he would not concede that idols such as Clint Eastwood could make a mediocre film. But we shared the pleasure of interpreting great films for a new generation of cinephiles.

Although Michel rarely laughed with gusto, he adored the eccentric aspect of British cinema, notably Ealing comedies and the work of Powell and Pressburger. He enjoyed visiting London for short trips, always finding a moment to inspect the latest exhibition at the National Gallery. Michel was a connoisseur of the history of painting, and could relate that, and the other arts, to the development of film culture in the 20th century.

During the Berlinale, where we both stayed at the Hyatt on Potsdamer Platz, we would enjoy breakfast together. His order remained the same across the years: two soft-boiled eggs and English Breakfast tea. Michel crossed swords with the head of the festival, Dieter Kosslick. Their temperaments were so different, although Dieter respected Michel's vast knowledge of world cinema. In the early years of his stewardship, Dieter established an ad hoc "advisory committee" consisting of Michel, Hiam Abbass, the Palestinian actress and director, and myself. We met at an Italian restaurant in Berlin, and Michel had the courage to voice his concerns about the quality of films in the competition. Dieter listened with good humour, but was clearly not on the same wavelength as Michel, and soon the committee was dissolved. Michel regretted the tendency of festival screenings proliferating out of control. "I must see the Competition films," he would say, "and for the rest, I have to make a choice."

We also shared dismay at the "cancelling" of directors like Roman Polanski and Woody Allen. Michel liked to invoke the example of Caravaggio, who in the late 16th and early

17th century painted one masterpiece after another and yet was reputed as an incorrigible brawler and murderer. "Do we remove all his paintings from the museums?" asked Michel rhetorically. "Of course not."

What I admired most about Michel was an almost indomitable will to survive as a cinephile. Afflicted by health problems in later life, and (unfortunately) reluctant to take exercise, he found it harder and harder to attend the festivals he loved. But he did so to the very end, sustained by the respect of his peers and his boundless curiosity for unearthing new films and new auteurs. I sent him an email some ten days before his death in hospital in November 2023. "Too good to hear from you," he responded. "Merci cher Peter, merci beaucoup. Amitiés. Michel."

On the first of my two trips to the Telluride Festival, in 1991, I found myself standing in line for screenings with Laura Dern and Renny Harlin, seated alongside Mimi Rogers at one of the festival's informal dinners, and serving on a panel with crime novelist Elmore Leonard and *The Silence of the Lambs* star Jodie Foster. Krzysztof Kieślowski was there with Irène Jacob, fresh from the triumph of *The Double Life of Veronique*, along with regulars at the Colorado event, Annette Insdorf, Laurie Anderson and documentarist Ken Burns, basking in the afterglow of his immense visual and oral history of the Civil War. Ten years later, I presented "The Ultimate DVD Show," a discussion about a technology that was then in rapid expansion. The late Roger Ebert was one of my panellists, and we spoke optimistically of the access to foreign-language films thanks to the new medium. Salman Rushdie, the festival's guest director in 2001, revealed a lifelong passion for cinema, and presented Satyajit Ray's children's film, *The Golden Fortress*, as well as science fiction favourites including *Metropolis*.

Telluride owed its success to four individuals: the co-founders, James Card, Tom Luddy, Bill Pence and Bill's wife Stella, who until her retirement managed the day to day affairs with rigour and charm. Card, the lynchpin of the Eastman-Kodak Film Preserve, was an archivist without peer. Tom Luddy had propelled the Pacific Film Archive in Berkeley to global renown, and Bill Pence had proved a vital element in the rise of Janus Films during the 1970s. Together they originated a formula unique among film festivals. No free accreditations, no advance announcement of programme, no reserved seats. Telluride thus became a truly democratic event, where the great and the good stood in line with couples who hailed from as far away as Florida and would happily pay up to $3,000 for the privilege of watching a Labor Day weekend stuffed with remarkable films, both new and classic.

Since 1946, the Locarno Film Festival has flourished—with some ups and downs—as the premier gathering for the Swiss cinema trade and for cinephiles in and beyond the country. But in 2005 a rival event was launched in Zürich. Karl Spoerri, an astute neophyte film producer at the time, founded the Zürich Film Festival as a shop-window for films from around the world, and which reached the German-speaking population of Switzerland (Locarno being in the Italian-speaking Ticino). But Spoerri shrewdly introduced an industrial element into the festival, with its awards accorded primarily to major stars and charismatic directors. Locarno continued with its more esoteric programming policy, and basked in official support. Zürich, however, had to fend for itself financially, and did so with considerable success.

Christine Dorn, with whom I had worked at the Berlinale Talent Campus, invited me to host some ambitious master classes at the Zürich event. Over the years, I talked onstage with filmmakers as diverse as Mike Leigh, Alejandro González Iñárritu, Miloš Forman, Claire Denis and Terry Gilliam. Equally fascinating were the personalities of Sylvester Stallone, the composer Tan Dun (*Crouching Tiger, Hidden Dragon*), the cinematographer Vilmos Zsigmond, and the producer Greg Shapiro, who had shared the Academy Award for Best Picture with *The Hurt Locker*. Stallone in particular held us in thrall with his thoughtful analysis of writing screenplays as well as directing pictures.

I arranged to meet with most of these guests before we went onstage, and in September 2009, I was scheduled to have breakfast with Terry Gilliam at the eminent and rather pompous Hotel Baur au Lac. The minutes slipped by, and after half an hour of waiting in the dining room, I asked the head waiter to call Terry's room. In fact, he had already come downstairs, but had been refused permission to enter the dining area because of "inappropriate footwear." I hastened to the lobby, where a bemused Terry Gilliam sat flexing his flip flops. I warmed to his manner immediately, and the master class proved very popular.

Christine and I collaborated one last time at a European Film Academy event near Düsseldorf. She asked me to moderate a master class with Danny Boyle, attended by young filmmakers and technicians. Danny was riding the crest of a wave, having directed *Slumdog Millionaire* in 2008 and having won the Academy Award for Best Director. He missed his early morning plane from London to Düsseldorf, and I was despatched to the airport to meet him as he arrived on the next flight. We then rushed back to the conference centre, and Danny hit the ground running, answering everyone's questions cheerfully and cogently. In the car he had talked to me about his early days at the BBC in Belfast, producing the searing documentaries of Alan Clarke, and his stint at the Royal Court Theatre, where he directed plays by Edward Bond and Howard Brenton. Restless, passionate, and almost consciously unpretentious, Danny was a man possessed, intent on seizing the day and whatever fresh challenge it offered. Few film directors could have produced the Opening Ceremony of the 2012 London Olympics with such commitment and originality. If any one film communicated the electric energy of Boyle's personality, it was *Trainspotting*, a rollercoaster ride through a Britain blighted by Thatcherism and drug abuse.

Flashback: Roman Polanski

A little before 1 a.m. on Sunday September 27th, 2009, the phone rang in my hotel room in Zürich. Roman Polanski had just been arrested on arrival in Switzerland, in response to a warrant for his arrest issued by the U.S. justice department. I had been due to meet him for breakfast, and then later that morning conduct a master class with him at the Zürich Film Festival.

Apparently, Polanski was allowed to make two calls after his arrest. He phoned his wife in Paris, and then he called the director of the festival, Karl Spörri, to apologise for the inconvenience caused. Everyone was stunned and outraged.

Ivan Butler's book about Polanski, published in 1970 by Tantivy.

Stunned, because for some years Polanski had travelled without difficulty in Europe, to Poland, Austria, and of course to Switzerland, where he had a chalet in Gstaad and visited frequently. ("Such a nice man," said the baker down the hill from his chalet, "always in a good humour.")

Outraged, because the arrest had occurred in Switzerland, that fabled neutral land that has been for so long a haven for the great and the good, the refugee and the notorious. The irony was that the head of the Federal Office of Culture (there are no "ministers" as such in Switzerland) had been preparing to make a speech in his honour when

Polanski would have been presented with his lifetime award that same Sunday evening at the festival. Almost next door, however, the Federal Councillor in charge of the Department of Justice and the Police had already been apprised on the Friday that Polanski would be seized on his arrival in the country.

This incident became a cause célèbre within a matter of days. An initial wave of anger swept through cultural circles in Europe. Everyone, from the European Film Academy to the French Minister of Culture, deplored the arrest, asking why it had occurred at exactly this moment in time when Polanski could have been arrested by U.S. authorities on dozens of other occasions during the past thirty years.

But then came the backlash. Conservative bodies (as well as the Society of Socialist Women in Switzerland) applauded the Swiss for their role in apprehending a rapist and a paedophile—in short, a menace to civilised society. Luc Besson announced that he would not sign a petition supporting Polanski, even though his daughter was friends with the filmmaker's own daughter, because he could not help feeling how appalled he would be if his 13-year-old had been forced to have illegal sex. Daniel Cohn-Bendit, champion of the Greens and the rebel who manned the barricades in Paris in 1968, denigrated Frédéric Mitterrand, the French Minister of Culture, for daring to intervene so swiftly on behalf of Polanski. "This is justice…" he intoned.

So began a witch hunt. All too many of those who were enthralled by *The Pianist*, let alone Polanski's earlier masterworks like *Knife in the Water*, *Repulsion* and *Chinatown*, turned against him with knee-jerk predictability, just as their parents did in 1969 when Polanski was widely suspected of satanism in the wake of *Rosemary's Baby* and the horrific murder of his wife Sharon Tate by the Manson gang. Most never studied the facts of the rape charges against him or considered the role of the original judge. Nor did they realise that Polanski had been incarcerated for 42 days in Chino State Prison for psychiatric evaluation, at the end of which a suspended sentence was recommended. Nor that he had been "forgiven" by Samantha Geimer, his partner in sex that ill-fated day in the home of Jack Nicholson.

Film history is strewn with such depressing episodes, from Fatty Arbuckle to Charlie Chaplin (even if Lita Grey was 16 while Samantha was 13), by way of Ingmar Bergman, who was dragged from the stage of the Royal Dramatic Theatre in 1976 on charges of alleged tax evasion.

Polanski is a member of the Académie française, France's most eminent body of artists and cultural personalities. He has lived and worked there for decades, coming and going at will for the simple reason that, thank goodness, the French do not extradite individuals in sex cases unless they have been convicted of rape in the first degree—and Polanski had pleaded guilty in Santa Monica to "unlawful sex with a minor."

The irony is that only several months earlier Polanski had been informed that if he were to return to make a court appearance in California, the case against him would probably be dismissed (in view of Judge Rittenband's misconduct in handling the original proceedings, which triggered Polanski's flight from Los Angeles Airport in 1978). But this was on one condition: that his appearance in court should be televised. That's show business, folks!

The auteur theory never engrossed me. The validity of the theory may be demonstrated in the distinctive signature of a director throughout his work; it does not mean that all his films are on the same high level. Even the greatest filmmakers have failed on certain occasions, and it little serves their reputation to acclaim each new production as a masterpiece.

Whenever I sense artifice, smugness, or objectivity, I shy away from a film, however illustrious its director. Jean-Luc Godard, Peter Greenaway, Chantal Akerman and Lars von Trier all leave me cold, with the exception of the odd film. I cringe when confronted by whimsy, which rules out the work of Frank Capra and Jacques Feyder, and by cynicism, which dispenses with George Cukor and Ernst Lubitsch.

I have often been drawn to the work of directors who have been damned with faint praise by the intellectual critics of their time. Michael Mann, Tom Tykwer, Volker Schlöndorff, Alan Parker and Costa-Gavras come immediately to mind. All four men were fiercely interested in their society, and also recognised the importance of controlling a good narrative on screen.

Flashback: Costa-Gavras

He has the remorseless, steely gaze of an advocate, homing in on malfeasance and injustice. He has found his subject matter not just in his native Greece (*Z*, *Adults in the Room*), but also in Chile (*Missing*), Uruguay (*State of Siege*), Czechoslovakia (*The Confession*), Nazi Germany (*Amen*) and the United States (*Betrayed*, *Music Box*). With his uncanny flair for editing, Costa-Gavras endows all his films with a powerful undercurrent of suspense. Perhaps because they are thrillers, they have been underestimated when lists of "the best films of all time" emerge in the press.

On May 20, 1993, I was invited to the world premiere of *Cliffhanger* at the Cannes Festival. Immediately after the screening the guests were whisked up to the Moulin de Mougins for a charity dinner. I climbed into the front seat of a crowded limousine, and from the darkness behind me a hand stretched out in greeting: "Costa-Gavras." The voice was so deep and forceful that the sound and image linger to this day.

With Costa-Gavras.

But it was a few years later, in the summer of 2009, that I could really talk with Costa, during a European Film Academy "Think Tank" in a castle near Düsseldorf. During one of the panels I moderated that weekend, Costa spoke with passion and conviction of the need for European identity and the screening of films in schools. Then on January 8th, 2015, I sat down with him in the main screening theatre of the Cinémathèque française. It was the morning after the ghastly terrorist attack on the offices of *Charlie Hebdo* in Paris. Amid the general consternation, someone suggested to Costa that the interview should be cancelled. He demurred, and we began to discuss one of his best films, *State of Siege*, that was about to be issued on DVD by Criterion in New York. He talked of his interest in the CIA and its "little sister," AID (Agency for International Development), and confided that the communists were reluctant to collaborate with him, given his trenchant critique of communist society in *The Confession*. The success of *Z*, however, had given Costa significant credibility among groups like the Tupamaros.

Costa's technique was always to avoid the explicit. Greece is not formally identified in *Z*, nor is Czechoslovakia in *The Confession*, nor Uruguay in *State of Siege*. "If you give the audience all the information," he told me, "they want to think about something else." Another characteristic of his approach was to create a claustrophobic mood, often using long lenses and underlining the control exerted by the army, or the police, or faceless authorities, over a particular society at a particular moment. Costa has regularly flecked the sombre tone of his political films with instants of humour. "It's like life," he says, "we are not always serious in life, we have moments of laughter too."

Every movie is political, he asserted. When he was a young boy, his image of America was coloured by the films of Esther Williams, with their beautiful girls and big swimming pools and pink cars and so on. "They were political in that they made me form an opinion about America that was not accurate, a very positive image of the Americans. Only later did I discover that American life was much more complex," he said. "My philosophy of the movies is that when you go to a movie, you don't go to listen to a political speech, you go for the show, because a movie is a show. You want to have emotions, to laugh, to love, to hate. So in all my movies, whatever the story, I also just trying to make a show!"

Just after Christmas 2019, the phone rang at my house in Montreux. It was Costa, who had seen my piece about *Z* that the *Wall Street Journal* had published to mark the fiftieth anniversary of the film and its devastating critique of the Colonels' regime in Greece during the 1960s. He spoke warmly about the article, and said how much it meant to him. The call was typical of this most humane of auteurs who as I write these lines is still at work—in his nineties.

My introduction to Venice was unexpected and fleeting. In early September 1997, I was asked to fly to Italy to moderate a conference arranged by the RAI and entitled "Can Europe and America Produce Together?" I already had met some of the participants: Saul Zaentz, Jan Mojto, Stewart Till, Krzysztof Zanussi, Adrienne Mancia. But the fly in the ointment proved to be the Minister of Culture in the Romano Prodi government of the time, Walter Veltroni. In the tradition of so many lofty functionaries, he arrived late—and we were working within strict time constraints. Late became later, and later... Finally he strode up to the dais, gave me a perfunctory greeting, and launched into a diatribe concerning the failure of European films to penetrate the American market. He had been asked to limit his speech to a few minutes, but he warmed to his task, and went on speaking for so long that I had abandoned all hope of even a snack lunch. Then, abruptly, he stopped, and without another word left the stage and the Sala Visconti as swiftly as he had come.

In 2005, Marco Müller, then director of the Festival, asked me to join the jury for the Opera Prima prize, which my friend Jörn Donner had won in 1963 for his first feature, *A Sunday in September.* By the time I came aboard it was referred to as the Luigi De Laurentiis Award for a Debut Film. Our president was the maverick and congenial Canadian artist-cum-filmmaker Guy Maddin. We were lodged in the late-lamented Hotel des Bains on the Lido. Its faded luxury was reflected in the endless corridors with their creaking parquet floors, the elegant baroque furnishings, and the immense salons, many long disused. This was the hotel where Thomas Mann had stayed in 1911, and had set his novella, *Death in Venice.*

Competitions, prizes, juries—film festivals have debated their value for decades. There is no question, however, that a competition attracts media coverage and adds a strong bass line to events like Cannes, Berlin, and Venice. The very word "jury" has a legal ring to it, and seems inappropriate for an art form. One cannot pronounce one film guilty, and another innocent. The only punishment inflicted by a festival jury amounts to neglect; the film that receives no prize or "honourable mention" has indeed been cast into a kind of darkness. I have served on juries at all these top festivals, but my most intriguing memories stem from my days as a juror in minor, offbeat film gatherings.

A glamorous Russian almost derailed the Best First Film jury of which I was a member at Venice in 2005. She seemed to be the staple Rent-a-Russian-Juror of the period, for she had also participated alongside me on the main Competition jury at Berlin in 2002, and was reputedly a friend of Vladimir Putin. We noted that she was attending fewer and fewer of our screenings on the Lido, and often spoke at length on her cell phone while watching the films. About three days from the end of the Mostra, she announced that she would have to see the remaining films in her room, on DVD. When our final voting took place, she seemed disinterested, and continued to take phone calls.

I had not been able to attend Venice as regularly as I had Cannes, quite simply because the *International Film Guide* was, in late August, in the throes of final production and proof-reading. Now, unfettered, I could enjoy the laid-back charm of the Mostra, a festival where you could always find a seat, and where the mood was not so business-oriented as at Cannes. I suggested to Marco that we should have some panels during the Mostra, and had the chutzpah to offer my services as moderator. He accepted, and we started what would become an annual fixture over the ensuing two decades.

The panels in Venice focused on industry issues, and, when the Biennale College Cinema project was launched by Alberto Barbera in 2012, I led an annual discussion on the feature films financed by this programme. I persuaded some leading American film critics to come to the Lido for the festival—a difficult

challenge because Venice takes place almost at the same time
as two influential North American gatherings, in Telluride and
Toronto. Some, like the late Richard Corliss, of *Time* magazine,
remained faithful to Venice year after year.

Flashback: Richard Corliss

Few critics have had such an encyclopaedic knowledge of
the movies that matter, and few could express their enthusiasm or their aversion with such eloquence as Richard
Corliss. He was younger than I, but we were both born
during the Second World War, and, if too young to be children of Carné's *Paradise*, we were, like so many others of
our generation, children of *The Seventh Seal*. We shared a
fondness for early Bergman and the arthouse achievements
of the 1960s.

Richard and I first corresponded in the early 1970s,
soon after he had become editor of *Film Comment*. But
although we would enjoy a passing acquaintance during the
hurlyburly of Cannes over the years, it was only in the early
2000s that we began to spend more time together. I asked
Richard if he would take part in the first panel I moderated
for the Venice Film Festival, in 2006. The subject was European films in the United States, and Richard sat alongside
Molly Haskell and Jonathan Rosenbaum as we discussed
the role of festivals in promoting foreign-language films
among other things.

Richard could hold forth (though he never pontificated)
on almost any topic, and did so frequently in my encounters
with him in Venice in the ensuing years. During one of my
panels, he talked about the spaghetti Western and its influence on Tarantino, and discussed the characteristics of Sergio
Corbucci's work at length and without a hint of condescension. In 2009, we celebrated, a few months in advance, the
centenary of Kurosawa's birth, and in 2012 we extolled the
virtues of micro-budget filmmaking, with Richard discussing
Maya Deren and Stan Brakhage alongside such less experimental, if equally low-budget, movies as *The Immoral Mr.
Teas*, *El Mariachi* and *The Blair Witch Project*, which had
struck it rich at the box office.

When we viewed the first fruits of the Biennale College Cinema programme in 2013, Richard, in company with his fellow U.S. critics, brought a sympathetic eye to bear on the four films presented, always admiring the skill with which they had been made, for the equivalent of a mere $175,000 or so. He was committed, he said, even with such a mass-market platform as *Time* magazine, to talking about films made on the slimmest of budgets.

His wife of more than forty years, Mary, had become a legend at the Museum of Modern Art's stills archive before it was cruelly dismantled. Mary, Richard, my wife Françoise and I would have annual dinners on the Lido, where he would talk about his erstwhile colleagues Pauline Kael and Andrew Sarris, his love for Ernst Lubitsch and Samson Raphaelson, and his fears for the future. Shooting movies on celluloid was a disappearing act, he conceded. "Venice, Cannes and the rest may have to change their names to the Moving Image Festival," he said with a laugh.

Richard could don a black tie with the best of them, but in everyday life he was remarkably modest. We would see Mary and him enjoying a late-night pizza at one of the humble snack bars along the Gran Viale Santa Maria Elisabetta, far from the glitz of the red-carpet screenings further up the Lido, and often after attending an offbeat classic in the festival's Retrospective. Richard rarely relaxed in public; he was forever bustling hither and thither. "I'm on deadline," he would apologise as he hastened to the hotel garden, opened up his laptop, and began to write. He always found time to acknowledge his friends, however. When my book on Louise Brooks appeared in 2006, he praised it with affection in his column at Time.com.

Richard prized Venice above all festivals, I think, because the city itself and the atmosphere it exudes seemed to accord with his vision of cinema—rooted in an enchanted past and yet open to new directions. When *Gravity* opened the 2013 festival, Richard's enthusiasm was second to none. Speaking of his experience on the selection committee of the New York Film Festival, he used to reflect that festivals can discover films but not invent them, and that a great festival must lead by example.

Writing to me after Venice in 2014, he referred to our "magical" dinner in the garden of the Hotel Quattro Fontane, adding, "We must do it again next year—as Richard Roud used to say, 'If we're spared.'" But alas, this "very parfit gentle knight" left us all too soon.

Over the years, I invited critics from all over the United States to Venice, and among those who relished returning year after year were Mick LaSalle of the *San Francisco Chronicle*, Stephanie Zacharek (at first of *The Village Voice*, and later of *Time*), Glenn Kenny, Chris Vognar and Michael Phillips. Some came on just one occasion, but contributed memorably to the discussions: Kenneth Turan, Ty Burr, Justin Chang and distinguished European critics like Michel Ciment and Derek Malcolm.

The filmmakers would sit in the audience and listen to their work being dissected, praised and occasionally criticised by the journalists on the dais. The mood was not one of antagonism, however, but rather of encouragement; often our critics could offer practical advice about gaining distribution or at least festival screenings, in the U.S. and elsewhere. Some of these Biennale College films reached a wider public than they might have at first imagined: Tim Sutton's *Memphis*, Lemohang Jeremiah Mosese's *This is Not a Burial, It's a Resurrection* and Shuhashish Bhutiani's *Hotel Salvation*, to cite just three examples.

Despite the image of glamorous stars arriving in water taxis, the Venice Film Festival is actually quite sober. It takes place on the Lido, that 12km-long finger of land between the Venetian Lagoon and the Adriatic Sea. Soon after 8 a.m. each morning, you leave your hotel in a leafy side-street to walk up the island to the festival centre. Behind forbidding gates and fences, period villas nestle in luxuriant and faintly neglected gardens. Silence prevails; a gate creaks open and a man appears, taking his dog for a stroll. Women cycle past quietly, perhaps aiming for the stores on the island's only major shopping thoroughfare, the Gran Viale Santa Maria Elisabetta. Only when you emerge into the vast open space in front of the Palazzo del Casino do the sound and bustle of the Mostra take over. Even the main Palazzo del Cinema, with its principal theatre seating more than a thousand spectators, has a discreet, intimate atmosphere.

I have always felt relaxed during the Venice Festival, but mostly stressed during Cannes and Berlin.

In 2018, I was commissioned by the Biennale to write a small book about the Mostra, entitled *Happy 75th: A Brief Introduction to the History of the International Film Festival.* I spent many hours in the Biennale's archives across the lagoon in Mestre, and was lucky enough to earn the blessing of that most visionary of Biennale presidents, Paolo Baratta. I well remember his having read my first draft, and how he then embarked on a learned and eloquent disquisition on the rise of Mussolini and the early "ideals" of his Fascist movement. Paolo Lughi, head of press for the festival, revealed a profound knowledge not merely of the Mostra, but of cinema history itself. He went through my manuscript with a fine-tooth comb, correcting a date here, a name there, an omission here, a misspelling there. Late at night or during weekends, Paolo would ply me with his invaluable comments. His tireless head of foreign press, Michela Lazzarin, became a friend to Françoise and myself, and encouraged me each year to continue with my panels. The entire team behind the Venice Film Festival has proved extraordinarily resilient, efficient, and enthusiastic. By the end of the two weeks of the event they are ready to sleep for a year, something that applies to anyone who works for a film festival.

I accompanied Don Groves, *Variety*'s bureau chief for Asia-Pacific, to Tokyo in the late 1990s. We spent most of our days in smoke-filled offices, where executives in white shirts and black suits listened courteously to our pitch for advertising support. Most were too polite to refuse openly, and I quickly learned that this was an element in Japanese business culture. So returning to Japan as a tourist in 2004 offered an altogether different experience. We discovered the temples of Kyoto and the memorials of Hiroshima, the voracious deer in Nara's parkland, and the hot spring resorts of Hakone.

Inspired by this visit, I decided to write a book about my preferred Japanese director, Akira Kurosawa. In the wake of two coffee-table books for Rizzoli in New York, on Louise Brooks and Joan Crawford, I received a green light for a similar volume on Kurosawa. The writing phase was straightforward, but seeking permissions for the images in such a lavish book proved more laborious. I found that Toho, who controlled the rights to most of the stills from the films, agreed to help me, but that to gain access to Kurosawa's immense archive of images, including shots of him off-set, demanded considerable negotiating skill and patience. Thanks to Marty Gross, a Canadian and a born fixer, I not only gained entree to those who made the decisions in such matters but also to the photographer Akihide Tamura, who had covered the shoot of Kurosawa's later films. Marty introduced me to the International House of Japan, in Roppongi, where I enjoyed the status of academic researcher and access to the IHJ's library.

My first research trip for the Kurosawa project brought me finally face to face with Donald Richie, a man of great wisdom to whom I dedicated my next book on Japan in 2022. His publisher in California, Stone Bridge Press, commissioned me to write what was eventually called *A Personal Journey Through Japanese Cinema*. Without speaking the language, I felt a profound kinship with Japanese life and culture, and have never tired of returning to the country, discovering fresh facets of the society on each occasion.

Flashback: Donald Richie

Donald Richie and I first corresponded in 1966, when I asked him to contribute an article on Japanese cinema to my annual *International Film Guide*. His flawlessly-typed copy arrived on that flimsy, durable rice paper we all used in the days when airmail letters were expensive, long before faxes or email. When Donald returned to the States to serve as Curator of Film at MoMA, we lost touch, and it was not until 2007 that we again exchanged letters. Donald could not have been more supportive of my plans for a book about Kurosawa, furnishing me with recommendations here there and everywhere in Tokyo. He also agreed to write the introduction, doing so on time and without in the slightest trotting out the familiar comments he had often made about the master with whom he drank so much whisky in the 1950s and '60s.

For practically everyone during the past half century, Donald was almost a synonym for Japanese cinema. His numerous books made him not just the pre-eminent guiding light on the subject, but also exemplified a kind of fluent prose that eludes the zillions of bloggers in today's cyber-world of film criticism. He wrote without affectation, engaging his reader in a cool, analytical discourse. The clarity of his thought, if not the waspishness of some of his judgments, stemmed from a profound self-confidence that, alas, failed him in private life. Donald was indeed an intellectual, but an intellectual for whom film theory, and terms like "semiotics" and "structuralism" were anathema. His fuel was enthusiasm—a simmering allegiance to life as expressed through literature (authors as diverse as Lafcadio Hearn, Nagai Kafu and Henry Green), through film, through Japanese theatre, and above all through the human personality he observed so keenly. Never a sentimentalist, he was, however, not afraid of emotion, and talking about Bresson, or Ozu, or his failed marriage to Mary Evans, could bring a tear to his eye.

Although we still turn fondly to his definitive studies of Kurosawa and Ozu (not forgetting the lucid commentaries for so many Criterion DVDs), Donald's private sanctum may best be found in *The Inland Sea*, his account of a solitary journey (one might almost say pilgrimage) around the seafaring communities bounded by three of Japan's four major islands. Written in 1971 and reissued with an afterword in 2002, this fascinating book mentions the cinema only in passing, and focuses on the individuals of every age and denomination whom Donald encountered by day, and by night, in this region of Japan unfamiliar to the regular tourist.

As his travel writings attested, Donald remained a loner all his life. He enjoyed the company of friends and visitors, but felt happiest on his own in his small Tokyo apartment, reading, writing, pottering around and, until the final, frail months of his life, watching DVDs. During my trips to Japan, we would meet for a sherry in his apartment overlooking Ueno Park, and then wander the nearby streets in search of fresh eel at one of his quiet, preferred restaurants. How well I remember chatting with Donald at a Korean café in Azabu-Jūban, and admitting that as I grew older, I thought about death at least once a week. "Once a week?" quipped Donald. "I think about it every day, sometimes every hour..."

With Teruyo Nogami

In 2009, I invited Donald to appear on a panel at the Venice Film Festival. The topic was Akira Kurosawa, the centennial of whose birth in 1910 loomed on the horizon. The journey from Tokyo to Rome and then, after a frustrating delay, on to Venice, proved fatiguing even in Business Class.

Donald was then 85 years of age, and accompanied by the indefatigable Teruyo Nogami, Kurosawa's script assistant for almost five decades. They arrived on the Lido late at night. But early next morning, in the breakfast salon of the Hotel des Bains, Donald greeted us as cheerfully as though he had been in residence for a week, his blue blazer and neatly-knotted tie giving him the aura of an eminent academic.

The panel attracted considerable attention, not least from Japanese television, and Donald basked in the limelight. We enjoyed a congenial dinner together with Marty Gross and Teruyo Nogami, and when the time came to say our farewells, Donald informed me, with a puckish smile, that he had sought out the room in which Thomas Mann had stayed while developing *Death in Venice*. He said so with an air of closure as though he, like Mann's alter ego, had come to Venice for the last time. Donald, who had attended all the world's major festivals, seemed ready to draw his curtains for the impending night.

In 2018, I was invited to read a paper at a conference to celebrate Bergman's centenary at the University of Lund. Meeting several other Bergman scholars fired my enthusiasm once more, and I decided to embark on a full-scale biography of Bergman.

When I wrote my first critical biography, Bergman was still alive. Although he reacted kindly to the book, I'd had no access to the sources of Bergman's art—to his annotated screenplays, to his workbooks, to the letters he had exchanged with countless individuals through the years. By 2018, however, all that had changed, and I was able to consult his letters and workbooks in the Swedish Film Institute. Out of this wealth of raw material came *God and the Devil: The Life and Work of Ingmar Bergman*, which Walter Donohue, my indefatigable editor at Faber and Faber, kept alive as a project through the turmoil of the Covid years.

For years I had thought of visiting Fårö, the island where Bergman spent the happiest days of his later life. It's a complicated journey—flight to Stockholm, then a bus to the ferry at Nynäshamn, a three-hour crossing by sea to Gotland, then a car to Fårö, which is guarded by yet another ferry. And in the summer of 2022 I was at last invited to the island to attend

Bergman Week. I was billeted in a small cottage built by Bergman to accommodate guests. It was in the midst of dense woodland, and no human sound could be heard by night or even by day, unless you were dropped or picked up by a driver from the festival. I had the luck to be shown Bergman's own home, with its immense library (including some of the earliest editions of the *International Film Guide*, I was chuffed to see).

But I was not enamoured of the island, which struck me as austere and un-beautiful. The gnarled pine trees, the feature-less fields and the grey brooding sea may have evoked *Shame* or *Through a Glass Darkly*, but they seemed unwelcoming and far from the sun-struck islands of the Stockholm archipelago that give such warmth to films like *Summer Interlude* and *Summer with Monica*. As I gazed down at the great boulder that served as Bergman's gravestone, I thought back to 1959, when I had first fallen in love with his work. My life would have been very different had I not encountered *The Seventh Seal* at that juncture. I owed Bergman a lot, and in visiting Fårö, I felt, as it were, that I had achieved some closure. My biography of Bergman appeared in 2023, as a final act of respect and affection. I left the island after three days and resumed my research in the Bergman Foundation in Stockholm.

Envoi

As I write this, I am thinking of Donald Richie, who died in Tokyo in 2013 at the age of 88. Someone sent me the details of his cremation, which sounded functional and unemotional in the extreme. It triggers memories of other friends and relatives who have passed away during the past fifty years.

First was a schoolmate, carried off by a rare cancer in his early twenties. And yet of all those dead individuals, I think regularly of only a handful. I am not religious, and nurse a grudging admiration for those who believe in an after-life. If I were to die, then awake in some form of existence thereafter, I would not be surprised in the least, any more than I would be if a ghost were to stand before my bed in a haunted house. But that is far removed from belief. As the Knight says in Bergman's *The Seventh Seal*: "What about those who want to believe, but cannot?" The precise instant of death may, one hopes, resemble that elusive moment when one falls asleep at the end of a long day. The mind races with worries and concerns but suddenly one is asleep, and next morning, try as one may, it's impossible to pin down the exact border between consciousness and slumber—life and death, if you like.

Thanks to the internet, one's writings may linger on for a generation or two, if only in references. Few reputations achieve real longevity; the most fortunate are those like Antonio Gaudí, whose Sagrada Familia in Barcelona will gradually reach completion over the coming years, and certainly more than a century after he first commenced work on the most spectacular cathedral of our epoch. The human personality (a more down-to-earth concept than "soul") can endure beyond physical death, as proved by a few of my friends whose charisma seemed independent of their body, and the memory of whom burns like a bright flame in the minds of those fortunate enough to have known them. They are not necessarily the most famous or the most successful of one's acquaintances. So for at least a couple of generations their identity will remain relevant, even vibrant.

In late 1954, I saw one of the early CinemaScope epics, *The Egyptian*, in London's West End. I was beguiled by the dangerous beauty of Bella Darvi as Nefer and bemused by the acting of Victor Mature as Horemheb. At the age of 15, I did not know who Mika Waltari was, let alone Michael Curtiz. Many, many years later I read Waltari's novel and was engrossed. Some of the closing words of *The Egyptian* seem a good way to end this little book of mine: "I, Sinuhe, am a human being. I have lived in everyone who existed before me and shall live in all who come after me. I shall live in human tears and laughter, in human sorrow and fear, in human goodness and wickedness, in justice and injustice, in weakness and strength. As a human being I shall live eternally in mankind. I desire no offerings at my tomb and no immortality for my name." Some would dismiss such thoughts as presumptuous, others might find them perceptive… as do I.

Personal Favourites

For fun, I have picked forty films, listed here in chronological order, that have either profoundly impressed me, or that I just love unashamedly; films that I can re-view with pleasure year in, year out.

The Outlaw and His Wife (1918)
Perhaps the greatest of early silent directors, Victor Sjöström would prove an important mentor for Bergman, and although *The Phantom Carriage* was his most famous achievement, and a Criterion DVD on which I worked, I still have a fondness for *The Outlaw and His Wife*. From his early breakthrough with *Terje Vigen* to *The Wind*, his finest work in Hollywood, Sjöström used physical movement and exertion to reflect mental turmoil. He himself played Berg-Ejvind, the Icelandic outlaw forced to climb ever higher into the mountains to evade capture by the region's sheriff. Sjöström captured the rhythm of pastoral life, and the pleasures and pain accompanying it. His location shooting in northern Sweden underlined man's struggle against a relentless adversary — Nature herself. Three years after its premiere in Stockholm, *The Outlaw and His Wife* opened in Paris, to rapturous praise. Louis Delluc, the foremost critic of the time, exclaimed: "Here without doubt is the most beautiful film in the world. Victor Sjöström has directed it with a dignity that is beyond words."

City Lights (1931)
Chaplin's most moving film ends, as usual, with the tramp abandoned by the world, but Chaplin the director was never more sensitive than in his arrangement of the closing sequence. As the flower-girl presses a coin and a rose with charity into Charlie's hand, she abruptly realises that this is the man who helped her in her blindness. Charlie gnaws desperately at the flower, his expression a rapturous blend of tears and joy. *City Lights* features some of the funniest passages in all Chaplin — the

boxing match in which the little man sports his bowler hat and bounces around the ring as though on springs, and the party scene when he swallows a whistle and peeps like a chaffinch as a pompous baritone attempts to perform. Quintessentially human, the Chaplin of *City Lights* may scale the peaks of fortune and plumb the depths of misery, but in the end he seems as bereft as when he entered the film, snoring in the lap of a statue dedicated to... prosperity.

La grande illusion (1937)

After seeing Jean Renoir's film at university, I returned to it in the mid-1980s, when Janus asked me to write and deliver the commentary for a laser disc release. The stylised nostalgia, the warmth of the sentiments, and the courage of its faith in human friendship have always fascinated me. Renoir manages to make his characters empathetic, whether aristocrat, bourgeois or even the redoubtable Rauffenstein (Erich von Stroheim) as commander of the fortress in Alsace, where the French soldiers are held as prisoners of war. Renoir, a confirmed pacifist, adumbrates the idea of mutual respect among those involved in conflicts such as the Great War of 1914–1918, irrespective of national or racial distinctions. He achieves this with humour, realism and a touch of romance. Boeildieu (Pierre Fresnay) helps his friend Maréchal (Jean Gabin) to escape, with a gesture of chivalry that transcends the bitterness of the war. Renoir's *La règle du jeu* may be held in higher esteem by critics, but the humanism of *La grande illusion* is for me more engaging.

Double Indemnity (1944)

Film noir gained momentum during and after World War II, often overlapping with other genres—the gangster film, the thriller, the private eye movie. Billy Wilder and Raymond Chandler endowed *Double Indemnity* with a feast of crackling dialogue, and Wilder's direction exploits the feverish, nocturnal energy of southern California. John F. Seitz, Wilder's cinematographer of choice, was at the peak of a career that ran from 1916 to 1960. His lighting of Barbara Stanwyck's home is a miraculous meld of shadow and shafts of moonlight. At the heart of the film stands an undeclared duel between Fred MacMurray as the insurance salesman intoxicated by a scheming Stanwyck and

Edward G. Robinson as the cigar-chomping investigator who will bring him down as surely as Pacino brings down De Niro in *Heat.*

Mildred Pierce (1945)

The Hollywood film noir in its heyday owed much to producers like Val Lewton, Mark Hellinger and Jerry Wald. *Mildred Pierce*, which won Joan Crawford her one and only Oscar for Best Actress, puts all the right ingredients in the blender: ambition, lust, jealousy, betrayal and, of course, crime. James M. Cain was the "noir" novelist par excellence, with *The Postman Always Rings Twice* and *Double Indemnity* to his credit as well as *Mildred Pierce*, all three books using a first-person narration, which Michael Curtiz maintained for this film. If the essence of film noir is the conflict between darkness and light, then Ernest Haller's jet-black shadows in *Mildred Pierce* communicate perfectly the sense of malice that lurks beneath the sunny streets of Glendale and Malibu. Curtiz draws the villainy out of each character, ranging from the oleaginous charms of Jack Carson as Mildred's would-be beau to the duplicity of Zachary Scott as the lover who sponges off Mildred's success as a restaurateur. However, neither man matches the venomous scheming of Mildred's spoiled daughter Veda, whose portrayal by 17-year-old Ann Blyth earned her an Academy Award nomination for Best Supporting Actress.

My Darling Clementine (1946)

I came first to the cinema via the Western. The authentic Hollywood Western, not the pastiche world of Old Shatterhand or "The Man with No Name." Once nourished by the Westerns of John Ford and Anthony Mann, one cannot take seriously the "modernist" variations on the genre by Sergio Corbucci and Sergio Leone, or the even more flagrant "post-modernist" work of Quentin Tarantino. For not only the myth matters, but also the emotional kick and the richness of character one associates with the great classic Westerns. Pacing, too, was important, which may explain why the leisurely Westerns of Howard Hawks have always remained something of a blind spot for me.

Although he made some disappointing movies, Ford put scarcely a foot wrong when it came to Westerns. In 2003,

I visited Monument Valley and the locations for films like *The Searchers* and *Cheyenne Autumn*. The result was a book on the affinities between Ford's images of the west and the paintings of Frederic Remington, Charles M. Russell and Charles C. Schreyvogel. The essential core of Ford's work, however, dealt with human relations—not just between men and women, but between brothers, families and among the Navajos whom Ford respected and cherished. *My Darling Clementine* appealed to me because of the emotional authority and poignancy of two memorable scenes: when Henry Fonda plucks up courage to ask Cathy Downs on to the alfresco dance floor; and when Victor Mature, for once not over-acting, shares with Alan Mowbray a recital of "To Be and Not To Be" in a crowded, hostile saloon.

Out of the Past (1947)
The film noir genre reached its apogee with the release of *Out of the Past* in 1947. The production was blessed with a rare constellation of talent: director Jacques Tourneur, cinematographer Nicolas Musuraca, composer Roy Webb, and actors Robert Mitchum, Kirk Douglas and 22-year-old Jane Greer. A retired private eye, Mitchum unexpectedly finds himself sucked into the quicksands of duplicity prepared by a scheming Douglas, and his fate unfolds in a dense yet lucid pattern of flashbacks. The architecture of film noir, with its inky-dark buildings, rain-slicked streets and human silhouettes, is captured to perfection by Musuraca's camerawork, notably in San Francisco and Acapulco. This is a film that you slip into again and again, like a pair of comfortable shoes, and you marvel at the hard-boiled dialogue and the mesmerising performances by Mitchum and Greer. *Out of the Past* proves that Tourneur had a talent as versatile as anyone's in Hollywood during the 1940s. The horror film *Cat People*, the superb Western *Canyon Passage*, and *Out of the Past* are all the work of a master.

Sunset Boulevard (1950)
Billy Wilder enjoyed his finest years at Paramount, and *Sunset Boulevard* remains a delight, from the sheer outrageousness of the opening scene, as William Holden's struggling screenwriter addresses the audience from beyond the grave, and the film's long central flashback begins. Writing with Charles Brackett for

the sixth time, Wilder delivers a sizzling satire on Hollywood past and present, lacing his narrative with a genuine degree of affection towards his characters. Who can forget Gloria Swanson as the star of yesteryear, telling Holden that "I am big. It's the pictures that got small." Or Erich von Stroheim as the imperturbable butler who guards all the secrets of his mistress's past with loyalty and elegance? Or the appearance of names by 1950 mostly unremembered: Buster Keaton, H. B. Warner, Anna Q. Nilsson and, of course, Cecil Be DeMille, who is persuaded to work just one more time with Swanson?

Summer Interlude (1950)

Seeing this early Bergman gem at the National Film Theatre in 1959 revealed the exquisite radiance of the Swedish summer, fleeting though it may be. I learned later that *Summer Interlude* had been inspired by Bergman's first encounter with love, during the 1930s. The complex weave of flashbacks manifested Bergman's technical mastery, and proved an augury of his suite of great films of the 1950s. As did his use of mirrors in the interior sequences, and his idiosyncratic, playful sense of humour that keeps the shadow of death at bay. Maj-Britt Nilsson as the ballerina haunted by the tragic loss of her young lover was the first actress to weather Bergman's insistence on the most ruthless of close-ups. The film also confirmed the stature of Gunnar Fischer as Bergman's cinematographer, a maestro of monochrome if ever there was one.

Shane (1953)

A child's introduction to the struggle between good and evil arrives via the playground or the movies, and this eternal conflict has never been better expressed than in the classic Hollywood Western. As I wrote much later in the *Wall Street Journal*, "*Shane* boasted an impeccable pedigree: a much-praised maiden novel by Jack Schaefer; a screenplay by Pulitzer Prize winner A. B. Guthrie, who had himself grown up in Montana; the flawless Alan Ladd as the hero; and George Stevens at the helm, having won an Academy Award a few months earlier for *A Place in the Sun*." The villains in *Shane* are not the "Injuns" but a rapacious cattle baron and his henchmen who seek to drive Van Heflin's Joe Starrett off his modest ranch in Wyoming.

Ladd as Shane, the mysterious bounty hunter who drifts into the valley, embodies the knight in shining armour, a one-man Cavalry, and a righter of wrongs whose own past leaves him in search of redemption. I identified with young Joey as he gazes in admiration at Shane's skills with the fist and the Colt, and I already admired the laconic dialogue, and the sinister, vulpine charm of Jack Palance's baddie. Should I already have surmised that such adulation might lead to a Trumpist America where everyone has a gun and the devil take the hindmost?

Ugetsu (1953)

My friend John Gillett once introduced a screening of *Ugetsu* at London's National Film Theatre and emphasised Kenji Mizoguchi's refusal to use a zoom lens. But this magician of the Japanese cinema could direct his camera with bewildering dexterity. Genjuro the potter is forced to flee his village by marauding troops of the Shibata clan in the late 16th century, and finds himself forever separated from his wife and little son after being attacked by pirates on Lake Biwa. He falls under the mesmeric influence of the mysterious Lady Wakasa, who is a spirit from the dead. Genjuro may never be reunited with his wife, but Mizoguchi recounts his story with poetic sensibility, and the cinematography of the great Kazuo Miyagawa furnishes the potter's tragic destiny with a haunting, spectral beauty. Mizoguchi directed almost a hundred films, but only a few have been distributed in the West. His creative partnership with the actress (and later director) Kinuyo Tanaka underscored his appreciation of a woman's all too often submissive role in Japanese society.

Senso (1954)

For years and years, *Senso* was unavailable on any platform. But to discover Visconti's masterpiece in middle life was prodigious. Camillo Boito's slender story has been expanded into a complex, sumptuous, and tightly-wound descent into emotional perdition. Set in Venice on the brink of the Risorgimento, *Senso* follows a countess' infatuation with a feckless Austrian army officer. Flouting the social conventions of their day, these lovers feed on stolen moments and clandestine meetings. Betrayed, the countess exacts her revenge. Visconti shows the fading beauty

of Venice as a metaphor for the decay, decadence, and chaos of
Italian civilisation in the 1860s. The struggle between destruction and construction remained a dialectic dear to Visconti
throughout his career: the destruction of the old order in society,
and the construction of a new, more democratic way of life.
Dominating the soundtrack, the languorous, serpentine chords
of Bruckner's *Symphony No. 7* underline the tragic destiny of
both Italy and the film's ill-matched lovers.

Floating Clouds (1955)

Mikio Naruse may at first appear the most detached, even severe,
of the great Japanese directors, but in *Floating Clouds* he made
a film governed by suppressed emotion. Yukiko and Kengo are
brought together by war, but their illicit love unravels in the
aftermath of Japan's defeat. "For us," sighs Yukiko, "the past is
the only reality." I adore the way in which Naruse expresses the
melancholy of the affair—mournful skies, furtive meetings, the
cold weather that not even the warmth of the *kotatsu* (a portable
electric heater under the table in many a Japanese home) can
alleviate. The locations contribute to the mood, notably in the
final part of the film, on the subtropical island of Yakushima,
with its incessant rain and precipitous mountain trails. The
legendary Hideko Takamine endows the character of Yukiko
with feline sensitivity, while Masayuki Mori (already a star in
Rashomon and *Ugetsu*) brings his usual finesse to the part of
Kengo.

The Seventh Seal (1957)

We all cite Bergman's breakthrough movie as a landmark in
world cinema. But why, exactly? Looking back to my first
discovery of the film, I realise that what struck me most was
the convincing way Bergman used a medieval framework in
which to pose fundamental questions that, in a modern context,
might have seemed banal. Fears and virtues thus took on human
form, from a flour-faced, black-cloaked Death to the innocence
embodied in the clown and his wife, Jof and Mia. Bergman,
although already almost forty years of age, could touch young
people's emotions to a remarkably vivid degree in scenes like
the Knight's reunion with his wife after long years away on the
Crusades, and in his anguished soliloquy in the rural church,

seeking the nature of God. And it was a "God" in the most abstract sense. I think that most of my generation who were moved by *The Seventh Seal* were troubled not so much by religious doubts as by a need to explain the wonder of the universe, in a way that Terrence Malick would dwell on much later.

Ashes and Diamonds (1958)

Andrzej Wajda convinced me from the first time I saw *Ashes and Diamonds* of his stature as the most versatile, most lyrical, and most sensitive of all the directors to emerge from Eastern Europe during the 1950s. As a reflection of a country morally and physically shattered by years of conflict, *Ashes and Diamonds* is unparalleled. The film also introduced a charismatic new star, Zbigniew Cybulski, who would die in a needless train accident in 1967, thus inspiring one of Wajda's most searching films, *Everything for Sale*. In *Ashes and Diamonds*, Cybulski plays Maciek, the young, handsome intellectual whose university aspirations have been frustrated by the war. A member of the underground resistance to the Nazis, Maciek is betrayed by his procrastination. His love for a young barmaid, coupled with the gathering disillusion that accompanies the final stages of a war, dissuades him from assassinating the Communist party secretary. Like the fireworks that pierce the sky at the climax, Wajda's flamboyant masterpiece assumes the form of a grand gesture, revelling in its short-lived romantic agony.

Vertigo (1958)

Tantivy's publication of Robin Wood's book on Hitchcock contributed to a revival of esteem for *Vertigo*, which had not performed well on first release. By 2012 it had risen to first place in the *Sight and Sound* poll for the Greatest Films of All Time. Inspired by a French thriller entitled *The Living and the Dead*, by Boileau-Narcejac, Hitch and his screenwriters developed and enriched the doppelgänger theme into a subjective thriller, following James Stewart as the retired detective inveigled into shadowing a beautiful woman who seems to be in contact with the spirit of a long-dead aristocrat, Carlotta Valdes. The treachery that eventually engulfs him renders Stewart a tragic figure, well-meaning if slow on the uptake, while Kim Novak becomes the most archetypal of Hitchcock's mysterious blondes. San Francisco and the coast of northern California are filmed in gorgeous VistaVision by Robert Burks, who had already won an Academy Award for Hitchcock's *To Catch a Thief*. What makes *Vertigo* so mesmerising to watch, however, is Hitchcock's meticulous blocking of each shot, and the editing that allows no escape from the sinister spiral of deceit at the core of the film.

Hiroshima mon amour (1959)

Almost a full year before Godard's *Breathless*, *Hiroshima mon amour* effected a revolution in the narrative technique of cinema. Not just because the editing took so many risks, turning conventional screen chronology on its head, but also by virtue of its emotional force. While Godard would follow Brecht in distancing the audience from romance and anguish, Resnais and the novelist Marguerite Duras did the opposite. The fleeting love affair between a Japanese architect and a French film actress on location in Hiroshima has a fervour heightened by memories of the Occupation in France. Emmanuelle Riva's off-screen reflections owe their strength to Duras' lapidary, almost incantatory prose. In *Varsity*, the Cambridge weekly paper, I concluded my review by saying that "[Riva's] excitement and anguish are conveyed with perfect timing and intensity, and within all the staggering audacity and beauty of its exposition, *Hiroshima mon amour* remains a love story both plaintive and magnificent."

L'avventura (1960)

Before *L'avventura*, all movies advanced at high speed. Or so it seemed when Antonioni decided to stretch time like elastic— not filming in slow motion but rather dwelling on the ooze of daily life. His characters were forever on the brink of boredom, their emotions hovering in the face of decisions. *L'avventura* deals with every aspect of infidelity—its impetuousness, its recklessness, its reverberations, its implications—while also perceiving the green shoots of love emerging from the seemingly aimless journey through Sicily undertaken by Monica Vitti and Gabriele Ferzetti. In the 1962 *Sight and Sound* poll for the Greatest Films of All Time, *L'avventura* came second only to Renoir's *Rules of the Game*. In a review of the film that year,

I noted that "Antonioni tends to 'write' more with his images than with his dialogue." The allusiveness, the exquisite sensitivity, and the visual architecture of this masterpiece have been unjustly forgotten in the intervening decades.

The World of Apu (1960)

The original negatives of Satyajit Ray's great trilogy were seriously damaged in a London fire in 1993. Thanks to more than eight months of meticulous application, the Academy Film Archive in Hollywood and the Criterion Collection managed to restore the films from, literally, a pile of ashes. The result is dazzling in 4K; the monochrome image gleams with life, the blacks intense and the whites refulgent. In the final film of the trilogy, Apu has become an indolent and feckless intellectual who survives on his gracious demeanour. Coerced into marriage in almost farcical circumstances, he finds himself beguiled by his young bride. When she dies abruptly during childbirth, Apu is distraught. He leaves Calcutta on a journey of atonement, his despair expressed in a magniloquent image as he casts away the sheets of his novel on a remote hillside. Thanks to his school mate, Pulu, he returns from the wilderness, as it were, and seeks out his 5-year-old son. The secret of Ray's creative genius stems from an accumulation of details and gestures; his characters live within their environment, rather than against its backdrop. As an undergraduate and aspiring writer when *The World of Apu* appeared, I identified vividly with Apu and all that Ray sought to convey.

La dolce vita (1960)

Fellini captured the accidie of the late 1950s with his supremely confident caricature of the chattering classes of Rome and invoked the wrath of the Vatican, who scorned his "vulgar and grotesque satire." Writing in *Varsity* in October 1961, I said that "the film seems to excel in three departments. First, as a devastating report on Italian High Society (Fellini wanted to call it Babylon, 2000 A.D.); secondly, as a splendid model of imaginative and entertaining film technique; and thirdly, as the detailed examination of a man's inability to come to terms satisfactorily with his community." The swagger and scope of Fellini's camera movements in *La dolce vita* have been imitated (notably by

Paolo Sorrentino), but never matched. Marcello Mastroianni as the world-weary journalist who wanders through night-clubs and into the arms of beautiful women became an international star thanks to this box-office triumph.

Jules and Jim (1962)

The two salient factors that made the French New Wave so innovatory involved image and music. In Truffaut's early classic, *Jules and Jim*, Raoul Coutard's camera conveys all the energy and spontaneity of the story. Georges Delerue's music has an infectious, effervescent zest that captures both the optimism and the melancholy of this ménage à trois in the France of the Belle Epoque and the Great War. Truffaut was fascinated by the writings of Henri-Pierre Roché, 74 years of age when he published *Jules and Jim*. Truffaut even claimed that it was his discovery of the novel, when he was a 21-year-old film critic, which made him determined to take up directing. With this film, Jeanne Moreau established herself as an icon of French cinema. Catherine captivates Jules and Jim with her capricious nature, and neither has the strength or the authority to contain her. Forever convinced of her own innocence, Catherine declares that one only loves truly for a single moment in life. The pursuit of that moment animates the entire film. Truffaut described it as "a hymn to love, and perhaps a hymn to life itself," and its freewheeling brio still shines with a welcome sincerity.

Lawrence of Arabia (1962)

Once a cherished project of Anthony Asquith's, *Lawrence of Arabia* became an epic for the ages under David Lean's inspired direction. No other film has caught the desert's dangerous beauty so persuasively. I can still remember the very first press screening, at the Odeon in Leicester Square, on the morning of December 10, 1962. The film looked and sounded magnificent, of course, but for me the personality of T. E. Lawrence elevated the narrative. Robert Bolt's screenplay had somehow condensed *Seven Pillars of Wisdom* into a thrilling odyssey across the Middle East, revealing Colonel Lawrence in all his flawed, flamboyant glory. Thanks to Peter O'Toole's performance, one is never surprised by the mesmeric hold that this eccentric officer exercised over the Bedouin forces between

1916 and 1918, but also over his superiors in the British army, including General Allenby. Lean's team combined to formidable effect—the camerawork of Freddie Young, the editing of Anne Coates, and the stirring score by Maurice Jarre. In the mid-1990s, I met Young at a reception and told him proudly that I had just acquired *Lawrence* on laser disc. "It looks better on a 92-foot screen," he growled, quite rightly!

An Autumn Afternoon (1962)

This was Ozu's final film, and distils his abiding themes with discreet equanimity. For me, Ozu was the Chopin of the cinema; his works are often melancholy, even heart-rending, yet they also contain moments of wit and joy. I was not even aware of Ozu when I was at university, but now, after watching his films through the decades, I greet his actors like old friends. Each has a distinctive personality—Nobuo Nakamura sly and malicious, Haruko Sugimura disgruntled, Eijiro Tono wistful and downcast, Chishu Ryu the most emblematic of all Ozu's actors. The fear of loneliness runs like a leitmotif through Ozu's greatest films, and Ryu's widower in *An Autumn Afternoon* must come to terms with his daughter's inevitable marriage and departure from home. Male companionship serves as a solace, as does nostalgia fuelled by the ceaseless sipping of sake. The eloquence of empty rooms in Ozu, and the serene, almost breathtaking beauty of Ryu's daughter Michiko (Shima Iwashita), shows a kinship with Vermeer's paintings. As I write these lines in 2024, Shima Iwashita is still alive, one of the last links with the world of Yasujirō Ozu.

Le feu follet (1963)

Louis Malle was always a guilty pleasure of mine, ever since I saw *Les amants* in my first year at Cambridge and heard the Brahms Sextet with its sensual chords accompanying the pretty explicit love scene (for the late 1950s at least). Malle, independently wealthy, was never properly accepted by the more radical members of the New Wave, but went his own happy way, exploring various genres, up to the striking later works like *Atlantic City* and *Damage*. *Le feu follet* offers a portrait of Alain Leroy, a man on the verge of suicide who decides to pay a farewell visit to his friends and enemies in the bourgeois-bohemian circles of Paris. Maurice Ronet plays the part in a single register, giving an everyday careless cadence to what, in the novel, is the incantatory language of Drieu La Rochelle. Alone, he scrutinises the minutiae of his surroundings. In company, he behaves with a languid, contemplative nonchalance. "Life flows too slowly in me," he mutters to himself as he caresses the gun he keeps wrapped fastidiously in a silk scarf. Alain's male friends reproach him for being trapped in adolescence, refusing the certainty that comes with adulthood. Former mistresses, however, reassure him. The one woman who might save him, Solange (Alexandra Stewart, who would share Malle's life for several years), is already wrapped and numbered in a golden bourgeois cage, with a husband as vigilant as a viper. *Le feu follet* lingers like a Spätlese wine, sweet and not quite over-ripe, full of regret, tenderness, and a yearning for love.

Chimes at Midnight (1966)

Welles was in pre-production on *Chimes at Midnight* when I first met him, so when the film appeared at Cannes in 1966, I was excited to find that it contained some of the finest sequences Welles ever directed, with his instinctive genius for camera placement as well as close-ups. The Battle of Shrewsbury conveys the authentic savagery of medieval warfare, and Fritz Mueller's editing gives the sequence a rhythm and agitation worthy of Eisenstein. Welles takes dialogue from Shakespeare's *Henry IV Pt 1* and *Pt 2*, *Henry V*, *Richard II* and *The Merry Wives of Windsor*. The figure of Falstaff (played, of course, by a paunchy Welles) dominates the film and its concern with death—the death of the king, the death of Falstaff, and the death of "Merrie England." The eloquence of Shakespeare elevates the most poignant scenes in *Chimes at Midnight*, with John Gielgud superb as Henry IV, and Keith Baxter a frosty Prince Hal, who dismisses Falstaff with the words, "I know thee not, old man. Fall to thy prayers. How ill white hairs become a fool and jester."

The Conformist (1970)

On the fiftieth anniversary of the release of Bertolucci's finest work, I wrote in *The Wall Street Journal*: "It is a tale of treachery and self-loathing and yet, clothed first in the elegant, sensual

prose of Alberto Moravia's 1951 novel, and then in the exhilarating mise-en-scène of Bernardo Bertolucci, it seizes one by
the throat and maintains its grip throughout what is nothing
less than a visual and psychological roller-coaster ride worthy
of Orson Welles and Josef von Sternberg at their best." Bertolucci captures the malodorous essence of fascism, as the sinister
Marcello (Jean-Louis Trintignant) struts and frets his way
around the stage of Mussolini's new Rome, betraying friends
and ideals alike, before stumbling into a state of subservience.
The predominant tone of Vittorio Storaro's cinematography is
an icy blue that matches Marcello's coldness and indifference.
An intricate web of flashbacks is knitted with breathtaking skill
into a narrative both intimate and reflective of issues such as
political commitment, marital fidelity, and the influence of the
Catholic church.

Five Easy Pieces (1970)
Despite its tiny budget (less than $1 million dollars, according
to the director, Bob Rafelson), *Five Easy Pieces* captured the
mood of the United States in that watershed period between the
idealism and innocence of the 1960s and the encroaching materi-
alism of the 1970s. Jack Nicholson's flash-bulb charisma makes
Bobby Dupea almost a tragic figure, the world-weary scion of
a privileged musical family who feels himself a failure at every
level. Shot on location on and around Vancouver Island, the
film exudes melancholy and compassion for a man whose talent
as a pianist has been numbed by life and his narcissistic liaisons
with women. Carole Eastman's screenplay crackles with wit to
offset the poignancy and despair of Bobby's drift through the
chilly, autumnal wasteland of the American northwest. I have
watched this movie again and again in different decades, but it
reveals new facets at each fresh viewing.

The Godfather (1972), The Godfather Part II (1974)
Until I saw *The Godfather*, I had always assumed that a massive
commercial hit could not have the depth and richness of a great
European movie. But Coppola's first masterpiece did not just
offer a panoply of fascinating and engaging characters, it also
achieved the sumptuousness of grand opera. At the time of its
opening, we were unaware of the upheavals that had afflicted

the production from start to finish. We could only marvel at the teamwork that had yielded such an engrossing experience: the music of Nino Rota, the cinematography of Gordon Willis, the production design of Dean Tavoularis, Marlon Brando's majestic performance, and above all the screenplay by novelist Mario Puzo and Coppola himself. And then the joy of watching the sequel in 1974, which to some degree surpassed the original. By that stage we empathised with so many of the actors who had come to the fore in *The Godfather*: Al Pacino, Robert Duvall, John Cazale, Talia Shire and others. Numerous films and TV series (notably *The Sopranos*) have sought to equal the passion and narrative skill of *The Godfather*, but Coppola's films remain beyond reach after more than half a century.

The Discreet Charm of the Bourgeoisie (1972)
Luis Buñuel deserves his place as the greatest of all Spanish directors (despite the fine achievements of Saura and Almodóvar), but ironically some of his best and most likeable work was made in France. In *The Discreet Charm of the Bourgeoisie*, Buñuel showed his diabolical skill in deflating the pretensions of a group of friends, headed by a corrupt Ambassador (the suave and malicious Fernando Rey), as they stride out in search of a dinner. They are thwarted in the most unexpected ways and confronted by hypocritical members of the established order: the police, the army and the church. With his ever-reliable screenwriter Jean-Claude Carrière, Buñuel mocks their "discreet charm" with a steady flow of trenchant witticisms, keeping his audience on its toes with dream sequences as surrealistic as they are implausible and underlining the lust and greed that drive those in power.

Illumination (1973)
Krzysztof Zanussi is the most underrated director of his generation, a brilliant analyst who develops ideas on screen with the same rigour as others develop characters. A lapsed physicist, he has a rare grasp of the problems and dilemmas faced by scientists in the postwar world. *Illumination* follows the life and career of a young physics student with a density and concision that speak not only of personal involvement but also of artistic maturity on the part of the Polish director himself. Like all men in Zanussi's

world, Franciszek does not succumb to self-pity, but he yearns for an interlude in which to assess his progress, to question the values by which he lives, and to find a moral justification for his behaviour. This engrossing film illuminates the high points of Franciszek's life: an affair with a mature woman, marriage, the birth of his first child, his army service, and a climbing expedition during which a close friend falls to his death.

Kagemusha (1980)

Many academics tend to damn Kurosawa with faint praise. Too many swordfights, too much grunting and roaring from Toshiro Mifune. Easy to forget, however, that Kurosawa opened the windows on to the Japanese cinema when *Rashomon* won the Golden Lion in Venice in 1951. Also that he pioneered the high-speed travelling shot that's an essential component of modern cinema technique. His narrative verve was applied not just to period dramas (jidai-geki) but to contemporary subjects in films as varied as *Ikiru*, *High and Low* and *Dersu Uzala*. Despite the formal brilliance of masterpieces like *Seven Samurai* and *Ran*, I have a soft spot for *Kagemusha*. Tatsuya Nakadai plays the unfortunate thief whose resemblance to the real-life Shingen Takeda, a samurai daimyo, renders him indispensable in a 16th-century clan war. When the warlord is killed in battle, his double or "kagemusha" finds himself obliged to fight for the honour of his clan. Wounded, unmasked and disgraced, he staggers towards the river and his corpse drifts downstream, accompanied by the bedraggled pennants of his former lord and master. One of the finest and most poignant closing sequences in all cinema.

Three Brothers (1981)

Rosi's political fury is tempered by an emotional warmth and tenderness, exemplified by *Three Brothers*. This masterpiece, alongside his adaptation of Carlo Levi's literary classic, *Christ Stopped at Eboli*, demonstrated in Rosi an understanding of the need for tolerance in a society torn apart by economic extremes. Charles Vanel played the widowed father in *Three Brothers* at the age of 89. Each of his sons affords a distinctive perspective on life: Philippe Noiret, the judge under threat from the Mafia; Michele Placido, the militant factory worker; and

Vittorio Mezzogiorno, the counsellor who deals with unruly boys. Rosi describes the poverty of the region with unobtrusive ease, finding an everyday poetry in the life of the remote village where the boys grew up. And from the arguments between these brothers there emerges a wisdom that leaves you profoundly moved.

The Silence of the Lambs (1991)

One of only four films to have won all the major Academy Awards (Best Picture, Best Director, Best Actor, Best Actress), *The Silence of the Lambs* was remarkable in that it opened in January, and yet retained its buzz throughout the year until Oscar-voting time. I saw it in Santa Monica while attending the American Film Market for *Variety*. I knew from the wintry, baleful chords of Howard Shore's music over the opening shots of Jodie Foster running through the woods that there would be no escape from the clutches of this thriller. Anthony Hopkins as the cannibalistic Hannibal Lecter wields a psychological hold over Foster's plucky Clarisse Starling, the FBI apprentice on the track of a serial killer. Their quiet scenes together exude as much menace as the most violent moments in the film. Jonathan Demme's range as a director was remarkable, from sexploitation movies like *Caged Heat* to comedies like *Melvin and Howard*, and social dramas such as *Philadelphia*. Along with *The Exorcist* and *Se7en*, *The Silence of the Lambs* ranks as one of the most sophisticated horror stories ever to have emerged from mainstream Hollywood.

The Double Life of Véronique (1991)

Only the most discerning critic had seen or heard much of Krzysztof Kieślowski when his spell-binding *The Double Life of Veronique* premiered at Cannes in May 1991. Irène Jacob served as muse to Kieślowski even as she was his Galatea. In the performance of a lifetime, she makes of her two characters a delicate blend of vivacity and introspection. She acts with the flawless candour born of total confidence in her director: her look transcends the words she utters. She confides in the camera and, by extension in us, her audience. Slawomir Idziak's camera bathes the film in a golden light, and Zbigniew Preisner's music, high-pitched and often choral, raises the psychological tension as each "Véronique" becomes aware of the other's spiritual existence. Kieślowski controls the many locations in Paris and Kraków with such ease that what might otherwise be regarded as science fiction seems anchored in an everyday reality. The result is a film that addresses love and grief with singular intimacy and intensity.

Basic Instinct (1992)

I had known Paul Verhoeven slightly from the very early 1960s, when I first toured Holland for an article on Dutch cinema in *The Financial Times*. I enjoyed his cocky, nothing sacred approach to cinema in features like *Turkish Delight* and *Katie Tippel*, but I was startled when, in 1987, his first Hollywood production, *RoboCop*, proved a corrosive satire on American society and its love of weapons. He would go on to pillory the U.S. military (*Starship Troopers*), Las Vegas (*Showgirls*) and the excesses of scientific experiment (*Hollow Man*). *Basic Instinct* opened the Cannes Festival in 1992, and deservedly so, for it was as smoothly constructed as a great machine, and excelled in three areas: the cinematography of Jan de Bont, the music of Jerry Goldsmith, and the production design by veteran Terence Marsh (who had been the art director on *Doctor Zhivago*). Each time I watch *Basic Instinct*, I find that it's compelling by virtue of Verhoeven's flair for what I might term obsessional narrative. Michael Douglas' detective finds himself dazzled by Sharon Stone's femme fatale, and plunges headlong into an affair that overwhelms his life. Suddenly, at the age of 34, Stone became a major star and a film buff's guilty pleasure par excellence.

Heat (1994)

In his seminal account of the Vietnam War, *Dispatches*, Michael Herr referred to the "icy sound" of The Doors. "Icy" can be applied to Michael Mann and his Manichean vision of urban crime: the icy blue that dominates the imagery of *Heat*; the icy music by Elliot Goldenthal; and the icy performance of Robert De Niro as the master criminal at the core of the story. It's a film that one revisits with pleasure almost every year. Al Pacino revels in his role as the stressed-out cop determined to bring down De Niro, the bank robber in whom he senses a kindred spirit. Somehow Mann merges scenes of ferocious violence with moments of surprising tenderness. Jon Voight and Val Kilmer are just two among a supporting cast that make *Heat* the most compelling heist movie of its period.

The Lord of the Rings (2001-2003)

Most of my intellectual friends damn the *LOTR* trilogy with faint praise. Some dismiss the films as aimed at youngsters; others find the action-driven plot too simplistic. Yet Peter Jackson remained faithful to the spirit, and for the most part to the letter, of Tolkien's monumental fantasy opus. By using the unfamiliar landscape of New Zealand, Jackson could create Tolkien's "Middle Earth" with convincing realism. Working with Richard Taylor and his Weta Workshop, Jackson presented such fanciful structures as Minas Tirith, Helm's Deep, and Isengard, and a panoply of dreadful creatures as the Orcs, Trolls, the monstrous spider Shelob, and the Balrog that almost drags the genial wizard Gandalf to his doom. Andrew Lesnie's cinematography, Howard Shore's majestic score, and the costumes and makeup all seem inspired by the ambition of the project. I have seen the three films in the cinema, on DVD, on Blu-ray, and most recently on 4K, and I still find myself immersed in a world at once more evil and more idealistic than our own.

Mulholland Drive (2001)

The polymath David Lynch directed the first great film of the new millennium, the perfect example of what in my youth we referred to as the "cinéma d'art et d'essai"—a work rich in ideas and experimental style. In a coming-of-age role, Naomi Watts plays the wide-eyed Midwesterner arriving in Hollywood in search of stardom, but her ambitions are sidelined by a series of weird developments that eventually lead her, like Alice, down the rabbit hole. Lynch sows his territory with any number of McGuffins, from a mysterious man in a gorilla suit to a sinister cowboy who intimidates Justin Theroux's irascible film director. And for seasoning, he scatters moments of antic wit into his narrative, skewering the pretensions of Hollywood executives along the way. The brunette Laura Harring is a deformed mirror image of Watts' blonde, and the two women's personalities converge like Alma and Elisabet in *Persona.* Angelo Badalamenti's eerie chords are harnessed by Lynch to the smooth, often furtive movements of Peter Deming's camera, creating a dreamlike mood in which even the most incongruous situation acquires a logic of its own.

The Master (2012)

There Will Be Blood had already startled me with its relentless power, but seeing *The Master* on its premiere in Venice confirmed that Paul Thomas Anderson was the most original American filmmaker of his generation. Rumour suggested that the jury wanted to give three major prizes, including the Golden Lion, to *The Master*, but compromise prevailed and the film had to be content with awards for Best Actor (Philip Seymour Hoffman) and director. At the Academy Awards the following spring, both Hoffman and Joaquin Phoenix were nominated, the former for Best Supporting Actor the latter for Best Actor, and Amy Adams for Best Supporting Actress. Strongly akin to L. Ron Hubbard, Hoffman's "Master" is a prince among charlatans, and takes under his wing a U.S. navy veteran (Phoenix) suffering from post-traumatic stress disorder—as it would come to be called. The dialectical struggle between these two extravagant individuals gradually takes you in its coils, laying bare the misleading hocus-pocus of so many cults, notably Scientology. More relevant than ever, it underlines the dangers of society's adulation of a strong male figure, in life or in politics. With its ravishing cinematography (in 65mm) by Mihai Malaimare, the music by Radiohead's Jonny Greenwood, and fine supporting performances by Adams and Jesse Plemons, *The Master* is the work of a true visionary.

An Officer and a Spy (2019)

I had admired Polanski's *Knife in the Water* in the early 1960s, and for him to make a film so perfectly paced, so controlled, so relevant as *J'accuse!* (the original and more appropriate French title) some six decades later was quite extraordinary. Brimming with ideas acutely relevant to the present geo-political arena, *J'accuse!* confronts the theme of anti-Semitism in the France of the 1890s, with the hapless army officer Alfred Dreyfus exiled to Devil's Island for a crime he did not commit. Polanski and the writer Robert Harris also expose the corruption and repression endemic in the highest echelons of the French army. Further-more they underline the courage of writers like Emile Zola, whose defence of press freedom resonates today. Jean Dujardin excels as the head of military intelligence who unearths the plot to discredit Dreyfus and have him condemned for treason. The fluency of the narrative, involving flashbacks, matches that of Polanski's finest work in *Rosemary's Baby*, *Chinatown* and *The Pianist*. The chilling first sequence, as Dreyfus is stripped of his military colours and his sword is broken in pieces, sets the tone for what is one of the finest historical dramas of the new century.

Acknowledgements

Many of the "flashbacks" in this book first appeared on the Criterion website, and I am very grateful to Peter Becker, president of Criterion, for permission to use them in an adapted form here. I have been amazed and delighted by Paul Cronin's enthusiasm for this project, and for his belief that there is a readership for my memoirs. I also wish to thank Daniel Rosenthal for his copy editing of the manuscript, as meticulous as his work alongside me for the *International Film Guide* in the late 1990s and early 2000s.

Most of all, my gratitude goes to those relatives, friends and colleagues who, across so many decades, have enabled me to write, edit, and publish so many books; as well as to all those at Criterion, *Variety*, and the Berlin and Venice Film Festivals with whom I have worked, and continue to work, in such harmony. I dedicate the book to them:

Ioan Allen, Kim Aubry, Alberto Barbera, William Becker†, Peter Becker, Sandrine Bentata, Françoise Buquet, Gerry Byrne, Sedgwick Clark, Elisabeth Cowie†, Nicholas Crane, Stefan Dreja, Walter Donohue, Hervé Dumont, Derek Elley, John Evans, Allen Eyles, Bengt Forslund, Christine von Fragstein, Christer Frunck†, Eric Gibson, Don Groves, Murray Grigor, Robert F. Hawkins†, Liz Helfgott, Kim Hendrickson, Gilles Jacob, Diane Jacobs, Margot S. Kernan†, Dieter Kosslick, Bob Krakoff†, Michela Lazzarin, Tom Luddy†, Torborg Lundell, Abbey Lustgarten, Anna-Maija Marttinen, Peter J. Meyer, Eric Mika, Laura Morris, Marco Müller, Julia Palau, Elizabeth Pauker, Michel Perrier, Eva Prinz, Anne Richardson†, Patrizio Rossi†, Shelley Ruston, Alan Rutsky†, Johanna Schiller, Howard Shore, Hy Smith, David Steavenson†, David Stratton, David Streiff, Thomas Struck, Ove Svensson†, Fumiko Takagi, Olli Tuomela†,

Jonathan Turell, Saul J. Turell†, Kari Uusitalo†, Dick Vriesman†, S.I. van Nooten†, Alice Waters, John Webber†, Thomas Yoseloff†.

Appendix

A Gap-Filling "Filmography"
Saul Kahan
Los Angeles Times, 22 November 1970

LONDON—With movies and books about movies reaching new horizons of popularity and prestige in this age of ever-mixing media, it was probably inevitable — a "World Filmography" listing the complete credits of virtually every theatrical film ever made.

This gargantuan answer to a cinema scholar's dreams is the crowning project of the Tantivy Press, a rapidly growing London publishing firm that puts out film books and film books only. The swift success story of Tantivy and its creator Peter Cowie parallels the dynamic growth of movies themselves in the last decade.

Cowie, a lanky, red-haired Englishman, started the Tantivy Press in 1962 in a minuscule office just off Oxford Street. From the outset it was the world's only English-language publishing firm devoted totally to books about movies. (The only similar operation was the French *Premier Plan* series, even then a much smaller house.)

The ground-breaking success of Tantivy, long before the peak of the current movie book boom, rested on the company's first publication, *The International Film Guide*, now in its seventh annual edition.

This 400-plus-page paperback offers information on everything from the year's film production in 33 countries to up-to-date lists of film archives, magazines, schools, art theaters and bookshops.

Reads Like Film Romance
With all the data, neither advertising nor editorial opinion are
avoided. Cowie reviews major movies, plugs obscure ones and
chooses five "directors of the year" for career surveys. For the
growing market of film buffs like himself, Cowie provides material such as director George Dunning's notes on the making of
Yellow Submarine, a survey of the world's top twenty cameramen, or a report on Hungary's three new female directors.

The birth of the *IFG* reads like a sequence from a movie
romance of behind-the-scenes publishing struggles. Young
movie buff, fresh out of Cambridge and cash, takes over father's
publishing firm; good name but no assets. Talks printers into
turning out one book on deferred payment. Grad sells ads
(San Francisco Film Festival, Mai Harris' subtitling company,
Cinema des Champs Élysées, Laterna Studio, Copenhagen,
etc.) and works long hours, aided by his wife.

The book comes out. The advertisers pay on time, and the
printers are paid. English sales go well and American distributor sells 3,000 copies in a few months. The National Library
Assn. of America adopts *IFG* as a standard reference book,
ensuring placement in hundreds of libraries.

Pan shot: tall, red-haired fellow ambling down Oxford
Street with paperback book under arm, happily oblivious to
traffic, shopping crowds, fog and mini-skirts. Fade Out.

His experience, says Cowie, 30, disproves a too-common
British publishing myth, that large amounts of capital are
needed to start something new. With the success of the *Film
Guide* came his well-received monographs on directors
Michelangelo Antonioni, Ingmar Bergman and Alain Resnais.
They appeared when the New Wave was still new and interest
was high in this formidable trio of foreign film artists.

Directed Mainly at Students
The following year saw the release of the second *IFG* and
the first edition of another gap-filling Tantivy paperback,
A Dictionary of the Cinema by Peter Graham. In 1965, Tantivy
Press published its first books devoted to specific directors—
Robin Wood's *Alfred Hitchcock's Films* and Cowie's *Orson
Welles*.

These, like the *IFG*, and all Tantivy books are square-ish (16x135 cm.) paperbacks directed mainly at students. Their reasonable prices and serious approach keep them out of what Cowie calls the "coffee table" class.

Later came the fourth *IFG* and Allan Eyles' book on the Marx Brothers, the latter issued just as Groucho travelled to the Vienna Film Festival for a Marx Brothers retrospective.

Subsequent Tantivy Press publications include an affectionate historical catalog of *The Musical Film*, *Buster Keaton*, *Science Fiction in the Cinema*, *Suspense in the Cinema*, *Religion in the Cinema*, *The Cinema of Alain Resnais*, *Four Great Comedians*, *The British Cinema: An Illustrated Index* and Allan Eyles' index to Westerns.

Authors David Robinson, John Baxter, Charles Higham and Joel Greenberg broke new ground in the fertile movie book boom with their critical histories of Hollywood in the '30s, '40s and '50s. And Cowie himself edited a "coffee table" book, *Seventy Years of Cinema*, for A. S. Barnes.

He recently brought out a new film magazine, *Focus on Film*, featuring in the first issue a large career article on the late Edward Everett Horton. In association with the London Film School, Tantivy is preparing a highly technical series of textbooks utilizing interviews with the world's leading film technicians.

Perhaps most impressive of all, Cowie has also embarked on the editorship of a "World Filmography," in which a worldwide research team will provide the complete credits of every feature film theatrically released in the history of the cinema. This mammoth work will take years and will comprise more than 70 volumes of approximately 600 pages and 300 illustrations each.

Nina Hibbin has compiled the first authoritative reference book on the films of Eastern Europe. Other forthcoming Tantivy titles include studies of Stanley Kubrick, Pier Paolo Pasolini and Carl Dreyer, as well as an index to gangster films, including references to the biographies of real gangsters. Plus: Paul O'Dell's *Griffith and the Rise of Hollywood*, Tom Vallance's *The Musical* and Anthony Slide's *The Rise of the American Cinema*.

All of the early writers of Tantivy books came to Cowie with their ideas. All of them, he reports, were willing to write for less guaranteed payment than they might have gotten from larger firms because they knew that their books, often labors of love, would be produced as they wished.

Gerald Pratley, a veteran reporter for the Canadian Broadcasting Co., authored Tantivy's recent book on the films of John Frankenheimer, Graham Petrie, a lecturer at Ontario's McMasters University, is writing a book on François Truffaut.

New Yorker Paul Jensen is doing one on Fritz Lang. Nebraskan Ken Wlaschin, director of the London film festival, is writing *Italian Cinema Since 1946.* Lucerne journalist Felix Bucher is doing German cinema, and Arne Svensson is covering Japanese films.

None of this increasing activity fazes Cowie, who still attacks his work with the zeal of a movie buff at a film festival. Most of the early work at Tantivy was done by Cowie, editorial assistant Eyles, and Cowie's wife, until the birth of their daughter. A cineaste dropping in at the Oxford Street cubicle for a chat might be asked to help pack books while he talked.

The adoption by Barnes has enabled Cowie to take on a staff of six. Friends are no longer enlisted as book packers, but Cowie has precious little time for talk.

Research in national film archives, printing in Holland, and ad hunting everywhere keep him traveling. He regularly attends at least two of Europe's many film festivals, Cannes and Oberhausen, Germany, the world's largest for short films. Last year he was an invited guest at the new Sydney Film Festival.

The last reel of our publishing romance finds our hero in his large new offices looking down on fashionable Bond Street. The phone rings, someone wants to do a book on *Citizen Kane.* British phones being what they are, he is cut off. But he'll call back. Fade out. But not the end.

Framed: Peter Cowie
Alan Stanbrook
Sight and Sound, Summer 1989

On 3 January this year, having turned 49 on Christmas Eve, Peter Cowie became a salaryman for the first time in his life. Known till then as a critic and as editor and publisher of the *International Film Guide*, Cowie joined *Variety* as its new European manager, with a brief to identify its role on the Continent and the means of getting there by 1992. As part of the deal, the *Film Guide* itself will now come out under the *Variety* banner.

It looks on the surface like one of those mid-career moves that make no sense to the outside world. What can Cowie, author of a biography of Ingmar Bergman, expert on Scandinavian cinema and advocate of the work of Francis Ford Coppola, have in common with a journal whose literary aspirations (as reflected in a recent comment on *Dangerous Liaisons*) stop at "stealing into 42 boudoirs for sexy $145,000, 15th lap, after $212,324 in 14th at 48"?

The answer, surprisingly, is quite a lot. By family background, inclination and sheer unflagging energy, Cowie is a unique combination of writer, businessman and advertisement salesman — an aesthete who never takes his eye off the bottom line. Americans can relate to somebody like him.

Born in 1939, Peter was the son of Donald Cowie, who founded the Tantivy Press after the war to publish books on specialist interests like antiques and farming. Peter grew up watching his father do the paste-up for his most successful title, an *Antiques Yearbook*, so the practical side of publishing held no terrors for him.

Educated at Charterhouse, Cowie became editor of the school magazine, the *Carthusian*, but at that time showed no interest in film. He can date his conversion precisely. It happened in 1959, when he went with his father and grandmother to the old Royal Cinema in the Edgware Road to see *I Am a Camera* because Cowie père was an Isherwood fan. But it was the second half of the bill that bowled him over. It was *The Seventh Seal*, which drove Cowie's grandmother out of the cinema because there was "too much talk about death" but opened his eyes to an art form of whose existence he had hitherto been largely ignorant.

Cowie went up to Cambridge in 1959 and quickly found fellow enthusiasts. Charles Barr became a close friend; so did Peter Graham, who widened Cowie's horizons by introducing him to *Cahiers du Cinéma*. There was another film buff there, too, at that time: David Frost. He edited *Granta* and Cowie became its business manager. Between them they published a special issue on cinema, which shared the same sense of discovery as work also being done at that time in *Oxford Opinion*. "You felt you were in on something expanding at the speed of light," says Cowie. Later, he worked under Philip Strick, films editor of *Varsity*, and succeeded him when he left. They ran two full pages a week on cinema without advertisements and Cowie did everything from editing to make-up and proof reading.

He came down from Magdalene College, Cambridge in 1962 with a 2:1 in history and convinced his father that there was a future in film publishing. Father made son a gift of the Tantivy Press as a vehicle with which to get started. Cowie had his sights set on what, in 1963, became the first of the Tantivy *International Film Guides*, now in its 27th year. From the start he declined to turn the product over to a design house, "which would have wrecked the finances," but did it himself. A tight rein on money is one of Peter Cowie's most celebrated traits.

Cowie had begun writing about films while he was at Cambridge. In 1960, he approached *Films and Filming*, then edited by Peter Baker, and wrote what was to be the first of many pieces for that publication—a profile of Spencer Tracy. Baker made him a studio correspondent, and on four days a month, young Cowie was whisked round the sets by studio car and got to see the tedious reality of how films are made— so different from academic theory. It's a practical grounding that has stood him in good stead and saved him from becoming too highfalutin. That, too, goes down well with his new employers.

As a critic he responds chiefly to those films that help to define the language of cinema, such as *Hiroshima, Mon Amour* and *L'Avventura*, although he admits that it took more than one viewing to persuade him in each case. And he is frank about blind spots—Godard, Ruiz and Greenaway. What he misses, in the cinema of the 1980s, is the commitment to the art of the film that was uppermost in the 1960s. He likes to quote Lindsay Anderson's observation that the '60s are both a threat and a reproach to the '80s.

At the same time, there are contradictions in Peter Cowie. He can be a champion of both rigorous intellectual cinema and its polar opposite. "Intensity of feeling," he says, "means more to me than the brilliance of technique. I respond to emotion in the cinema. I like Bergman's films of the '50s, for example, more than the later cerebral ones. And I can identify with directors like Truffaut and Cassavetes."

Cassavetes? There's a name that wouldn't be on the tip of every critic's tongue nowadays. What Cowie admires in him is not the American flavour, the improvisational hit-or-miss quality of early films like *Shadows*, but what he sees as a strong European undertow in his work—linking him to Welles, Coppola, Hitchcock, Kubrick and Michael Curtiz, all firm favourites.

Welles has been a particular influence on him. He was so struck with the use Welles made of what is now the Musée d'Orsay in *The Trial* that he resolved to write a book about him. The snag was that Welles never gave interviews, but Cowie wangled one by a white lie when the great man was staying at the Ritz, pretending to have a message for him from Spain, where Welles was to film next. They subsequently corresponded extensively.

An interesting, though far from definitive book came out of it. In his books on Welles and Coppola it is hard not to feel that Cowie is trying to appropriate them into a tradition which they only partly fit. His approach to Coppola, for instance, breaks down because the recurring theme that Cowie claims to find in his work (crisis within the family) maddeningly refuses to apply to many of the films— *Apocalypse Now,* for instance, and *Peggy Sue Got Married.*

Looking at the films in this way now smacks of an older, rather fusty critical method that Cowie seems not to have outgrown with the years. By the same token, is his regret for the ebullient 1960s, when there was a thirst for knowledge he does not find among filmgoers today, a sign of encroaching rage?

All this adds up to one very good reason why Cowie made the leap into management at the start of the year. He would never, perhaps, say so—not even to himself—but he may be approaching the end of a rich and productive period as a critic. The relative failure of his Coppola study as a critical assessment, coupled with its incisiveness as an account of what went wrong with the commercial structure of the Zoetrope studios, suggests that it marked a watershed in his career. So the *Variety* offer may have come at an opportune moment. "After 25 years," he says, "you feel you need a new challenge. If it had come a year earlier or a year later I probably wouldn't have done it."

His major contribution in those 25 years has been to put film publishing on the map. Along with Ian Cameron at Studio Vista, he pioneered the notion of film books in this country. He was in at the birth of auteur studies in Britain and throughout the 1960s and 1970s the name of Tantivy led the pack.

At the hub of the operation was the *International Film Guide*, planned originally as a small book about the state of art cinemas, but expanding into an ambitious survey of world production. Cowie says that he never imagined this would develop into the engine-room of the entire book. His aim, he says, is to have something from every country in the world but without a political slant.

The *Guide* was more influential overseas than at home, which has always niggled him. For many years Cowie focused in each edition on five directors—an idea lifted from Wisden, along with a strict taboo on second appearances. "After a hundred I got browned off," says Cowie; but Zanussi was one director who claims to have once got a visa on the strength of it. When he pointed out his own name on the cover as one of the directors of the year, he sailed through immigration. Till then, he reports (perhaps apocryphally) they had taken him for a washing machine salesman.

Did Cowie ever have film ambitions of his own? Apparently not; he always knew his limitations. He is a writer, not an artist—just as, though he loves music, he cannot play. The composers he admires most are those such as Berlioz and Sibelius who broke the mould. This interest in music encouraged him to start an *International Music and Opera Guide*, one of a fistful of Tantivy guides on various topics, including cycling and athletics.

These publications essentially mirrored Cowie's own enthusiasms (he's a keen cyclist and, these days, an armchair athletics fan—"I know all the world records and distances for athletics"). But although some were relatively successful, none sold as well as the *Film Guide* and they were discontinued when it became clear that the profits from the film book were going to pay the salaries of those working on the others.

One publication that was a huge success, though, was a *Scandinavian Guide*, not least because Cowie was able to persuade major companies, such as the airline SAS, to take 2,000 copies. This reflects Cowie's long and amicable association with Scandinavia dating back to 1963, when he went to Sweden to write a story about *The Silence* for the *Financial Times*. He fell immediately under the Swedish spell, became friendly with Jörn Donner, Bo Widerberg and other directors, and won a deserved reputation as the leading British writer on Scandinavian films. To this day a third of his friends are Scandinavian.

He later felt equally at home among the Dutch and for a time blazed a trail in writing about Dutch filmmakers such as Paul Verhoeven years before they won international reputations. Cowie, indeed, has always felt a greater rapport with foreigners than with the British. He did some lecturing in the United States in the early 1970s and found that he liked the American eagerness for new things. "They respect knowledge on a specialist subject," he says, "and if they feel you have new ideas they'll come up and listen." But he prefers to work for the Americans in Europe.

Long-standing *Variety* staff knew there was a keen wind blowing as early as the Berlin festival in February; in the interests of a fresh perspective, Cowie overturned traditional territorial preserves and reassigned them for the festival to films other than from their native countries. It caused a rumpus that took even Cowie by surprise. Who did he think he was? A cottage publisher grown too big for his boots? Or the coolest thing that's blown through the *Variety* hothouse? Time will tell, but in the meantime, in his neat Newman Street offices, Cowie sharpens his pencils and writes himself a memo listing what he plans to do that day—conscientious, compulsive, rather Scandinavian really.

Bibliography

Books by Peter Cowie

Ingmar Bergman, Motion Publications, London (pamphlet), 1961.

International Film Guide (editor), published annually by Tantivy
    Press from 1963 until 2003 (with distribution from 1993 to
    2003 by Hamlyn, then André Deutsch, and finally Faber
    and Faber), then other publishers (final edition 2012). Retired
    as Editor in 2003.

Antonioni-Bergman-Resnais, Tantivy Press, London; A.S. Barnes
    & Co., New York, 1963.

The Cinema of Orson Welles, Tantivy Press, London; A.S. Barnes
    & Co., New York, 1965. Revised 1973 as *A Ribbon of
    Dreams*. Reissued in late 1980s by Da Capo Press under
    original title.

Korda, Anthologie du Cinéma, L'Avant-Scène du Cinéma, Paris,
    1965.

Swedish Cinema, A. Zwemmer, London, 1966.

Seventy Years of Cinema, Tantivy Press, London; A.S. Barnes
    & Co., New York, 1967. Reissued as *Eighty Years of
    Cinema,* 1977.

Sweden 1 and 2, two volumes, Tantivy Press/A. Zwemmer,
    London, 1970.

Finnish Cinema, Tantivy Press, London; A.S. Barnes, New Jersey,
    1975. Enlarged. Revised edition 1990, VAPK-Publishing,
    Helsinki.

50 Major Film-Makers, A.S. Barnes, New Jersey, 1975.

Film in Sweden: Stars and Players, Tantivy Press, London,
    in co-operation with SFI, 1977.

Dutch Cinema, Tantivy, London; A.S. Barnes & Co., New York, 1979.

Ingmar Bergman: A Critical Biography. Scribner's, New York; Secker and Warburg, London, 1982. Reissued by Limelight, 1993.

Swedish Cinema from Ingeborg Holm to Fanny and Alexander, Svenska Institutet, Stockholm, 1985.

Max von Sydow, from The Seventh Seal *to* Pelle the Conqueror, Chaplin, Stockholm. Published simultaneously in Swedish and English, 1989.

Coppola, Scribner's, New York; André Deutsch, London, 1989; Faber and Faber, 1990). Revised and expanded edition André Deutsch, London, 2013; Applause Books, New York, 2014.

Le Cinéma des Pays Nordiques, Centre Georges Pompidou, Paris, 1990. Translated in English and published by the various Nordic film institutes in 1992.

World Cinema: Diary of a Day (editor), Mitchell Beazley, London, 1994.

Icelandic Films, Icelandic Film Fund, Reykjavik, 1995. Revised edition 2000.

Annie Hall, BFI Classics, London 1996.

The Godfather Book, Faber and Faber, London, 1997.

Straight from the Heart, Modern Norwegian Cinema 1971-1999, Kom Forlag, Kristiansund, 1999.

The Variety Almanac (editor), Boxtree Publishing, London, 2000.

The Apocalypse Now Book, Faber and Faber, London; Da Capo Press, New York, 2000.

Revolution! The Explosion of World Cinema in the Sixties, Faber and Faber, London; Farrar Straus & Giroux, New York, 2004.

John Ford and the American West, Harry N. Abrams Inc., New York, 2004.

Cool and Crazy: Modern Norwegian Cinema, Oslo, Norwegian Film Institute, 2005.

Louise Brooks – Lulu Forever, Rizzoli, New York, 2006.
    Translated into German and published by Schirmer-Mosel,
    2006.

*Projections: A Celebration of 20 Years of the European Film
    Awards*, with Pascal Edelmann, Faber and Faber, London, 2007.

The Ingmar Bergman Archives, Taschen, Cologne, 2008.
    Contributing editor.

Joan Crawford – The Enduring Star, Rizzoli, New York, 2009.

Akira Kurosawa, Master of Cinema, Rizzoli, New York, 2010.

The Berlinale. The Festival, Bertz und Fischer, Berlin, 2010.
    In German and English.

The Godfather Treasures/Archives, Carlton Books, London/
    Insight Editions, U.S.A., 2012.

*Happy 75: A Brief Introduction to the History of the Venice
    International Film Festival,* La Biennale, Venice, 2018.

Japanese Cinema, A Personal Journey, Stone Bridge Press,
    California, 2022.

God and the Devil, The Life and Work of Ingmar Bergman,
    Faber and Faber, London, 2023.

Ray Dolby, Engineer, Businessman, Pilot, edited by Dagmar
    Dolby, based on an oral history by Peter Cowie (DD Ops,
    San Francisco, 2024)

Contributions to The Criterion Collection

Persona (visual essay)
Summer Interlude (essay)
Summer with Monika (interview with Harriet Andersson)
Cries and Whispers (interview with Harriet Andersson)
Smiles of a Summer Night (conversation with Jörn Donner)
The Magician (visual essay)
The Virgin Spring (essay)
Night and Fog (visual essay)
The Element of Crime (essay)
Children of Paradise (essay)
Knife in the Water (essay)
Senso (visual essay)

I Am Curious (visual essay)
Miss Julie (visual essay)
The Phantom Carriage (visual essay)
Le feu follet (essay on Maurice Ronet)
Seven Samurai (essay)
Insomnia (essay)
Bo Widerberg (essay)
The Double Life of Véronique (essay on Irène Jacob)
Scenes from a Marriage (on-screen interview)
The Silence (on-screen interview)
Winter Light (on-screen interview)
Through a Glass Darkly (on-screen interview)
The Magic Flute (essay)
Sawdust and Tinsel (audio commentary)
The Seventh Seal (audio commentary)
Wild Strawberries (audio commentary)
Hiroshima mon amour (audio commentary)
Salvatore Giuliano (audio commentary)
Tokyo Olympiad (audio commentary and extras)
Diary of a Country Priest (audio commentary)
Grand Illusion (audio commentary on LD and DVD)
Casque d'or (audio commentary)
The Leopard (audio commentary)
Fanny and Alexander (audio commentary)
Autumn Sonata (audio commentary)
Z (audio commentary)
Here Is Your Life (interview with Jan Troell)
The Emigrants and *The New Land* (interviews)
State of Siege (interview with Costa-Gavras)
A Special Day (interview with Sophia Loren)
Visions of Eight (associate producer)
Ingmar Bergman's Cinema (box-set, consulting producer)
100 Years of Olympic Films: 1912–2012 (box-set, producer, and
    author of accompanying book)
Moonrise (interview with Hervé Dumont)
History is Made at Night (interview with Hervé Dumont)
Elvira Madigan (interviews with Jörgen Persson and
    Thommy Berggren)

Essays included in academic anthologies

"The Study of a Colossus, *Citizen Kane*" in *The Emergence of Film Art*, edited by Lewis Jacobs, Hopkinson and Blake, New York, 1969.

"Ingmar Bergman, The Middle Period" in *Focus on The Seventh Seal*, edited by Birgitta Steene, Prentice-Hall, New Jersey, 1972.

"The Study of Persecution, *The Trial*" in *Focus on Orson Welles*, edited by Ronald Gottesman, Prentice-Hall, New Jersey, 1976.

"Bergman's Passion: Dream and Reality" in *Film and Dreams, An Approach to Bergman*, edited by Vlada Petric, Redgrave Publishing, South Salem, NY, 1981.

Introduction for *Hiroshi Tasogawa's All the Emperor's Men: Kurosawa's Pearl Harbor,* Applause Books, New York, 2012.

"Bergman and the Switching Off of Lights" in *Death in Classic and Contemporary Film, Fade to Black*, edited by Daniel Sullivan and Jeff Greenberg, Palgrave Macmillan, New York, 2013.

"Ingmar Bergman on the International Scene" in *Ingmar Bergman: An Enduring Legacy*, edited by Erik Hedling, Lund University Press, 2021.

Books published by the Tantivy Press 1963–1981

A Dictionary of the Cinema, by Peter Graham, 1964.

Hitchcock's Films, by Robin Wood, 1965; second enlarged edition, 1969.

The Marx Brothers, Their World of Comedy, by Allen Eyles, 1966.

French Cinema since 1946, Volume 1, The Great Tradition; Volume 2, The Personal Style, by Roy Armes, 1966. Second enlarged edition, 1970.

Buster Keaton, by J.-P. Lebel, translated from French by P.D. Stovin [Peter Graham], 1967.

The Western, An Illustrated Guide, by Allen Eyles, 1967. Revised and expanded edition, 1975.

The Horror Film, by Ivan Butler, 1967. Second enlarged edition 1970, as *Horror in the Cinema*.

The Cinema of Joseph Losey, by James Leahy, 1967.

The Musical Film, by Douglas McVay, 1967.

Animation in the Cinema, by Ralph Stephenson, 1967.
    Second enlarged edition 1973, as *The Animated Film.*

The Cinema of Alain Resnais, by Roy Armes, 1968.

British Cinema, An Illustrated Guide, by Denis Gifford, 1968.

Four Great Comedians: Chaplin, Lloyd, Keaton, Langdon,
    by Donald W. McCaffrey, 1968.

Hollywood in the Twenties, by David Robinson, 1968.

Hollywood in the Thirties, by John Baxter, 1968.

Hollywood in the Forties, by Charles Higham and
    Joel Greenberg, 1968.

Suspense in the Cinema, by Gordon Gow, 1968.

The Cinema of Fritz Lang, by Paul M. Jensen, 1969.

Religion in the Cinema, by Ivan Butler, 1969.

The Cinema of John Frankenheimer, by Gerald Pratley, 1969.

Screen Series: Eastern Europe, by Nina Hibbin, 1969.

The Cinema of Roman Polanski, by Ivan Butler, 1970.

Science Fiction in the Cinema, by John Baxter, 1970.

Early American Cinema, by Anthony Slide, 1970.

Griffith and the Rise of Hollywood, by Paul O'Dell, 1970.

The Cinema of François Truffaut, by Graham Petrie, 1970.

Screen Series: Germany, by Felix Bucher, 1970.

Screen Series: The American Musical, by Tom Vallance, 1970.

Screen Series: The Gangster Film, by John Baxter, 1970.

Screen Series: Sweden 1 by Peter Cowie with Arne Svensson, and
    Sweden 2, by Peter Cowie, 1970.

Screen Textbooks: Practical Motion Picture Photography,
    compiled and edited by Russell Campbell, 1970.

*Screen Textbooks: Photographic Theory for the Motion Picture
    Cameraman*, compiled and edited by Russell Campbell, 1970.

The Cinema of Carl Dreyer, by Tom Milne, 1971.

Screen Series: France, by Marcel Martin, 1971.

Screen Series: Japan, by Arne Svensson, 1971.

Hollywood in the Fifties, by Gordon Gow, 1971.

Hollywood Today, by Pat Billings and Allen Eyles, 1971.

The Cinema of Otto Preminger, by Gerald Pratley, 1971.

The Cinema of John Ford, by John Baxter, 1971.

Patterns of Realism, A Study of Italian Neo-Realist Cinema, by Roy Armes, 1971.

A Concise History of the Cinema, Volume 1: Before 1940; Volume 2: Since 1940, edited by Peter Cowie, 1971.

The Cinema of Joseph von Sternberg, by John Baxter, 1971.

Ustinov in Focus, by Tony Thomas, 1971.

Hollywood in the Sixties, by John Baxter, 1972.

Ray Harryhausen's Film Fantasy Scrapbook, 1972. Revised and expanded edition, 1974.

Z is for Zagreb, by Ronald Holloway, 1972.

James Bond in the Cinema, by John Brosnan, 1972. Second expanded edition, 1981.

Screen Textbooks: Directing Motion Pictures, compiled and edited by Terence St John Marner, 1972.

The Cinema of Luis Buñuel, by Freddy Buache, translated by Peter Graham, 1973.

The Cinema of Andrzej Wajda, by Boleslaw Michalek, translated by Edward Rothert, 1973.

Cinema in Britain, by Ivan Butler, 1973.

The Griffith Actresses, by Anthony Slide, 1973.

The Hollywood Professionals, Volume 1: Michael Curtiz, Raoul Walsh, Henry Hathaway, by Kingsley Canham, 1973.

The Hollywood Professionals, Volume 2: Henry King, Lewis Milestone, Sam Wood, by Kingsley Canham, Clive Denton and Tony Thomas, 1974.

Screen Textbooks: Film Design, compiled and edited by Terence St John Marner, 1974.

The Hollywood Professionals, Volume 3: Howard Hawks, Frank Borzage, Edgar G. Ulmer, by John Belton, 1974.

The Hollywood Professionals, Volume 4: Todd Browning, Don Siegel, by Stuart Rosenthal and Judith M. Kass, 1975.

Puppet Animation in the Cinema, History and Technique, by L. Bruce Holman, 1975.

The Making of King Kong, by Orville Goldner and George E. Turner, 1975.

Cagney, The Actor as Auteur, by Patrick McGilligan, 1975.

The Vampire Film, by Alain Silver and James Ursini, 1975.

The Hollywood Professionals, Volume 5: King Vidor, John Cromwell, Mervyn Leroy, by Kingsley Canham, 1976.

The Music of Joseph Haydn: The Symphonies, by Antony Hodgson, 1976.

Hollywood 1920-1970, compilation edited by Peter Cowie, 1977.

World Filmography 1967, edited by Peter Cowie and Derek Elley, 1977.

World Filmography 1968, edited by Peter Cowie and Derek Elley, 1977.

The Music of Johannes Brahms, by Bernard Jacobson, 1977.

The Samurai Film, by Alain Silver, 1977.

Hollywood Renaissance, Altman, Cassavetes, Coppola, Mazursky, Scorsese and Others, by Diane Jacobs, 1977.

International Music Guide, published annually from 1977 to 1981, edited by Derek Elley.

Close-Ups, from the Golden Age of the Silent Cinema, edited by John Richard Finch and Paul Elby, 1978.

The Music of Dimitri Shostakovich: The Symphonies, by Roy Blokker with Robert Dearling, 1979.

John Wayne, by Allen Eyles, with an introduction by Louise Brooks, 1979.

The Hollywood Professionals, Volume 6: Frank Capra, George Cukor, Clarence Brown, by Allen Estrin, 1980.

Paramount Pictures and the People Who Made Them,
    by I.G. Edmonds and Reiko Mimura, 1980.

Olympiad – A Graphic Celebration, by Brett R. Thompson, 1980.

The Cinema of Sidney Poitier, by Lester J. Keyser and
    Andre H. Ruszkowski, 1980.

The Dark Side of the Screen: Film Noir, by Foster Hirsch, 1981.

Wings on the Screen, A Pictorial History of Air Movies,
    by Bertil Skogsberg, 1981.

International Music Guide, published annually from 1982
    to 1985, edited by Jane Dudman.

International Music & Opera Guide 1986, edited by
    Catriona Hall.

International Music & Opera Guide 1987, edited by
    Hugh Canning.

International Cycling Guide, edited by Nicholas Crane,
    published annually from 1980 to 1986.

International TV & Video Guide, edited by Olli Tuomola,
    published annually from 1983 to 1987.

International Running Guide, edited by Cliff Temple (1983-1984)
    and Mel Watman (1985-1987), published annually from 1983
    to 1987. Final edition entitled *International Athletics Guide*.

The Scandinavian Guide, edited by Peter Cowie,
    published annually from 1986 to 1990.

Index

Steinberg, David 73
Steiner; Max 210
Stenklev, Jon 172
Stephenson, Ralph 83
Steene, Paprika 214
Sterling Films 200
Sternberg, Josef von 264
Stevens, George 113, 255
Stevens, Roger L. 197
Stevens, Stella 116
Stewart, Alexandra 198-199, 263
Stewart, James 74, 258
Stockhausen, Adam 207
Stockholm 18, 13, 131-132, 134, 137, 139, 143, 146, 243, 251
Stockholm Film Festival 210
Stone, Sharon 88, 222, 268
Stone Bridge Press 240
Storaro, Vittorio 180, 203, 264
Storey, David 55
Story of Adèle H., The (Truffaut) 26
Straight from the Heart (Cowie) 172
Stranger, The (Welles) 67
Stranger, The (Ray) 121
Strangis, Jean-Louis 169
Stratton, David 64, 273
Straub, Jean-Marie 225
Straume, Unni 173
Straw Dogs (Peckinpah) 172
Streep, Meryl 207
Streiff, David 273
Stroheim, Erich von 255
Struck, Thomas 206, 273
Studio Acacias 42
Studio des Ursulines 42
Studio Vista 79
Sub 4 167
Suecia hotel (Madrid) 67
Sugimura, Haruko 262
Summer Interlude (Bergman) 137, 139, 244, 255
Summer with Monika (Bergman) 134, 139-140, 146, 149, 244
Sunday Bloody Sunday (Schlesinger) 74
Sunday in September, A (Donner) 153, 234
Sunday Telegraph (newspaper) 118
Sunday Times, The (newspaper) 53, 123
Sundgren, Nils Petter 135
Sunset Boulevard (Wilder) 254

Surrealism and the Cinema (Gould) 26
Sutherland, Donald 164
Sutton, Tim 238
Svensk Filmindustri 138, 142, 146, 148
Svensson, Arne 49
Svensson, Ove 273
Swanson, Gloria 255
Swedish Film Institute 132, 151, 155, 173, 243
Swedish Institute 104
Swedish Radio Symphony Orchestra 150
Sweet Movie (Makavejev) 114-115
Switchboard Operator (Makavejev) 112
Syberberg, Hans-Jürgen 204
Sydney Film Festival 63,-64
Sydow, Max von 14-16, 22, 138, 142, 144, 149, 164, 194
Symphony Hall (San Francisco) 221
Syms, Sylvia 68
Szabó, István 222

Taking Off (Forman) 77
Taj Mahal 118, 12
Takagi, Fumiko 273
Takamine, Hideko 257
Take One (magazine) 121
Talbot, Dan 94
Talent Press programme 209
Tallier, Armand 42
Tamer of Wild Horses (Dragić) 52
Tampere Short Film Festival 151
Tamura, Akihide 240
Tanaka, Kinuyo 256
Tanović, Danis 214
Tantivy Press, The 3, 26-27, 49-50, 64, 69-71, 82-83, 89, 91-92, 98, 100, 121, 187, 275-283
Tarkovsky, Andrei 78
Tate, Sharon 230
Tati, Jacques 130-132
Tavernier, Bertrand 208
Tavoularis, Dean 175, 178, 180, 203, 265
Taylor, Elizabeth 36, 74
Taylor, Richard 269
Teacher, The (Sjöman) 133
Technicolor 217
Tehran Film Festival 74, 116
Telluride Film Festival 147, 163, 175, 226-227, 236
Terayama, Shuji 124

www.ingramcontent.com/pod-product-compliance
Lightning Source LLC
Chambersburg PA
CBHW060125130626
46556CB00006B/2239